Living Eng...

Englisch für Erwachsene

1

Jonathan Bygrave

Beratende Mitarbeit

Dr. Andrea Kreher, VHS Berlin Treptow-Köpenick

Karmen Heup, VHS Essen

Irene Ofteringer MA, VHS Köln

PEARSON
Longman

Das zeitgemäße Lehrwerk für Erwachsene

Living English A1 ist ein speziell auf die Bedürfnisse von erwachsenen KursteilnehmerInnen abgestimmtes Lehrwerk. Das Kursbuch ist zielorientiert und versetzt Sie in die Lage, die erlernten Sprachkenntnisse sofort im Alltag und beruflichen Umfeld aktiv einsetzen zu können.

Klar definierte Lernziele

Die Lernziele jeder Unterrichtseinheit sind als *Can do*-Statements formuliert und folgen dem GERR (Gemeinsamer Europäischer Referenzrahmen). So können Sie am Ende jeder Lektion mit konkreten Alltagssituationen umgehen, wie zum Beispiel einen Ort beschreiben, in ein Hotel einchecken oder ein Essen im Restaurant bestellen.

Grammatik selbst entdecken

Zu Beginn jeder Unit wird das Grammatikthema erwähnt, das Sie benötigen, um das Lernziel zu erreichen. Aber keine Sorge, Sie brauchen die Grammatik nicht „stur zu pauken", sondern entdecken sie spielerisch durch Übungen. Die *Active Grammar-Box* und die deutschen Erklärungen auf der *Suchen und finden*-Seite festigen schließlich das Gelernte.

Motivierende und vielseitige Themen

Dieses Kursbuch haben wir für Sie gemacht! Ihre Interessen und Ihr Spaß beim Lernen waren den Autoren in jedem Moment besonders wichtig. Die aktuellen, vielseitigen Themen, attraktiven Fotos und nicht zuletzt die moderne, ansprechende Gestaltung motivieren Sie zu einem lebendigen Umgang mit der englischen Sprache.

Balance in der Kommunikation

Living English A1 ist nicht irgendein Kursbuch, denn Sie profitieren von der langjährigen, praktischen Unterrichtserfahrung der Longman Autoren und gewinnen eine ausgewogene Balance in der Kommunikation, ob beim Schreiben, Lesen, Sprechen oder Hörverstehen.

Wir wünschen Ihnen viel Vergnügen und Erfolg. Ihr Longman Autorenteam und Ihre Redaktion!

Was wir tun, damit Sie Ihre Lernziele optimal erreichen

Damit Sie Ihre Lernzeit effizient nutzen können, stellen wir für jede individuelle Situation das geeignete Medium bereit. Wir wissen, dass Ihre Zeit kostbar ist.

Die **Audio CD** zum Üben des Hörverständnisses und mit zur Unterrichtseinheit passenden Themen. Wer will, kann den Text der CD im hinteren Buchteil nachlesen.

Wenn Sie eine Kursstunde versäumen, können Sie mit der **interaktiven CD-ROM** die verpasste Stunde nachholen.

In der **zweisprachigen Vokabelliste** finden Sie die Übersetzung der wichtigsten Wörter nach Units sortiert.

Das Kapitel **Texte verfassen** enthält viele zusätzliche Beispiele und Formulierungen, damit Sie mehr Sicherheit im schriftlichen Ausdruck bekommen.

www.longman.de/livingenglish

Auf unserer Website finden Sie Wissenswertes rund um **Living English** wie zum Beispiel ein Sprachenportfolio, mit dem Sie Ihren Lernfortschritt dokumentieren können, Hörproben zu allen Kursbüchern, Infos zum Autorenteam und vieles mehr.

Blick ins Buch

Living English A1 ist in zehn übersichtliche und klar strukturierte Units gegliedert. Sie finden in jeder Unit:

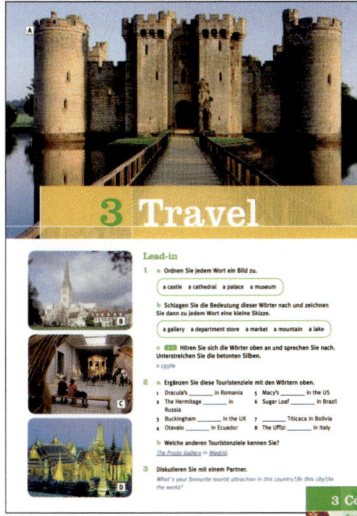

eine kurze Einführung in das Thema

und drei abgeschlossene Unterrichtseinheiten, die jeweils auf einer Doppelseite präsentiert werden,

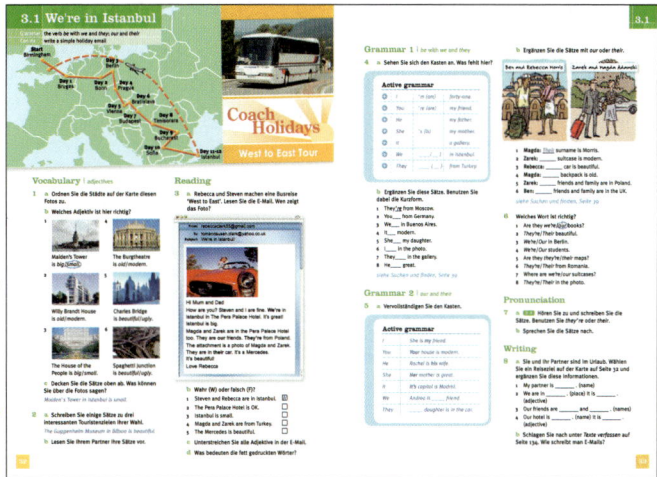

eine Grammatikübersicht auf deutsch mit Beispielen und Tipps

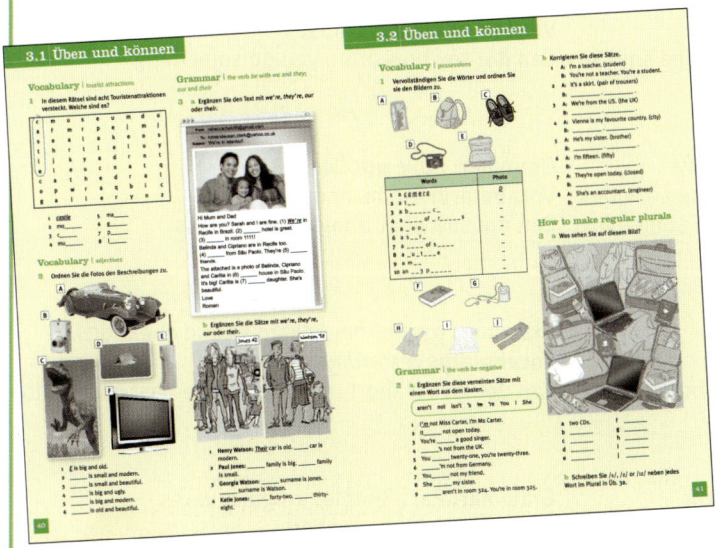

eine **Communication**-Seite mit zusätzlichen Sprachübungen, Rollenspielen,

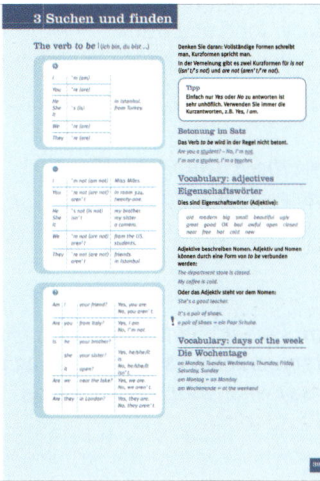

und einen Übungsteil für Zuhause oder den Unterricht. Pro Unterrichtseinheit gibt es eine Übungsseite (mit Antwortschlüssel zum Nachschlagen am Ende des Buches).

Living English und der Europäische Referenzrahmen

Ihr Kursbuch wurde nach den Richtlinien des GERR (Gemeinsamer Europäischer Referenzrahmen) entwickelt: Alle *Can do*-Statements sind am Anfang jeder Unit benannt. Auf diese Weise erfahren Sie sofort, welchen Fortschritt Sie am Ende einer Unterrichtseinheit gemacht haben. Die klar definierten Lernziele versetzen Sie in die Lage konkrete Alltagssituationen zu meistern.

Mit Hilfe der *Life Long Learning*-Boxen bekommen Sie wertvolle Tipps, wie Sie leichter und Zeit sparender den gewünschten Lernerfolg erreichen.

Living English unterstützt Sie beim selbstständigen Lernen. Das hilft Ihnen nicht nur später, wenn Sie im Beruf oder im Urlaub die Sprache ohne fremde Hilfe anwenden wollen.

Contents

Nützliche Ausdrücke im Unterricht

Excuse me, can you help me?
Entschuldigung, können Sie mir helfen?

Can you say that slowly, please?
Können Sie das bitte (noch einmal) langsam sagen?

Can you say that again, please?
Können Sie das bitte wiederholen?

Open your books.
Öffnen Sie Ihre Bücher.

What's this in English?
Wie heißt das auf Englisch?

What's this
Was ist das?

Which page/exercise is it?
Welche Seite/Übung ist das?

Close your books.
Schließen Sie Ihre Bücher.

I don't know.
Ich weiß nicht.

Sorry, I don't understand.
Es tut mir leid, das verstehe ich nicht.

Vokabeln Lerntipps

Englische Vokabeln begegnen Ihnen nicht nur im Englischbuch, sondern ebenso im Internet oder im Supermarkt. Es ist immer gut, sie zu notieren – nur wie, wenn man sie auch wiederfinden will? Das traditionelle Vokabelheft ist zwar handlich, aber eine Sortierung, die inhaltlich sinnvoll ist, gelingt Ihnen eher in einem Ringbuch: Sie können Blätter einfügen, umheften, ersetzen und die neuen Vokabeln dort einsortieren, wo sie hingehören.

Und was gehört auf ein Vokabelblatt? Wählen Sie ein Thema, z.B. *Familie*. Notieren Sie die Wörter mit Übersetzung. Ordnen Sie sie sinnvoll an, z.B. die weibliche und männliche Entsprechung jeweils gegenüber.

Sollte für die Schwiegereltern kein Platz sein, fügen Sie einfach noch eine Seite ein, wenn sie "drankommen". So landen neue Wörter an der richtigen Stelle.

Bilder lernen sich oft besser – beschriften Sie ein Bild Ihrer eigenen Familie mit den englischen Begriffen.

Farbliche Kennzeichnungen unterstützen Sie beim Lernen!

Wenn Sie sich nicht entscheiden können, ob die Katze zur Familie oder zu den Tieren gehört, schreiben Sie sie einfach beide Male dazu.

Das schönste Vokabelringbuch nutzt wenig, wenn Sie nicht regelmäßig reingucken. Zweimal täglich Zähneputzen, einmal täglich eine Portion Englisch!

Soll ich dir mal meine Englischsammlung zeigen?

Bunte Ideen, die nicht ganz so ins System passen, sammeln Sie im Portfolio – machen Sie eine Extra-Abteilung in Ihrem Ringbuch. Sammeln Sie Ihr "Wort der Woche"? Ob Postkarten, Cartoons, Witze, Liebesgedichte oder Songtexte – oder auch Ihre eigenen Meisterstücke: Sammeln Sie sie und sehen Sie immer wieder rein! Zeigen Sie Ihre Sammlung ruhig mal den anderen Menschen in Ihrem Kurs.

Sie kennen bereits viele englische Wörter. Können Sie diese Wörter im Rätsel finden?

tennis computer web update download radio camera hotel late-night show check-in model superstar international tv shampoo service love homepage date lotion email work fun size

q	w	m	e	u	e	t	e	r	z	u	h	g	r	d
h	c	o	m	p	u	t	e	r	f	h	g	h	a	j
o	l	d	l	d	k	e	c	a	m	e	r	a	d	k
m	o	e	n	a	s	n	b	v	c	u	x	y	i	a
e	t	l	a	t	e	n	i	g	h	t	s	h	o	w
p	i	s	f	e	r	i	h	g	f	v	o	o	d	s
a	o	h	t	g	v	s	u	p	e	r	s	t	a	r
g	n	a	e	v	i	j	j	u	z	t	t	e	t	e
e	r	m	r	b	c	h	e	c	k	i	n	l	e	m
o	o	p	s	n	e	w	f	h	l	l	o	s	d	a
f	w	o	h	d	o	w	n	l	o	a	d	q	c	i
u	o	o	e	n	n	e	e	o	x	f	e	w	v	l
n	r	n	v	s	i	z	e	v	h	k	u	e	w	b
e	k	l	e	c	e	n	s	e	r	u	c	b	i	o
n	i	n	t	e	r	n	a	t	i	o	n	a	l	t

1 Arrivals

Lead-in

1 **a** Welcher Dialog gehört zu welchem Foto?

A: Good morning.
B: Good morning.
A: Welcome to Easton Hotel.
B: Thank you.
Photo *A*

A: Hi, Nina.
B: Hi, James.
Photo ___

A: Hello. I'm Alonzo Moreno.
B: Hello. I'm Camila Diaz. Nice to meet you.
A: Nice to meet you, too.
Photo ___

A: Hello. I'm Maria Hofmann. What's your name?
B: I'm Helga Peters.
Photo ___

b **1.1** Hören Sie zu und überprüfen Sie Ihre Antworten.

2 **1.2** Decken Sie Üb. 1a ab. Hören Sie zu und antworten Sie richtig.
Welcome to Leonard Hotel.
You: *Thank you.*

3 Partnerarbeit: Stellen Sie sich den anderen Kursteilnehmern vor.
A: *Hello. I'm Adelina Garza.*
B: *I'm Nahid Golovina. Nice to meet you.*
A: *Nice to meet you, too.*

Vocabulary | numbers 0–9

1 **a** `1.3` Hören Sie zu und sprechen Sie nach.

b Schreiben Sie die Zahlen neben die Wörter.

four ___   eight ___   one ___   two ___
five ___   seven ___   six ___
three ___   zero ___   nine ___

2 Zeigen Sie auf eine Zahl. Kann Ihr Partner sie nennen?

3 **a** Lesen Sie den *How to*-Kasten und schreiben Sie die Zimmernummern aus.

> **HOW TO …**
>
> **say hotel room numbers**
>
> **329** : Room three two nine
>
> **406** : Room four oh six

1 **129**	4 **209**
Room *one* *two* *nine*	Room ___ ___ ___
2 **438**	5 **608**
Room ___ ___ ___	Room ___ ___ ___
3 **517**	6 **345**
Room ___ ___ ___	Room ___ ___ ___

b Wie spricht man die Zimmernummern aus?

Listening

4 `1.4` Hören Sie zu. Welches Anmeldeformular ist korrekt ausgefüllt?

1
NAME:	Cristina Bally
ROOM:	329

2
NAME:	Cristina Branco
ROOM:	329

3
NAME:	Cristina Branco
ROOM:	239

5 Partnerarbeit: Lesen Sie den *How to*-Kasten und spielen Sie mit Ihrem Partner eine Szene wie in Üb. 4a.

> **HOW TO …**
>
> **say names**
>
> Mr Smith : Mrs/Ms/Miss Jones

A: *Hello.*

B: *Hello. I'm Helmut Becker.*

A: *Welcome to Bally Hotel, Mr Becker. You're …*

Grammar | *I'm/you're*

6 Ergänzen Sie den Kasten unten mit *am* oder *are*.

Active grammar

I	———	*Cristina Branco.*
I	*'m*	
You	———	*in room 329.*
You	*you're*	

siehe Suchen und finden, Seite 15

7 **a** Ergänzen Sie die Dialoge mit *'m* oder *'re*.

1 **A:** Good morning. *I'm* Mateo Alvarez.
   B: Good morning, Mr Alvarez. You___ in room 121.

2 **A:** Hello. Welcome to Hotel Lux.
   B: Thank you. I___ Britney Black.
   A: You___ in room 820, Ms Black.

3 **A:** Good morning. I___ Mi Lei Ling.
   B: I___ Walter Mann. Nice to meet you.

4 **A:** Hello, Ms West. You___ in room 320.
   B: Thank you.

5 **A:** I___ Paul Wolf.
   B: Nice to meet you, Mr Wolf. I___ Rutger Krüger.
   A: Nice to meet you, too, Mr Krüger.

b Partnerarbeit: Üben Sie das Einchecken mit Hilfe der Namen und Zimmernummern unten.

A: *I'm Scott Wilson.*
B: *Hello Mr Wilson. You're in room two three five.*

1 Scott Wilson **2 3 5**
2 Jasmine Dudek **4 0 9**
3 Carlos Santos **1 2 6**
4 Elsa Richter **9 0 8**
5 Luca Rosa **2 1 7**
6 Marisa Gonzales **3 4 1**
7 Jane Cross **7 3 6**
8 Lara Bezmel **1 0 8**

Vocabulary | greetings

8 **a** Vervollständigen Sie die Begrüßungen mit den Wörtern aus dem Kasten.

> evening   afternoon   morning   night

1
Auguste: Good _____ .
Betty: Good _____ .

2
Auguste: Good _____ .
Camilla: Good _____ .

3
Auguste: Good _____ .
Daniel: Good _____ .

4
Auguste: Good _____ .
People: Good _____ .

b 🔊 1.5 Hören Sie zu und überprüfen Sie Ihre Antworten.

c Üben Sie mit einem Partner:
A: *Good afternoon.*   **B:** *Good afternoon.*

Speaking

9 Wählen Sie eine der beiden Rollen:

Partner A: Sie arbeiten an der Rezeption und begrüßen vier Gäste in Ihrem Hotel. Tragen Sie ihre Namen unten ein.

ROOM	NAME
504	
319	
428	
716	

Teilnehmer B: Gast. Checken Sie als Gast in vier verschiedene Hotels ein.

A: *Good evening. Welcome to Hotel California.*
B: *Thank you. I'm Gerik Pawlak.*
A: *Mr Pawlak. You're in room 504.*
B: *Thank you.*

Grammar	*he's/she's/it's*
Can do	greet someone at an airport

Vocabulary | letters

1 **a** `1.6` Hören Sie sich das Alphabet an.

a b c d e f g h i j k l m n
o p q r s t u v w x y z

b Hören Sie noch einmal zu und sprechen Sie nach.

c Partnerarbeit: Üben Sie das englische Alphabet.

2 **a** Wie spricht man die Laute unten aus?

b Ordnen Sie die Buchstaben des Alphabets den entsprechenden Lauten zu.

/eɪ/ (<u>eigh</u>t) = <u>a</u>__ ___ ___ ___
/iː/ (thr<u>ee</u>) = <u>b</u>__ ___ ___ ___ ___ ___ ___
/e/ (t<u>e</u>n) = <u>f</u>__ ___ ___ ___ ___ ___ ___
/aɪ/ (f<u>i</u>ve) = <u>i</u>__ ___
/əʊ/ (zer<u>o</u>) ___
/uː/ (tw<u>o</u>) <u>q</u>__ ___ ___
/ɑː/ (<u>a</u>re) ___

c `1.7` Hören Sie zu und überprüfen Sie Ihre Antworten.

3 Wie lauten die Flugnummern auf der Tafel?

A: *HD three four seven.*

B: *Delhi.*

Arrivals

Flight number	From	Arrival time	Comments
HD347	Delhi	14.00	landed
AR191	Sydney	14.05	landed
CT248	Buenos Aires	14.05	delayed
WG506	Tokyo	14.10	
MO793	New York	14.15	
JF820	Rio de Janeiro	14.15	on time
ML145	London	14.25	
PE706	Berlin	14.25	
IS003	Rome	14.30	cancelled
YI449	Warsaw	14.30	

Vocabulary | countries

4 **a** Ordnen Sie jeder Stadt auf der Flugtafel ein Land im Kasten zu.

> Argentina ~~India~~
> Germany Japan Italy
> Poland the UK
> Australia Brazil the US

	City	Country
1	Delhi	*India*
2	Sydney	_____
3	Buenos Aires	_____
4	Tokyo	_____
5	New York	_____
6	Rio de Janeiro	_____
7	London	_____
8	Berlin	_____
9	Rome	_____
10	Warsaw	_____

b `1.8` Hören Sie zu und überprüfen Sie Ihre Antworten. Sprechen Sie nach.

Pronunciation

5 **a** Hören Sie noch einmal zu. Wie viele Silben hat jedes Land?

In – di – a = 3

b Partnerarbeit: Nennen Sie eine Stadt. Ihr Partner nennt das entsprechende Land.

A: *Tokyo.* **B:** *Japan.*

c Welche Länder kennen Sie noch?

Lifelong learning

Englisch ist überall!

Ob auf der Shampooflasche oder im Lieblingslied. Nachschlagen, notieren – Neugier genügt!

Listening and reading

6 **a** [1.9] Hören Sie zu und ergänzen Sie die Sätze unten.

1 He's Sunny Deva. He's from India. He's in ____ .

2 She's Ana ____ . She's from Brazil. She's in ____ .

3 She's Nicole ____ . She's from Australia. She's in ____ .

b Hören Sie noch einmal zu und überprüfen Sie Ihre Antworten.

c Partnerarbeit: Lesen Sie den *How to*-Kasten. Begrüßen Sie Ihren Partner am Flughafen.

HOW TO …

greet someone at airport arrivals

A: *Mrs Cole?*

B: *Yes.*

A: *Hello, Mrs Cole. I'm Hans Adler. Welcome to Germany.*

B: *Thank you.*

Grammar | *he's/she's/it's*

7 Vervollständigen Sie den Kasten mit *is* oder *'s*.

Active grammar

He	is	
He	's	
She	_	from India.
She	_	from Argentina.
It	_	
It	_	

siehe Suchen und finden, Seite 15

8 **a** Ergänzen Sie die Sätze mit *he's*, *she's* oder *it's*.

1 He's from Australia. (Russell Crowe)

2 _____ from the US. (Hillary Clinton)

3 _____ in Italy. (Venice)

4 _____ in London. (Gwyneth Paltrow)

5 _____ from Germany. (Angela Merkel)

6 _____ in Australia. (Melbourne)

7 _____ from the UK. (Anthony Hopkins)

8 _____ from Argentina. (the tango)

b Partnerarbeit: Stellen Sie wahre oder falsche Behauptungen über verschiedene Städte auf.

A: *Sydney is in Argentina.*

B: *False!*

c Berichten Sie über andere Teilnehmer im Kurs.

She's Olga. She's from Russia.

Speaking

9 Was wissen Sie über die Prominenten auf den Bildern?

A: *She's Gisele Bündchen. She's from Brazil.*

1.3 Nice to meet you

Grammar	*Where ...?*
Can do	introduce someone; start a conversation

Vocabulary | common phrases

1 a Ordnen Sie diese nützlichen Wendungen den Bildern zu.

> Sorry!   Nice to meet you.   No, thank you.   Yes, please.   Pardon?
> Excuse me, ...

b **1.10** Hören Sie zu und überprüfen Sie Ihre Antworten.

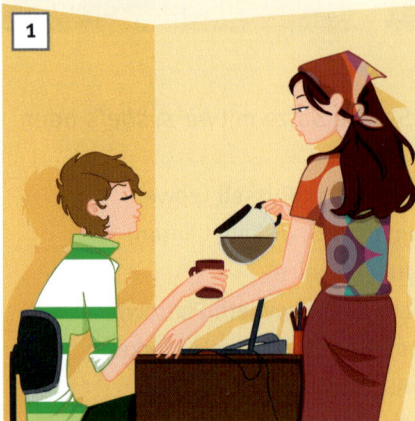

2 **1.11** Hören Sie zu und ergänzen Sie die Dialoge mit einer Wendung aus Üb. 1a.

1 _____
2 _____
3 _____

Boris

Listening

3 a **1.12** Hören Sie zu und bringen Sie die Sätze in die richtige Reihenfolge.

A: Hi, Boris. ☐ 1
L: Nice to meet you, too. ☐
B: Hi, Andy. This is Luisa. ☐
A: Nice to meet you, Luisa. ☐

b Hören Sie noch einmal zu und überprüfen Sie Ihre Antworten.

4 a Üben Sie das Gespräch in 3er-Gruppen.

HOW TO ...

introduce people

This is (Paul).
Nice to meet you.
Nice to meet you, too.

b Lesen Sie den *How to-*Kasten. Schließen Sie dann Ihre Bücher und stellen Sie sich einander vor.

A: *Hi, Britta.*
B: *Hi, Pedro. This is Roxana.*

5

a [1.13] Hören Sie zu und ergänzen Sie den Dialog zwischen Luisa und Andy.

Luisa: Where (1) *are* you from, Andy?
Andy: I'm from the US.
Luisa: (2) _____ are you from in the US?
Andy: I'm from New York. Where are (3) _____ from?
Luisa: I'm from Argentina.
Andy: Where are you (4) _____ in Argentina?
Luisa: I'm from Rosario.

b Wahr (W) oder falsch (F)?

1 Andy is from Argentina. ☑ F
2 Andy is from New York. ☐
3 Luisa is from New York. ☐
4 Luisa is from Buenos Aires. ☐
5 Luisa is from Rosario. ☐

6

a Partnerarbeit: Üben Sie den Dialog.

A: *Where are you from, Andy?*
B: *I'm from New York.*

b Nun fragen Sie Ihren Partner.

A: *Where are you from, Rainer?*
B: *I'm from …*

Grammar | questions with be

7 Ordnen Sie die Fragen im Kasten den entsprechenden Antworten zu.

> ### Active grammar
>
> **Questions**
>
> | | | | |
> |---|---|---|---|
> | 1 | *Where are* | *you* | *from?* |
> | 2 | *Where are* | *you* | *from in the US?* |
>
> **Answers**
>
> | | | | |
> |---|---|---|---|
> | a) | *I* | *'m* | *from Las Vegas.* |
> | b) | *I* | *'m* | *from the US.* |

siehe Suchen und finden, Seite 15

8

a Vervollständigen Sie die Dialoge.

A: (1) *Where* are you from?
B: (2) _____ from Turkey.
A: (3) _____ are you from in Turkey?
B: I'm (4) _____ Istanbul.

C: Where are (5) _____ from?
D: I'm (6) _____ Germany.
C: Where (7) _____ you from in Germany?
D: I'm (8) _____ Berlin.

b Ergänzen Sie die Fragen und Antworten.

1 A: *Where are you from?*
  B: I'm from the UK.
2 A: _____ in India?
  B: I'm from Delhi.
3 A: Where are you from?
  B: _____ São Paolo in Brazil.
4 A: _____ Australia?
  B: I'm from Sydney.

Pronunciation

9 **a** [1.14] Hören Sie zu und unterstreichen Sie die betonten Wörter.

1 *Where* are you *from*?
2 Where are you from in Germany?
3 I'm from Hamburg.

b Hören Sie zu und sprechen Sie nach.

Speaking

10 Arbeiten Sie in 3er-Gruppen:

Partner A: Stellen Sie B und C vor.
Partner B: Fragen Sie C, wo er/sie herkommt.
Partner C: Fragen Sie B, wo er/sie herkommt.

Find a phone number

1 **a** Ordnen Sie die Länder a–f oben den Ländern in der Tabelle zu.

b `1.15` Hören Sie zu und tragen Sie die internationale Vorwahl in die Tabelle ein.

Dial 00 + country code + telephone number	
COUNTRY	**CODE**
Australia	____
Brazil	+55
China	____
Japan	+81
Mexico	____
Russia	____
Spain	____
Turkey	____
UK	+44
US	+1

c Lesen Sie den *How to*-Kasten. Wie spricht man die Ländernamen und die dazugehörige Vorwahl aus?

HOW TO …

say phone numbers

55 = double five

o = oh 🇬🇧   o = zero 🇺🇸

2 `1.6` Hören Sie zu und ergänzen Sie die fehlenden Informationen.

1

HOTEL: *Hotel Lamden*
WHERE: _____ , *Italy.*
PHONE NUMBER: _____ .

2

HOTEL: **Hotel Kelem**
WHERE: _____ , **Turkey.**
PHONE NUMBER: _____ .

3 Partnerarbeit:

Partner A: Lesen Sie weiter auf Seite 127. Stellen Sie Fragen über das Hotel Miller.

Partner B: Lesen Sie weiter auf Seite 128. Stellen Sie Fragen über das Hotel Calmia.

1 Suchen und finden

Numbers 0–9
Die Zahlen 0–9

0	zero
1	one
2	two
3	three
4	four
5	five
6	six
7	seven
8	eight
9	nine

Bei Telefonnummern sagt man die Ziffern einzeln in Dreierblocks:

345 714 *three four five   seven one four*

99 = *double nine*

Aussprache der Null:

oh   oder *zero*

Letters
Die Buchstaben

a b c d e f g h i j k l m
n o p q r s t u v w x y z

Tipp

Buchstaben in der gleichen Farbe reimen sich, wenn man sie einzeln ausspricht.

/eɪ/ ('eight') = a h j k

/iː/ ('three') = b c d e g p t v

/e/ ('ten') = f l m n s x z

/aɪ/ ('five') = i y

/əʊ/ ('zero') = o

/uː/ ('two') = q u w

/ɑː/ ('are') = r

Verb *to be* | (ich bin, du bist ...)

I	am	
I	'm	
You	are	from China.
You	're	
He	is	in room 2 3 4.
He	's	Jennifer West.
She	is	in London.
She	's	
It	is	
It	's	

I am/you are/he is/she is/it is = die vollständige Form. Die vollständige Form **schreibt man** (außer in privaten Briefen).

I'm/you're/he's/she's/it's = die Kurzform. Die Kurzform **spricht** man.

Where ...?

Where are	you	from?
Where is	he	from?
Where is	she	from?
Where is	it	from?

Where is ...? kann man beim Sprechen zusammenziehen zu *Where's.*

Where are ...? kann man nicht zusammenziehen.

Common phrases
Nützliche Redewendungen

Mit *Sorry* bittet man um Verzeihung. (*Das tut mir Leid.*)

Mit *Excuse me* bittet man um Aufmerksamkeit, z.B. als Einleitung zu einer Frage oder Bitte. (*Entschuldigung, ...*)

Pardon? sagt man, wenn man etwas akustisch nicht verstanden hat (*Wie bitte?*).

Nice to meet you sagt man, wenn man jemandem zum ersten Mal begegnet (*Nett, Sie kennen zu lernen*).

Mit *No, thank you* lehnt man ein Angebot ab, mit *Yes, please* nimmt man es an.

Speaking

1 **a** Bringen Sie die Wörter in die richtige Reihenfolge.

1 Mr I'm Stewart

I'm Mr Stewart.

2 meet you to Nice

_____ .

3 Patrick is Wendy, this

_____ .

4 David Hello, Smith I'm

_____ .

5 name? your What's

_____ .

6 to Hotel Havana Welcome

_____ .

b Ordnen Sie zu:

A	B
1 Nice to meet you.	a) Hi, Rudi.
2 This is Stefan.	b) Nice to meet you, too.
3 Hi, Olga.	c) Thank you.
4 Welcome to The Palace Hotel.	d) Hello, Stefan.

1 _____
2 _____
3 _____
4 _____

Vocabulary | numbers 0–9

2 Füllen Sie das Kreuzworträtsel aus.

WAAGERECHT	c) 1 e) 5 g) 6 h) 3 i) 9
SENKRECHT	a) 2 b) 8 d) 4 f) 7

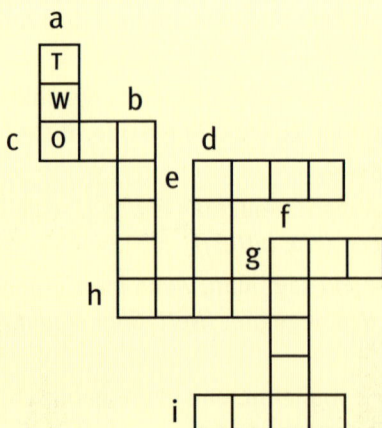

Grammar | I'm, you're

3 **a** Schreiben Sie diese Sätze mit der Kurzform.

1 A: I am Maggie May.
B: You are in room 511.
A: _I'm Maggie May._
B: _____ .

2 A: I am Ruby Tuesday.
B: You are in room 147.
A: _____ .
B: _____ .

3 A: I am Peggy Sue.
B: You are in room 312.
A: _____ .
B: _____ .

b Ergänzen Sie mit I'm oder You're.

1 A: Hello. Welcome to Hotel California.
B: Thank you. _____ Don Henley.
A: _____ in room 329, Mr Henley.

2 A: Hello.
B: Hello. I'm Ms Turner.
A: Welcome to Nutbush Hotel, Ms Turner. _____ in room 808.
B: Thank you.

3 A: Hello. Welcome to The Kelly Hotel.
B: Thank you. _____ Trina Cassidy.
A: _____ in room 415, Ms Cassidy.

c Schreiben Sie einen Dialog.

A: _Hello. Welcome ..._
B: _____ .
A: _____ .
B: _____ .

Vocabulary | letters a–z

1 Welche Buchstaben haben denselben Laut?

a	y
b	u
i	s
m	j
q	d

1 _a_ and _j_
2 ___ and ___
3 ___ and ___
4 ___ and ___
5 ___ and ___

Vocabulary | countries

2 a Korrigieren Sie die Fehler und unterstreichen Sie die betonten Silben.

1 Itily _Italy_
2 Polan _____
3 Mexica _____
4 Turkiy _____
5 Espain _____
6 Rusia _____

b Lösen Sie das Rätsel. Welches Land bildet hier das Lösungswort?

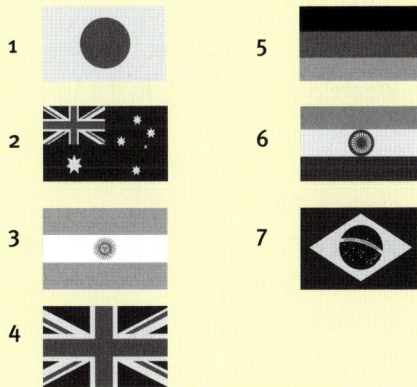

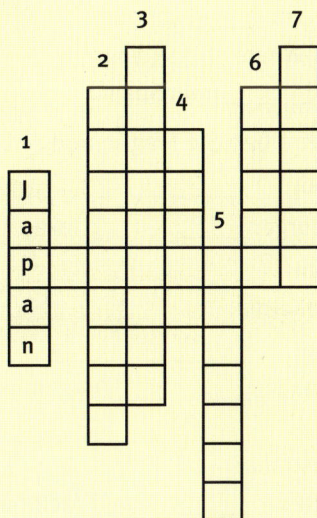

Grammar | he's, she's, it's

3 Woher kommen diese Prominenten?

1 Prince Charles: _He's from the UK._
2 Madonna: _____ the US.
3 Diego Maradona: _____ Argentina.
4 Takeshi Kitano: _____ Japan.
5 Claudia Schiffer: _____ Germany.
6 Pelé: _____ Brazil.
7 Sonia Gandi: _____ India.
8 Kylie Minogue: _____ Australia.

4 Schreiben Sie zwei Sätze zu jedem Bild.

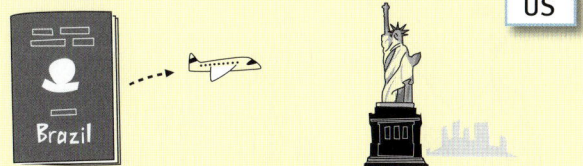

US

1 He's from Brazil. He's in the US.

the UK

2 She _____ .

Japan

3 He _____ .

Australia

4 He _____ .

India

5 She _____ .

Argentina

6 She _____ .

17

Vocabulary | common phrases

1 **a** Füllen Sie die Lücken aus.

1 S_rry.

2 P_rd_n?

3 N_, th_nk y_ _.

4 N_c_ t_ m_ _t y_ _.

5 _xc_s_ m_.

6 Y_s, pl_ _s_.

b Ordnen Sie die Wendungen aus Üb. 1 diesen Bildern zu.

How to introduce people

2 Stellen Sie Person A die gerade angekommene Person B vor.

1 **A:** Susan   **B:** George

Susan, this is George.

2 **A:** Luis   **B:** Murat

_____ .

3 **A:** Hans   **B:** Olga

_____ .

4 **A:** Bill   **B:** Nicole

_____ .

Grammar | *Where ...?*

3 **a** Bringen Sie die Wörter in die richtige Reihenfolge.

Tom: (is Ali. this Carol,) *Carol, this is Ali.*

Carol: (meet to Nice you.) _____

Ali: (meet to too. you Nice) _____

Carol: (from, Where Ali? are you) _____

Ali: (from UK. the I'm) _____

Carol: (you are from Where the UK? in)

_____

Ali: (from London. I'm) _____

b Ergänzen Sie die Dialoge.

1 **A:** Where _are_ you _____ in the US?
   B: I'm from Chicago.

2 **A:** _____ _____ you from?
   B: I'm from Tokyo in Japan.

3 **A:** Where are _____ _____ in Brazil?
   B: I'm from Curitiba.

4 **A:** Where are _____ _____ ?
   B: I'm _____ Australia.

5 **A:** _____ are you from in the UK?
   B: I'm _____ London.

6 **A:** Where _____ you _____ ?
   B: _____ from Spain.

c Schreiben Sie Fragen und Antworten.

1 **You:** _____ _____ _____ from in the US?
   George: _____ _____ Texas.

2 **You:** _____ _____ _____ _____ ?
   Mahatma: _____ _____ India.

3 **You:** _____ _____ _____ _____ ?
   Eva: _____ _____ Argentina.

4 **You:** _____ _____ _____ _____ in Australia?
   Cate: _____ _____ Melbourne.

A

Karen

John

Luke

Lucy

2 | My life

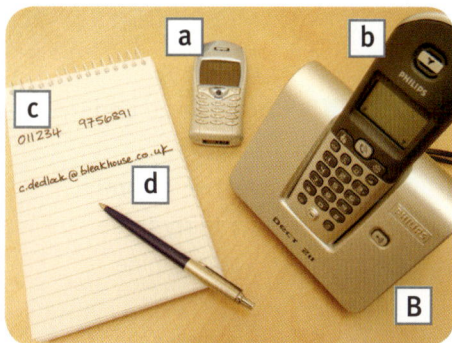

a
b
c 011234 9756891
d c.dedlak@blenkhouse.co.uk
B

e
g
f
h
C

i
j
k Edward Hamilton
27 High Street
LONDON
SE3 8NY
D

Lead-in

1   a   Ergänzen Sie mit den Wörtern aus dem Kasten.

> mother   husband   sister   daughter
> father   son   wife   brother

1   Karen – Luke = *mother – son*   4   John – Luke = _____ – _____
2   John – Lucy = _____ – _____   5   Karen – John = _____ – _____
3   Lucy – Luke = _____ – _____   6   Karen – Lucy = _____ – _____

b **2.1** Hören Sie zu und überprüfen Sie Ihre Antworten. Sprechen Sie nach. Unterstreichen Sie die betonten Silben.

mother

2   a   Ordnen Sie die Buchstaben a–k den Wörtern im Kasten zu.

> phone   email address   address   mobile phone   computer
> passport   first name   website   phone number   surname   photo

a = mobile phone

b **2.2** Hören Sie zu und überprüfen Sie Ihre Antworten. Sprechen Sie nach. Unterstreichen Sie die betonten Silben.

*email ad**dress***

3   Partnerarbeit:

Partner A: Zeigen Sie auf einen Gegenstand in Bild B–D.
Partner B: Nennen Sie das entsprechende Wort.
Wechseln Sie sich ab.

Grammar	Who ...?; my
Can do	give basic information about your family

Marek, _____

Tom, _____

Anna, _____

Sofia, _____

James, _____

Sabrina, 37

Carl, _____

Sarah, _____

Listening

1 a Sehen Sie sich die Fotos an. Wie sind diese Leute mit Sabrina verwandt?

a mother = *Sofia*
b father = _____
c brother = _____
d sister = _____
e son = _____
f daughter = _____
g husband = _____

b `2.3` Hören Sie zu und überprüfen Sie Ihre Antworten.

c Hören Sie noch einmal zu und schreiben Sie das richtige Alter neben die Namen auf den Bildern.

> 26 32 3 ~~37~~ 1 57 60 40

Vocabulary | numbers 10–99

2 a `2.4` Hören Sie zu und sprechen Sie nach.

b Schließen Sie Ihr Buch. Wie lauten die Zahlen 1–20?

10	11	12	13	14	15
ten	eleven	twelve	thirteen	fourteen	fifteen
	16	17	18	19	20
	sixteen	seventeen	eighteen	nineteen	twenty

3 a `2.5` Hören Sie zu und sprechen Sie nach.

20 twenty	21 twenty-one
30 thirty	33 thirty-three
40 forty	49 forty-nine
50 fifty	56 fifty-six
60 sixty	67 sixty-seven
70 seventy	74 seventy-four
80 eighty	88 eighty-eight
90 ninety	99 ninety-nine

b Partnerarbeit: Zeigen Sie auf ein Feld in der Zahlen-tabelle auf Seite 27. Ihr Partner nennt die Zahl.

c Lesen Sie den *How to*-Kasten. Wie alt sind die Leute auf den Fotos?

HOW TO ...

talk about age

How old is he/she?

He's	sixty-two	
She's	twenty-one	years old.

Grammar | *Who ...?; my*

4 **a** Ergänzen Sie den Kasten unten mit *he*, *she* und *my*.

Active grammar

	Who's (is)	*she?*
		___ ?
		Sofia?
Marek	*'s* (is)	___ *father.*
He		*my brother.*
___		___ *sister.*

b Vervollständigen Sie diese Dialoge.

A: Who's *he?*
B: He's _____ father.

A: _____ she?
B: _____ my mother.

A: Who's _____ ?
B: _____ _____ brother.

A: _____ he?
B: It's OK. _____ _____ friend.

siehe Suchen und finden, Seite 27

5 **a** Ergänzen Sie diese Sätze aus Sabrinas Sicht.

1 Carl is *my brother.*
2 Anna is _____ .
3 Marek is _____ .
4 Sofia is _____ .
5 Sarah is _____ .
6 Tom is _____ .
7 James is _____ .

b Schreiben Sie Fragen zu diesen Antworten.

1 *Who's Marek?*   He's my father.
2 _____ ?   He's my brother.
3 _____ ?   She's my mother.
4 _____ ?   She's my sister.
5 _____ ?   He's my son.
6 _____ ?   He's my husband.
7 _____ ?   She's my daughter.

Pronunciation

6 **a** **2.6** Hören Sie zu und unterstreichen Sie die betonten Silben.

(1) Cristina's my mother. (2) She's sixty-five.
(3) Janet's my daughter. (4) David's my son.
(5) He's fifteen. (6) Jeff's my brother. (7) Eric's my father. (8) Diana's my wife.

b Hören Sie noch einmal zu. Spricht man *'s* scharf /s/ oder weich /z/ aus?

1 */z/*   2 ___   3 ___   4 ___
5 ___   6 ___   7 ___   8 ___

c Lesen Sie die Sätze aus Üb. 6a laut vor.

Speaking

7 **a** Schreiben Sie eine Liste mit fünf Namen von Verwandten oder Freunden.

b Erklären Sie Ihrem Partner, wer die Personen auf Ihrer Liste sind.

A: *Who's Martin?*
B: *He's my brother. He's twenty-seven years old.*

Lifelong learning

Mäßig aber regelmäßig!

10 Minuten täglich – in der U-Bahn, vor dem Schlafengehen ... Finden Sie Ihr Sprachlernritual.

Grammar	*What's your ...?*
Can do	ask for and give personal details

Listening

1 **a** `2.7` Hören Sie zu. Kreuzen (x) Sie die genannten Adressen an.

1. a 59 Princes Street, Edinburgh ☐
    b 69 Princes Street, Edinburgh ☐
2. a 21 Globe Road, London ☐
    b 31 Globe Road, London ☐
3. a 18 Boulevard de Clichy, Paris ☐
    b 80 Boulevard de Clichy, Paris ☐
4. a 46 Lower Abbey Street, Dublin ☐
    b 26 Lower Abbey Street, Dublin ☐
5. a 17 Brook Street, Boston ☐
    b 70 Brook Street, Boston ☐

b Sprechen Sie die Adressen aus Üb. 1a nach.

2 **a** `2.8` Hören Sie zu und ergänzen Sie die Informationen a–f.

b Hören Sie noch einmal zu und überprüfen Sie Ihre Antworten.

a Name: Ben _____
b From: _____
c Age: _____ years old
d Address: _____, Kings _____, Angel, London.
e Phone number: _____
f Mobile phone number: _____

Vocabulary | *great, good, ok, bad, awful*

3 **a** Ordnen Sie jeweils eines dieser Wörter einer Person zu.

b `2.9` Hören Sie Auszüge aus einem Gesangswettbewerb und schreiben Sie in die Tabelle, was die Juroren von den Kandidaten halten.

	Judges	You
Ben	*He's awful.*	
Terri		
Vittoria		
Hans		
Sanjay		

c Partnerarbeit: Was halten Sie von den Kandidaten?

A: *Ben's awful.*

B: *Yes, he's awful. Terri's ok.*

A: *Terri's great!*

d Sprechen Sie über andere Sänger, die Sie kennen.

A: *Mariah Carey's great.*

B: *Mariah Carey? She's ok.*

Grammar | *What's your ...?*

4 **a** Ergänzen Sie die Fragen im *Active grammar*-Kasten unten mit diesen Wörtern:

> number   your   name   phone

Active grammar

What		your ____?
	's	____ address?
	(is)	your ____ number?
		your mobile phone ____?

b Ordnen Sie die Fragen im Kasten diesen Bildern zu.

? — Gloria Reed.

My mobile number is 0719 482 388.

?

12 Kenton Road, Manchester.

?

It's 01232 499 8211.

?

siehe Suchen und finden, Seite 27

5 **a** Schreiben Sie Fragen aus dem Kasten zu diesen Antworten.

1 A: *What's your phone number?*
   B: It's 0441 85263.

2 A: _____
   B: Finkenweg 3a.

3 A: _____
   B: My mobile number is 0170 8910104

4 A: _____
   B: Stephanie Baumann.

b Partnerarbeit: Lesen Sie die Dialoge in Üb. 5a mit verteilten Rollen.

Speaking

6 **a** Lesen Sie den *How to*-Kasten und ergänzen Sie den Dialog.

HOW TO ...

ask for spelling

A: *What's your name?*

B: *Julian Carax.*

A: *How do you _____ that, please?*

B: *C – A – R – A –X*

b **2.10** Hören Sie zu und schreiben Sie die genannten Namen und Adressen auf.

1 Simon _____

2 82, _____ _____, Rome

c Partnerarbeit: Fragen Sie einander nach Namen und Adresse.

7 **a** Wählen Sie *eine* Person unten aus, deren Rolle Sie übernehmen möchten. Lesen Sie die entsprechenden Informationen.

b Rollenspiel: Stellen Sie sich einander vor und tauschen Sie Informationen aus.

Name: Vittoria ____
Age: _____
From: _____
Address:_____
_____
Phone Nº: _____
Mobile Nº: _____

siehe Seite 128

Name: Hans _____
Age: _____
From: _____
Address:_____
Phone Nº: _____
Mobile Nº: _____

siehe Seite 130

Name: Sanjay _____
Age: _____
From: _____
Address:_____
_____
Phone Nº: _____
Mobile Nº: _____

siehe Seite 133

Name: Terri _____
Age: _____
From: _____
Address:_____
_____
Phone Nº: _____
Mobile Nº: _____

siehe Seite 127

A: *Hello. What's your name?*

B: *I'm Hans Mello.*

A: *How do you spell that, please?*

Reading and listening

1   **a**   Lesen Sie die Kurzprofile. Woher kommen die Leute?

> Canada   Japan   Germany

```
○○○                                                    ⬡
◀  ▶  ⟳  ✖  🏠  [ http://www.emailfriends.net ]          ○  (          )
```

e-mail Friends

Email address [   ]   [Sign in]
Password   [   ]

REGISTER HERE!

Friends Search

[ENTER FIRST NAME HERE]
[ENTER SURNAME HERE]
SEARCH [   ]

- School friends
- College friends
- University friends
- Work friends
- Team friends
- Neighbours

RESULTS

a) I'm Frieda _____ . I'm from Munich. I'm 52 years old.
I'm a _____ .
_____@teachernet.de

b) Hello. My name's _____ Mackintosh. I'm 34 years old.
I'm an _____ . I'm from Toronto.
_____@mackintosh.com

c) My name's _____ Nakamura. I'm from Kyoto. I'm 18.
I'm a _____ .
_____@jmail.jp

b   **2.11**   Hören Sie zu und vervollständigen Sie die Angaben zu jeder Person.

2   **a**   Lesen Sie den *How to*-Kasten. Wie spricht man die E-Mail-Adressen in den Kurzprofilen aus?

HOW TO …

say email addresses
john.smith@email.com

'john **dot** smith **at** email **dot** com'

b   Tauschen Sie E-Mail-Adressen mit einem Partner aus.

A: *What's your email address?*

B: *It's henrique99@vista.co.uk*

A: *How do you spell that?*

B: *Henrique: H – E – N …*

3   Schließen Sie das Buch und sprechen Sie über die drei Personen oben.

She's Guida Lang. She's a teacher. She's …

Vocabulary | *a/an* + jobs

4 a Ordnen Sie jedem Beruf ein Bild zu.

accountant actor engineer teacher
artist student manager sales assistant
police officer doctor

b [2.12] Hören Sie zu und überprüfen Sie Ihre Antworten. Unterstreichen Sie die betonten Silben.

1 *doctor*

c Partnerarbeit: Zeigen Sie auf ein Bild. Ihr Partner nennt den Beruf. Wechseln Sie sich ab!

A: *Picture 4.*   **B:** *Student.*

d Finden Sie weitere Berufe mit Hilfe Ihres Wörterbuches.

5 a [2.13] Hören Sie zu und ergänzen Sie.

1 He's _____ .   3 He's _____ .
2 She's an _____ .   4 She's _____ .

b Schreiben Sie die Berufe aus Üb. 4a in die richtige Spalte.

a	an
	accountant

c Partnerarbeit: Sprechen Sie über die Berufe von Freunden und Verwandten.

My sister's a teacher.

Grammar | *his/her*

6 a Ergänzen Sie den Kasten mit *his*, *he's*, *her* oder *she's*.

Active grammar

What's his name?
_____ *name's Tom.*
What's _____ job?
_____ *an accountant.*

What's _____ name?
_____ *name's Maria.*
What's _____ job?
_____ *a student.*

b Vervollständigen Sie die Sätze mit *his/her*.

A: What's *her* name?

B: _____ name's Rachel.

A: What's _____ email address?

B: _____ email address is ricky@starmail.com.

c Ergänzen Sie hier mit *his*, *he's*, *her* oder *she's*.

A: What's *his* name?

B: _____ name's Martin.

A: Where's _____ from?

B: _____ from the UK.

A: Who's she?

B: _____ Lucy Lane.

A: What's _____ job?

B: _____ an actor.

siehe Suchen und finden, Seite 27

Speaking

7 Partnerarbeit:

Partner A: Schlagen Sie Seite 127 auf.

Partner B: Schlagen Sie Seite 129 auf.

Stellen Sie sich abwechselnd Fragen zu diesen Personen. Ihr Partner gibt Ihnen die fehlenden Informationen.

Writing

8 a Erstellen Sie Ihr persönliches Kurzprofil für emailfriends.net.

b Tauschen Sie Ihr Kurzprofil mit Ihrem Partner aus. Berichten Sie anschließend der Gruppe über Ihren Partner.

His name's Sebastian. He's from ...

My favourite singer is ...

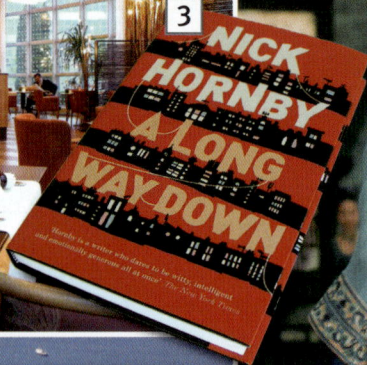

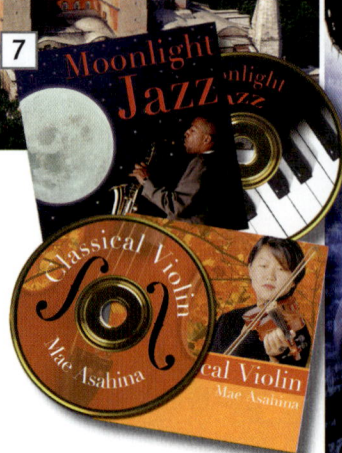

1 **a** Ordnen Sie diese Wörter den Bildern zu.

> singer   CD   city   actor   film   website
> book   restaurant

b Partnerarbeit: Decken Sie die Wörter im Kasten ab und sprechen Sie über die Bilder.

A: *What's number 2?*

B: *It's a restaurant. What's number 4?*

A: *She's an actor.*

2 **a** Finden Sie für jedes Wort drei weitere Beispiele.

Actor: *Al Pacino, Salma Hayek ...*

b Testen Sie Ihren Partner.

A: *Who's Salma Hayek?*

B: *She's an actor.*

A: *What's Toronto?*

B: *It's a city.*

3 Schreiben Sie Fragen.

What's Who's	your favourite	restaurant? website? actor? CD? city? singer? film? book?

c Partnerarbeit: Stellen Sie sich abwechselnd Fragen. Verwenden Sie *great*, *good*, *ok*, *bad* oder *awful* in Ihren Antworten.

A: *Who's your favourite singer?*

B: *Dido. She's great.*

A: *Dido? She's ok.*

4 **a** Stellen Sie Ihre Fragen drei anderen Kursteilnehmern. Schreiben Sie die Antworten in die Tabelle.

	1 _____	2 _____	3 _____
city			
restaurant			
singer			
film			
book			
CD			
actor			

b Berichten Sie Ihrem Partner, was Sie herausgefunden haben.

Number 1 is Ruth. Her favourite actor is ...

2 Suchen und finden

Questions
Fragen

Who fragt nach Personen.

Who is he?

Who is your best friend?

What fragt nach Dingen/Ideen.

What is Rachel's surname?/your email address?

What is 'Angestellte' in English?

What is your job?

Die vollständige Form *who is/what is* schreibt man.

Who's und *what's* sind Kurzformen. So spricht man Englisch.

Who's she? She's my boss.

Questions with *How ...?*
Fragen mit *How ...?*

How do you spell that?

How old are you?

How old is he/she?

Possessive pronouns: *my, your, his, her*
Die Possessivpronomen

Possessivpronomen (besitzanzeigende Fürwörter) zeigen an, wem etwas gehört.

Pronoun	Possessive pronoun
I am Robert.	*My name is Robert.*
You are 32.	*Your sister is 21.*
He is a singer.	*His brother is an actor.*
She is great.	*Her CD is great.*
It is in Europe.	*Its capital is Prague.*

a/an

a und *an* sind unbestimmte Artikel (ein, eine).

Chez Bruce is a restaurant.

The Sorbonne is a university.

She is an architect.

A steht vor gesprochenem Konsonanten.

An steht vor gesprochenem Vokal.

! *a university:* Man **schreibt** *u* (Vokal), aber man **spricht** /j/ (Konsonant).

Tipp

Berufsbezeichnungen stehen im Englischen immer mit dem unbestimmten Artikel!

Ich bin Architekt(in). = I am an architect.

Er/Sie ist Lehrer(in). = He/She is a teacher.

Die Berufsbezeichnung für Männer und Frauen ist gleich.

Numbers 10–99
Die Zahlen 10–99

				10
				ten
11	12	13	14	15
eleven	twelve	thirteen	fourteen	fifteen
16	17	18	19	20
sixteen	seventeen	eighteen	nineteen	twenty

20	21
twenty	twenty-one
30	37
thirty	thirty-seven
40	44
forty	forty-four
50	58
fifty	fifty-eight
60	65
sixty	sixty-five
70	76
seventy	seventy-six
80	82
eighty	eighty-two
90	99
ninety	ninety-nine

Vocabulary | My life

1   Schreiben Sie diese Wörter in das Rätsel. Wie heißt das Lösungswort?

9 Park Road
London
NW14 9IU

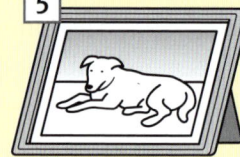

Tom Green

Numbers | 10–99

2   Ergänzen Sie jeweils mit den folgenden Zahlen.

1   two   four   eight   sixteen   *thirty-two*   *sixty-four*

2   eleven   twenty-two   thirty-three   forty-four   _____   _____

3   ninety   eighty   seventy   sixty   _____   _____

4   nineteen   eighteen   seventeen   sixteen   _____   _____

5   forty-nine   fifty-six   sixty-three   seventy   _____   _____

6   twenty-seven   thirty-six   forty-five   _____   _____

7   sixteen   twenty-five   thirty-six   forty-nine   _____   _____

Grammar | Who ...?; my

3   Sehen Sie sich den Familienstammbaum an und ergänzen Sie die Sätze.

1   Dieter: *Julia's my* daughter.
2   Konrad: _____ mother.
3   Julia: _____ brother.
4   Adele: _____ son.
5   Julia: _____ father.
6   Dieter: _____ wife.
7   Konrad: _____ sister.
8   Adele: _____ husband.

Dieter   Adele

Julia

Konrad

4   Schreiben Sie Fragen zu jeder Antwort in Üb. 3.

1   *Who's Julia*?
2   _____ ?
3   _____ ?
4   _____ ?
5   _____ ?
6   _____ ?
7   _____ ?
8   _____ ?

Pronunciation |

/s/ and /z/

5   Schreiben Sie /s/ oder /z/ neben jedes 's.

This is my family.
1   Vladik's my brother.
2   He's twenty.
3   Elga's my sister.
4   She's twenty-five.
5   Zack's my best friend.
6   Pavlov's my father.
7   Ivana's my mother.

Vocabulary | *Great, good, ok, bad, awful*

1 Ordnen Sie jedem Symbol ein Wort aus dem Kasten zu.

> bad   great   ~~good~~   awful   ok

1 ☺   *good*

2 ☹☹   _____

3 ☺☺   _____

4 😐   _____

5 ☹   _____

2 Beschreiben Sie die einzelnen Sänger.

1   *She's good.*

2   _____ .

3   _____ .

4   _____ .

5   _____ .

Grammar | *What's your ...?*

3 Bringen Sie die Wörter in die richtige Reihenfolge.

1   address   your   What's
What's your address?

2   phone   What's   number   your
_____ ?

3   number   your   mobile   phone   What's
_____ ?

4   are   How   you   old
_____ ?

5   you   Where   from   are
_____ ?

6   spell   How   please   that,   you   do
_____ ?

4 Vervollständigen Sie den Dialog mit Fragen aus Üb. 3.

A: (1) What's your name?
Joachim: Joachim Schmidt.
A: (2) _____ ?
Joachim: Schmidt: S – C – H – M – I – D – T.
A: (3) _____ ?
Joachim: I'm 22.
A: (4) _____ ?
Joachim: Erftstadt in Germany.
A: (5) _____ ?
Joachim: Kölner Straße, 110, 50374 Erftstadt.
A: (6) _____ ?
Joachim: 00 49 2235 973382
A: (7) _____ ?
Joachim: My mobile number is 0173 3428079.
A: Thank you Mr Schmidt.

Writing

5 Schreiben Sie die SMS aus.

R U from Germany?

My mob no is 07060 987885. Pls phone!

How old R U?

1   *Are you from Germany?*

2   _____

3   _____

What's yr name?

It's gr8!

4   _____

5   _____

Vocabulary | Jobs

1 Können Sie dieses Kreuzworträtsel lösen?

SENKRECHT

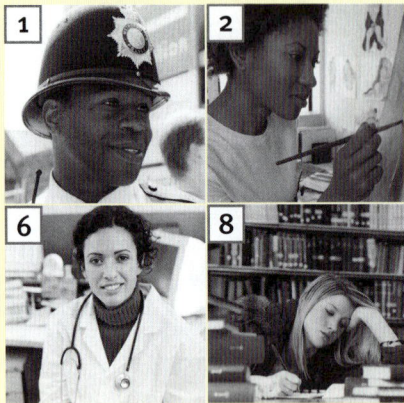

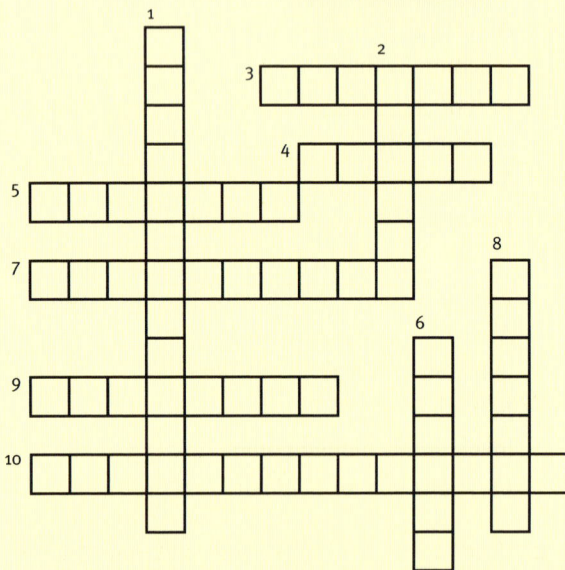

WAAGERECHT

a/an

2 Schreiben Sie Sätze zu jedem Bild in Üb. 1. Verwenden Sie *a/an*.

1 *He's a police officer.*   6 _____ .
2 _____ .   7 _____ .
3 _____ .   8 _____ .
4 _____ .   9 _____ .
5 _____ .   10 _____ .

Information

3 Ordnen Sie jedem Wort 1–6 ein Beispiel zu.

1	name	a) julia.mann@mail.net
2	job	b) Julia Mann
3	address	c) engineer
4	age	d) 023 896537
5	email address	e) 34
6	phone number	f) 12 King Street, London

Grammar | *his/her*

4 Welches Wort ist hier richtig?

This is Michael Douglas. (1) *He's/His* an actor. (2) *He's/His* from the US. (3) *He's/His* sixty-two years old. (4) *He's/His* wife is Catherine Zeta Jones. (5) *She's/Her* thirty-seven years old. (6) *She's/Her* an actor, too.

This is Michelle Douglas. (7) *She's/Her* a sales assistant. (8) *She's/Her* from the UK. (9) *She's/Her* twenty-six years old. (10) *She's/Her* husband is David Douglas. (11) *He's/His* twenty-seven years old. (12) *He's/His* a doctor.

5 Ergänzen Sie die Fragen und Antworten.

A: What's (1) *his* name?
B: (2) _____ name's Kemal Atlan.
A: Where's (3) _____ from?
B: (4) _____ from Turkey.
A: How old is (5) _____ ?
B: (6) _____ fifty-five.
A: What's (7) _____ job?
B: (8) _____ a manager.
A: What's (9) _____ email address?
B: (10) _____ kemal@freemail.com

A: What's (11) _____ name?
B: (12) _____ name's Alva Braun.
A: Where's (13) _____ from?
B: (14) _____ from Vienna in Austria.
A: How old is (15) _____ ?
B: (16) _____ forty years old.
A: What's (17) _____ job?
B: (18) _____ an engineer.
A: What's (19) _____ mobile phone number.
B: (20) _____ 07932 787221

3 Travel

Lead-in

1 **a** Ordnen Sie jedem Wort ein Bild zu.

> a castle   a cathedral   a palace   a museum

b Schlagen Sie die Bedeutung dieser Wörter nach und zeichnen Sie dann zu jedem Wort eine kleine Skizze.

> a gallery   a department store   a market   a mountain   a lake

c `3.1` Hören Sie sich die Wörter oben an und sprechen Sie nach. Unterstreichen Sie die betonten Silben.

a castle

2 **a** Ergänzen Sie diese Touristenziele mit den Wörtern oben.

1 Dracula's _____ in Romania
2 The Hermitage _____ in Russia
3 Buckingham _____ in the UK
4 Otavalo _____ in Ecuador
5 Macy's _____ in the US
6 Sugar Loaf _____ in Brazil
7 _____ Titicaca in Bolivia
8 The Uffizi _____ in Italy

b Welche anderen Touristenziele kennen Sie?

The Prado Gallery in Madrid.

3 Diskutieren Sie mit einem Partner.

What's your favourite tourist attraction in this country?/in this city?/in the world?

Grammar	the verb *be* with *we* and *they*; *our* and *their*
Can do	write a simple holiday email

Start
Birmingham

Day 3
Berlin

Day 1
Bruges

Day 2
Bonn

Day 4
Prague

Day 6
Bratislava

Day 5
Vienna

Day 7
Budapest

Day 8
Timisorara

Day 9
Bucharest

Day 10
Sofia

Day 11-12
Istanbul

Coach Holidays

West to East Tour

Vocabulary | adjectives

1 a Ordnen Sie die Städte auf der Karte diesen Fotos zu.

b Welches Adjektiv ist hier richtig?

1
Maiden's Tower
is *big*/*small*.

4
The Burgtheatre
is *old*/*modern*.

2
Willy Brandt House
is *old*/*modern*.

5
Charles Bridge
is *beautiful*/*ugly*.

3
The House of the
People is *big*/*small*.

6
Spaghetti Junction
is *beautiful*/*ugly*.

c Decken Sie die Sätze oben ab. Was können Sie über die Fotos sagen?

Maiden's Tower in Istanbul is small.

2 a Schreiben Sie einige Sätze zu drei interessanten Touristenzielen Ihrer Wahl.

The Guggenheim Museum in Bilbao is beautiful.

b Lesen Sie Ihrem Partner Ihre Sätze vor.

Reading

3 a Rebecca und Steven machen eine Busreise 'West to East'. Lesen Sie die E-Mail. Wen zeigt das Foto?

From: rebeccaclark55@gmail.com
To: tomandsusan.clark@yahoo.co.uk
Subject: We're in Istanbul!

Hi Mum and Dad
How are you? Steven and I are fine. **We're** in Istanbul in The Pera Palace Hotel. It's great! Istanbul is big.
Magda and Zarek are in the Pera Palace Hotel too. **They** are **our** friends. **They're** from Poland.
The attachment is a photo of Magda and Zarek. They are in **their** car. It's a Mercedes.
It's beautiful!
Love Rebecca

b Wahr (W) oder falsch (F)?

1 Steven and Rebecca are in Istanbul. [W]
2 The Pera Palace Hotel is OK. [ ]
3 Istanbul is small. [ ]
4 Magda and Zarek are from Turkey. [ ]
5 The Mercedes is beautiful. [ ]

c Unterstreichen Sie alle Adjektive in der E-Mail.

d Was bedeuten die fett gedruckten Wörter?

Grammar 1 | *be* with *we* and *they*

4 **a** Sehen Sie sich den Kasten an. Was fehlt hier?

Active grammar

⊕ I	'm (am)	forty-one.
⊕ You	're (are)	my friend.
⊕ He		my father.
⊕ She	's (is)	my mother.
⊕ It		a gallery.
⊕ We	____ (__)	in Istanbul.
⊕ They	____ (__)	from Turkey.

b Ergänzen Sie diese Sätze. Benutzen Sie dabei die Kurzform.

1 They*'re* from Moscow.
2 You____ from Germany.
3 We____ in Buenos Aires.
4 It____ modern.
5 She____ my daughter.
6 I____ in the photo.
7 They____ in the gallery.
8 He____ great.

siehe Suchen und finden, Seite 39

Grammar 2 | *our* and *their*

5 **a** Vervollständigen Sie den Kasten.

Active grammar

I	She is **my** friend.
You	**Your** house is modern.
He	Rachel is **his** wife.
She	**Her** mother is great.
It	**It's** capital is Madrid.
We	Andrea is _____ friend.
They	_____ daughter is in the car.

b Ergänzen Sie die Sätze mit *our* oder *their*.

Ben and Rebecca Morris   Zarek and Magda Adamski

1 **Magda:** *Their* surname is Morris.
2 **Zarek:** _____ suitcase is modern.
3 **Rebecca:** _____ car is beautiful.
4 **Magda:** _____ backpack is old.
5 **Zarek:** _____ friends and family are in Poland.
6 **Ben:** _____ friends and family are in the UK.

siehe Suchen und finden, Seite 39

6 Welches Wort ist richtig?

1 Are they *we're*/*our* books?
2 *They're*/*Their* beautiful.
3 *We're*/*Our* in Berlin.
4 *We're*/*Our* students.
5 Are they *they're*/*their* maps?
6 *They're*/*Their* from Romania.
7 Where are *we're*/*our* suitcases?
8 *They're*/*Their* in the photo.

Pronunciation

7 **a** [3.2] Hören Sie zu und schreiben Sie die Sätze. Benutzen Sie *they're* oder *their*.

b Sprechen Sie die Sätze nach.

Writing

8 **a** Sie und Ihr Partner sind im Urlaub. Wählen Sie ein Reiseziel auf der Karte auf Seite 32 und ergänzen Sie diese Informationen.

1 My partner is _____ . (name)
2 We are in _____ . (place) It is _____ . (adjective)
3 Our friends are _____ and _____ . (names)
4 Our hotel is _____ . (name) It is _____ . (adjective)

b Schlagen Sie nach unter *Texte verfassen* auf Seite 134. Wie schreibt man E-Mails?

| Grammar | negative of *be*; plural nouns |
| Can do | say what's in your suitcase |

Vocabulary | holiday things

1 **a** Ordnen Sie die Wörter aus dem Kasten den Zahlen in den Bildern zu.

> camera   book   skirt   pair of shoes   suitcase   pair of trousers
> MP3 player   top   map   backpack

b **3.3** Hören Sie zu und überprüfen Sie Ihre Antworten. Unterstreichen Sie die betonten Silben.

a suitcase

c Hören Sie noch einmal zu. Sprechen Sie nach.

Listening

2 **a** Lesen Sie den *How to*-Kasten.

HOW TO …

make regular plurals

| one suitcase | : | two suitcases |
| one MP3 player | : | three MP3 players |

b **3.4** Hören Sie zu. Was befindet sich in den Koffern? Ergänzen Sie die Listen.

Dialogue 1: a camera, two books

Dialogue 2: a backpack

Dialogue 3: a pair of trousers

c Hören Sie noch einmal zu und überprüfen Sie Ihre Antworten.

3 Partnerarbeit: Decken Sie einen der Koffer ab. Wissen Sie noch, was sich darin befindet?

Pronunciation

4 **a** **3.5** Hören Sie zu. Wie spricht man das *-s* aus: /s/, /z/ oder /ɪz/?

a   two suitcases

b   five maps

c   seven tops

d   three cameras

e   two pairs of shoes

f   four books

g   eight pairs of trousers

h   six skirts

b Hören Sie noch einmal zu. Sprechen Sie nach.

Lifelong learning

Der Schein trügt

Was (fast) gleich aussieht, klingt nicht gleich. Notieren Sie Betonung und Aussprache.

Japan, camera, address

/ə peər əv ʃuːz/

a pair of shoes = ein Paar Schuhe

Speaking

5 a Partnerarbeit: Beschreiben Sie den Inhalt eines Koffers aus Üb. 2. Kann Ihr Partner erraten, welchen Koffer Sie meinen?

A: *What's in the suitcase?*

B: *Two skirts, a pair of shoes, three books ...*

b Was packen Sie ein, wenn Sie verreisen? Berichten Sie Ihrem Partner.

Listening

6 a `3.6` Hören Sie zu und beantworten Sie diese beiden Fragen.

1 What is the woman's name?

2 What is in her suitcase?

b Hören Sie noch einmal zu und ergänzen Sie mit den genauen Worten.

Jane: _____ _____ Miss Miles.

Jane: _____ _____ a camera.

Jane: _____ _____ books.

Grammar | the verb *be*; negative

7 Vervollständigen Sie den Kasten mit *aren't* oder *isn't*.

Active grammar

–	I	'm not (am not)	Miss Miles.
–	You	're not (are not) _____	in room 324. twenty-one.
–	He	's not (is not)	my brother.
–	She	_____	my sister.
–	It	_____	a camera.
–	We	're not (are not) _____	from the US. students.
–	They	're not (are not) _____	friends. in Istanbul.

siehe Suchen und finden, Seite 39

8 a Wie heißt es hier richtig?

1 You *'m not/*(*'re not*) an actor.

2 I *'re not/'m not* from Brazil.

3 She *'re not/'s not* my sister.

4 It *'m not/'s not* my camera.

5 You *'re not/'s not* in room 232.

6 It *'m not/'s not* my favourite city.

b Ergänzen Sie diese Dialoge mit *'m not, 're not* oder *'s not*.

A: Hello Bob. This is my wife. Two tickets to New York, please.

B: *I'm not* Bob, I'm Bill. You_____ eighteen years old, you're eight. And she_____ your wife, she's your sister.

A: Is this your backpack, Mr Robson?

B: I_____ Mr Robson, I'm Mr Clark. And it_____ my backpack, it's his backpack.

9 a Wahr (W) oder falsch (F)?

	You	Your partner	Your teacher
From this city			
A good singer			
Between 18–25 years old			

b Partnerarbeit: Schreiben Sie Sätze mit Hilfe der Informationen aus Üb. 9a.

We're from this city. Our teacher isn't from this city.

Speaking

10 Partnerarbeit: Wie könnte das Gespräch zwischen Mr Boyle und Mrs Miles aus Üb. 6a weitergehen?

Mr Boyle	Mrs Miles
pair of trousers	skirt
top	pair of trousers
MP3 player	camera

Mr Boyle: *OK, an MP3 player.*

Mrs Miles: *It isn't an MP3 player, it's a camera.*

3.3 Tourist information

Grammar	*Yes/No* questions with *be*
Can do	ask for tourist information

Vocabulary | days of the week

1 a `3.7` Hören Sie zu und sprechen Sie die Wochentage nach.

> Monday   Tuesday   Wednesday   Thursday
> Friday   Saturday   Sunday

b Partnerarbeit: Nennen Sie einen Wochentag. Ihr Partner nennt dann den Folgenden.

A: *Thursday.*   B: *Friday.*

The Whitechapel Art Gallery

The Whitechapel Art Gallery is small and beautiful.
The photos and pictures are great.
It's <u>open</u> from Tuesday to Sunday.
It's <u>closed</u> on Mondays.
It isn't free.

The Whitechapel Art Gallery
80–82 Whitechapel High Street
London, E1 7QX
020 7522 7888

info@whitechapel.org

THE BRITISH MUSEUM

The British Museum is the <u>top</u> tourist attraction in London. (5,000,000 visitors every year!)
It's <u>near</u> Oxford Street.
It's open from Monday to Sunday
It's big and it's free!

The British Museum
Great Russell Street
London WC1B 3DG
020 7323 8299

visitorinformation@thebritishmuseum.ac.uk

HAMPTON COURT PALACE

Hampton Court
Palace
East Molesey
Surrey
KT8 9AU
0870 752 7777

Hampton Court is a beautiful palace.
It's near London, on the River Thames.
It's open from Monday to Sunday.
It isn't <u>free</u>.

info@hrp.org.uk

Reading

2 a Partnerarbeit: Wie spricht man die Adressen, Telefonnummern und E-Mail-Adressen im Text richtig aus?

b Was bedeuten die unterstrichenen Wörter im Text? Schlagen Sie im Wörterbuch nach.

c Lesen Sie die Texte. Wie muss es hier richtig heißen?

1 The British Museum *is/isn't* closed on Sundays.
2 The Whitechapel Art Gallery *is/isn't* big.
3 Hampton Court Palace *is/isn't* open on Sundays.
4 The British Museum *is/isn't* in London.
5 The Whitechapel Art Gallery *is/isn't* open on Mondays.
6 Hampton Court Palace *is/isn't* in London.

Listening

3 a `3.8` Hören Sie zu. Welcher Dialog bezieht sich auf welche Sehenswürdigkeit?

Dialogue 1 _____
Dialogue 2 _____
Dialogue 3 _____

b Lesen Sie den *How to*-Kasten.

> **HOW TO ...**
>
> **use *here* and *there***
>
> It's here.
>
> It's there.
>
> Here's a map.

c Hören Sie noch einmal zu. Kreuzen Sie an, welche Wörter Sie in jedem Dialog hören.

a here   b there   c Here's

4 Ergänzen Sie diesen Dialog mit *here*, *there* oder *here's*.

A: Where's the department store?
B: It's _____.
A: Where's the market?
B: It's _____. _____ a map.

Grammar | questions with *be*

5 a Vervollständigen Sie den Kasten mit *is*, *are* oder *am*.

b Sehen Sie sich den Hörtext 3.8 auf Seite 137 an und unterstreichen Sie alle Fragen mit *be*.

Active grammar

?	___	*I*	*your friend?*	*Yes, you are.* *No, you aren't.*
?	___	*you*	*from Italy?*	*Yes, I am.* *No, I'm not.*
?	___	*he* *she*	*your brother?* *your sister?*	*Yes, he/she/ is.* *No, he/she/ isn't.*
?	___	*we*	*near the lake?*	*Yes, we are.* *No, we aren't.*
?	___	*they*	*in London?*	*Yes, they are.* *No, they aren't.*

siehe Suchen und finden, Seite 39

6 a Ergänzen Sie die Fragen und Antworten.

1 Are you from China?
Yes, I _____ .

2 _____ it a cathedral?
No, it _____ .

3 _____ she your sister?
Yes, she _____ .

4 _____ we near Hampton Court?
Yes, we _____ .

5 Are _____ students?
No, they _____ .

6 _____ the museum closed today?
Yes, it _____ .

7 _____ they from the UK?
No, they _____ .

8 _____ you in room 324?
Yes, I _____ .

b Bilden Sie eine Frage und einen Satz. Benutzen Sie wenn möglich *'s* oder *'re*.

1 open is today it
a *Is it open today?* b *It's open today.*

2 you Germany are from
a _____ ?   b _____ .

3 the UK is from she
a _____ ?   b _____ .

4 a museum it is
a _____ ?   b _____ .

5 is open the shop
a _____ ?   b _____ .

6 you an actor are
a _____ ?   b _____ .

Speaking

7 Partnerarbeit:

Partner A: Schlagen Sie Seite 127 auf. Stellen Sie Fragen über Harrods. Geben Sie Informationen über den Louvre.

Partner B: Schlagen Sie Seite 129 auf. Geben Sie Informationen über Harrods. Stellen Sie Fragen über den Louvre.

See you on Friday

2 **3·9** Lesen und hören Sie das Telefongespräch zwischen Sara und Louis. Können Sie diese Fragen beantworten?

1	Where is Sara?	4	Is Marakesh hot?
2	Is she in Casablanca?	5	Is the hotel nice?
3	Is Marakesh beautiful?	6	Is the food nice?

Louis: Hello.

Sara: Hi, Louis. It's Sara.

Louis: Hi, Sara. How are you and Paul?

Sara: We're fine, thanks. And you?

Louis: Fine, thanks. Where are you?

Sara: We're in Morocco.

Louis: Are you in Casablanca?

Sara: No, we aren't. We're in Marakesh.

Louis: Is it beautiful?

Sara: Yes, it is. It's very beautiful.

Louis: Is it hot?

Sara: Yes, it is. It's very hot.

Louis: Is your hotel nice?

Sara: No, it isn't. It's very small and very old.

Louis: Oh dear! Is the food nice?

Sara: Yes, it's very nice. Are Mum and Dad OK?

Louis: Yes, they are. They're fine.

Sara: OK, see you on Friday.

Louis: See you on Friday. Bye.

Sara: Bye.

1 **a** Was bedeuten die Wörter im Kasten? Schlagen Sie im Wörterbuch nach.

> skirt   small   suitcase   book   food   old
> bad   beautiful   ugly   hot   cold   backpack
> good   nice   camera   modern   big   map
> awful   great   new   fine

b Tragen Sie die Wörter in die richtige Spalte ein.

Nouns	Adjectives
skirt	small

c Bezieht sich *very* auf Nomen oder Adjektive?

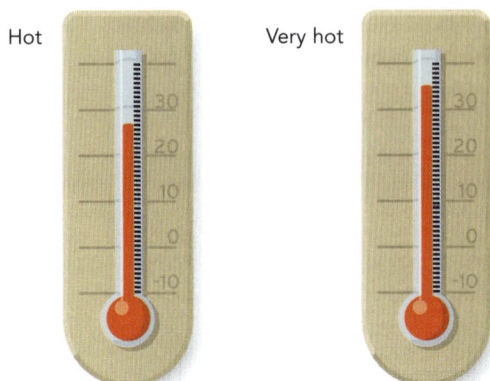

Hot

Very hot

3 **a** Partnerarbeit: Lesen Sie das Telefongespräch mit verteilten Rollen.

b Führen Sie das Telefongespräch noch einmal mit einem anderen Partner. Lesen Sie diesmal nicht den Text, sondern benutzen Sie nur die Wörter im Kasten als Hilfe.

Louis	Sara
Hello.	It's ...
How ...?	Fine ... you?
Where ...?	Morocco
Casablanca?	Marakesh
beautiful?	Yes
hot?	Yes
hotel nice?	No
food nice?	Yes. Mum and Dad?
fine	Friday
Friday. Bye	Bye

4 Schreiben Sie einen Dialog. Benutzen Sie andere Namen, Orte und Adjektive als in Üb. 2.

Esther: *Hello.*

Flavia: *Hi, Esther. It's Flavia.*

The verb *to be* | (ich bin, du bist ...)

+

I	'm (am)	
You	're (are)	
He She It	's (is)	in Istanbul. from Turkey.
We	're (are)	
They	're (are)	

−

I	'm not (am not)	Miss Miles.
You	're not (are not) aren't	in room 324. twenty-one.
He She It	's not (is not) isn't	my brother. my sister. a camera.
We	're not (are not) aren't	from the US. students.
They	're not (are not) aren't	friends. in Istanbul.

?

Am	I	your friend?	Yes, you are. No, you aren't.
Are	you	from Italy?	Yes, I am. No, I'm not.
Is	he	your brother?	
	she	your sister?	Yes, he/she/it is.
	it	open?	No, he/she/it isn't.
Are	we	near the lake?	Yes, we are. No, we aren't.
Are	they	in London?	Yes, they are. No, they aren't.

Denken Sie daran: Vollständige Formen **schreibt** man, Kurzformen **spricht** man.

In der Verneinung gibt es zwei Kurzformen für *is not* (*isn't/'s not*) und *are not* (*aren't/'re not*).

> **Tipp**
> Einfach nur *Yes* oder *No* zu antworten ist sehr unhöflich. Verwenden Sie immer die Kurzantworten, z.B. *Yes, I am.*

Betonung im Satz

Das Verb *to be* wird in der Regel nicht betont.

Are you a <u>student</u>? – No, I'm <u>not</u>.

I'm not a <u>student</u>. I'm a <u>teacher</u>.

Vocabulary: adjectives
Eigenschaftswörter

Dies sind Eigenschaftswörter (Adjektive):

> old   modern   big   small   beautiful   ugly
> great   good   OK   bad   awful   open   closed
> near   free   hot   cold   new

Adjektive beschreiben Nomen. Adjektiv und Nomen können durch eine Form von *to be* verbunden werden:

The department store is closed.

My coffee is cold.

Oder das Adjektiv steht vor dem Nomen:

She's a good teacher.

! *It's a pair of shoes.*

a pair of shoes = ein Paar Schuhe.

Vocabulary: days of the week
Die Wochentage

on Monday, Tuesday, Wednesday, Thursday, Friday, Saturday, Sunday

am Montag = on Monday

am Wochenende = at the weekend

Vocabulary | tourist attractions

1 In diesem Rätsel sind acht Touristenattraktionen versteckt. Welche sind es?

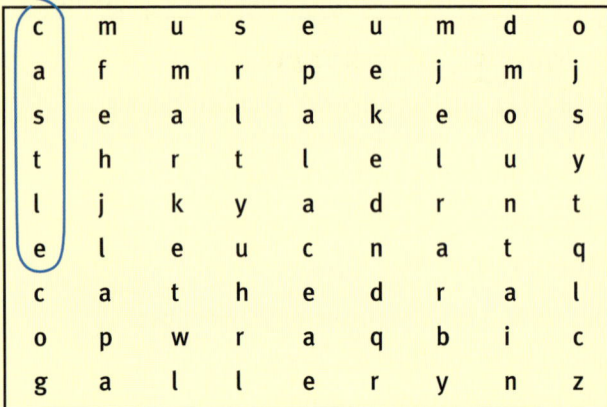

c	m	u	s	e	u	m	d	o
a	f	m	r	p	e	j	m	j
s	e	a	l	a	k	e	o	s
t	h	r	t	l	e	l	u	y
l	j	k	y	a	d	r	n	t
e	l	e	u	c	n	a	t	q
c	a	t	h	e	d	r	a	l
o	p	w	r	a	q	b	i	c
g	a	l	l	e	r	y	n	z

1 *castle*   5 ma_____
2 mo_____   6 g_____
3 c_____   7 p_____
4 mu_____   8 l_____

Vocabulary | adjectives

2 Ordnen Sie die Fotos den Beschreibungen zu.

A
B
C
D
E
F

1 *E* is big and old.
2 _____ is small and modern.
3 _____ is small and beautiful.
4 _____ is big and ugly.
5 _____ is big and modern.
6 _____ is old and beautiful.

Grammar | the verb be with we and they; our and their

3 a Ergänzen Sie den Text mit *we're, they're, our* oder *their*.

From: rebeccaclark55@gmail.com
To: tomandsusan.clark@yahoo.co.uk
Subject: We're in Istanbul!

Hi Mum and Dad
How are you? Sarah and I are fine. (1) *We're* in Recife in Brazil. (2) _____ hotel is great. (3) _____ in room 1111!
Belinda and Cipriano are in Recife too. (4) _____ from Sãu Paolo. They're (5) _____ friends.
The attached is a photo of Belinda, Cipriano and Carlita in (6) _____ house in Sãu Paolo. It's big! Carlita is (7) _____ daughter. She's beautiful.
Love
Roman

b Ergänzen Sie die Sätze mit *we're, they're, our* oder *their*.

Jones 42   Watson 38

1 **Henry Watson:** *Their* car is old. _____ car is modern.
2 **Paul Jones:** _____ family is big. _____ family is small.
3 **Georgia Watson:** _____ surname is Jones. _____ surname is Watson.
4 **Katie Jones:** _____ forty-two. _____ thirty-eight.

Vocabulary | possessions

1 Vervollständigen Sie die Wörter und ordnen Sie sie den Bildern zu.

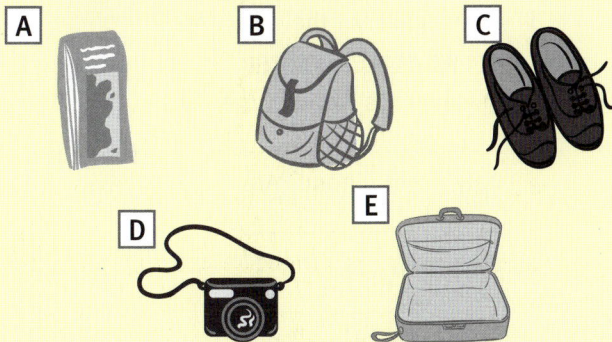

A

B

C

D

E

Words	Photo
1 a *c a m e r a*	*D*
2 a t _ _	_
3 a b _ _ _ _ _ c _	_
4 a _ _ _ _ of _ r _ _ _ _ _ s	_
5 a _ o o _	_
6 a s _ _ r _	_
7 a _ _ _ _ of s _ _ _ _	_
8 a _ u _ t _ _ _ e	_
9 a m _ _	_
10 an _ _ 3 p _ _ _ _ _	_

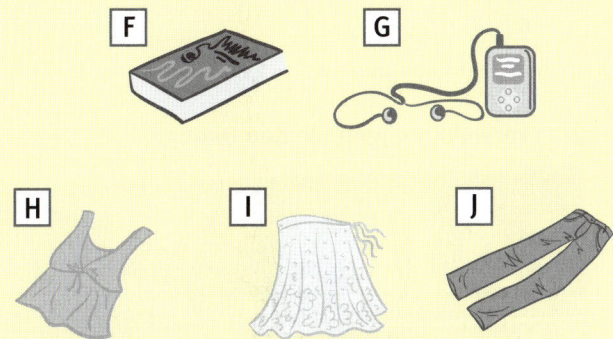

F

G

H

I

J

Grammar | the verb *be* negative

2 a Ergänzen Sie diese verneinten Sätze mit einem Wort aus dem Kasten.

> aren't not isn't 's ~~'m~~ 're You I She

1 I*'m* not Miss Carter, I'm Ms Carter.
2 It_____ not open today.
3 You're _____ a good singer.
4 _____'s not from the UK.
5 You _____ twenty-one, you're twenty-three.
6 _____'m not from Germany.
7 You_____ not my friend.
8 She _____ my sister.
9 _____ aren't in room 324. You're in room 325.

b Korrigieren Sie diese Sätze.

1 A: I'm a teacher. (student)
   B: You're not a teacher. You're a student.
2 A: It's a skirt. (pair of trousers)
   B: _____ . _____ .
3 A: We're from the US. (the UK)
   B: _____ . _____ .
4 A: Vienna is my favourite country. (city)
   B: _____ . _____ .
5 A: He's my sister. (brother)
   B: _____ . _____ .
6 A: I'm fifteen. (fifty)
   B: _____ . _____ .
7 A: They're open today. (closed)
   B: _____ . _____ .
8 A: She's an accountant. (engineer)
   B: _____ . _____ .

How to make regular plurals

3 a Was sehen Sie auf diesem Bild?

a two CDs.   f _____
b _____   g _____
c _____   h _____
d _____   i _____
e _____   j _____

b Schreiben Sie /s/, /z/ or /ɪz/ neben jedes Wort im Plural in Üb. 3a.

Vocabulary | days of the week

1 Vervollständigen Sie die Wochentage. Bringen Sie sie dann in die richtige Reihenfolge.

W _ _ n _ _ day
Th_ _ _ day
F _ _ day
M _ _ day
S_ t _ _ day
T_ _ _ day
S _ _ day

How to | use *here* and *there*

2 Wählen Sie die richtige Aussage zu jedem Bild.

  a The cathedral is here.
  b The cathedral is there.

  a Here's your mobile phone.
  b There's your mobile phone.

  a Here's the gallery.
  b There's the gallery.

  a Here are your shoes.
  b There are your shoes.

Grammar | questions with be

3 **a** Bilden Sie Fragen, indem Sie die Wörter in die richtige Reihenfolge bringen.

  1 near gallery the we Are
    Are we near the gallery?

  2 museum Is open the
    _____ ?

  3 Italy they from Are
    _____ ?

  4 she your Is friend
    _____ ?

  5 here the near lake Is
    _____ ?

  6 department stores Are today open the
    _____ ?

  7 we Are York Hotel in the
    _____ ?

 b Schreiben Sie Antworten zu jeder Frage in Üb. 3a.

  1 (✓) *Yes, we are.*
  2 (✗) *No, it isn't.*
  3 (✓) _____ .
  4 (✗) _____ .
  5 (✓) _____ .
  6 (✗) _____ .
  7 (✓) _____ .

4 Vervollständigen Sie den Dialog.

What:	a gallery
Open:	Monday–Sunday
Where:	London
Free:	Yes

A: Good morning. Can I help you?
B: (1) Yes. Is the Tate Modern _____ today?
A: (2) _____ , _____ _____ .
B: (3) Good. _____ _____ a museum?
A: (4) _____ , _____ _____ . It's a gallery.
B: (5) _____ _____ free?
A: (6) _____ , _____ _____ .
B: (7) _____ _____ near here?
A: (8) Yes, _____ _____ . Here's a map. We're here and the Tate Modern is there.
B: Great. Thank you. Goodbye.
A: Goodbye.

4 | In town

Lead-in

1 **a** Ordnen Sie die Wörter im Kasten den Buchstaben A–N in den Bildern zu.

E F G H I

J K L M N

> chemist   supermarket   café   bookshop   train station
> bus stop   bank   cinema   newsagent   car park   restaurant
> cashpoint   pub   market

b **4.1** Hören Sie zu und überprüfen Sie Ihre Antworten. Unterstreichen Sie die betonten Silben.

a *café*

c Partnerarbeit: Decken Sie die Wörter oben ab. Was sehen Sie auf den Bildern?

2 Partnerarbeit: Fragen Sie: *What's your favourite ...?*

A: *What's your favourite supermarket?*

B: *Quickbuy is my favourite.*

Grammar	*Can I have ...?*
Can do	order food in a café or coffee shop

Vocabulary | food and drink

1 **a** Sehen Sie sich *A Guide to Coffee* an und beschriften Sie diesen Führer mit den Wörtern im Kasten.

A GUIDE TO COFFEE

a _____ b c

d _____

e _____

f _____

g _____

h _____

> a black coffee   a white coffee   a cappuccino
> an iced coffee   an espresso   sugar
> an instant coffee   milk

b 4.2 Hören Sie zu und überprüfen Sie Ihre Antworten. Wo sind diese Zubereitungsarten von Kaffee besonders beliebt?

c Welchen Kaffee trinkt man in Ihrem Land am liebsten?

2 **a** Wie ist Ihr Geschmack? Ergänzen Sie die Sätze mit einem Kaffee Ihrer Wahl (ohne *a/an*).

1 _____ is my favourite.

2 _____ is very nice.

3 _____ is awful.

b Partnerarbeit: Lesen Sie Ihrem Partner Ihre Sätze vor.

Espresso is my favourite ...

3 **a** Sehen Sie sich die Fotos an. Ordnen Sie die Wörter im Kasten den Buchstaben in den Fotos zu.

> an orange juice   a mineral water
> a sandwich   a piece of cake   a salad
> a cup of tea

b 4.3 Hören Sie zu und überprüfen Sie Ihre Antworten. Ordnen Sie jeder Bestellung ein Bild zu.

4 **a** Hören Sie noch einmal zu und ergänzen Sie die Bestellungen unten mit den Wörtern aus dem Kasten.

> chicken   chocolate   large   ham   small

1 a *chicken* salad and

2 a _____ cappuccino, please.

3 a _____ sandwich

4 a _____ orange juice

5 a piece of _____ cake

b Partnerarbeit: Bestellen Sie Speisen und Getränke aus Üb. 1 und 3.

A: *Can I have a black coffee, please?*

B: *Sure. Anything else?*

A: *No, thank you.*

Grammar | *Can I have ...?*

5 **a** Ordnen Sie die Frageteile im Kasten einander richtig zu.

> ### Active grammar
>
> | Can I have a | orange juices, please? |
> |---|---|
> | Can I have an | ham sandwich, please? |
> | Can I have two | iced coffee, please? |
>
> Certainly/Sure. Anything else?
>
> No, thank you./Yes. Can I have?

b Ergänzen Sie die Dialoge mit den Wörtern aus dem *Active grammar*-Kasten.

A: Hello. Can I help you?

B: Yes. (1) _____ iced coffee, please?

A: Certainly. Anything (2) _____ ?

B: Yes. (3) _____ small chicken salad, too?

A: Sure.

C: (4) _____ large cappuccino, please?

A: Certainly. (5) _____ else?

C: No, (6) _____ .

c Lesen Sie den Dialog mit verteilten Rollen.

siehe Suchen und finden, Seite 51

Pronunciation

6 **4.4** Hören Sie zu und sprechen Sie nach.

Can I /kæ – naɪ/

Can I have a /kæ – naɪ – hæ – və/

Can I have a small coffee /kæ – naɪ – hæ – və – smɔːl – kɒ – fi/

Vocabulary | *prices*

7 **a** Lesen Sie die Tabelle.

49p			forty-nine	pence
80c			eighty	cents
£1.50	One	(pound)	fifty	
€1.99	One	(euro)	ninety-nine	
$2.20	Two	(dollars)	twenty	
€5.90	Five	(euros)	ninety	

b **4.5** Hören Sie zu und unterstreichen Sie die richtigen Preise in den Dialogen 1–5.

1 a £1.00 b £1.10 c £1.20
2 a €2.98 b €3.89 c €3.98
3 a $1.19 b $1.90 c $1.99
4 a €4.34 b €3.34 c €4.43
5 a £3.13 b £3.19 c £3.39

c Partnerarbeit: Nennen Sie einen Preis in Üb. 7b. Ihr Partner zeigt auf die richtige Zahl.

Speaking

8 **a** Lesen Sie den *How to*-Kasten. Schließen Sie dann Ihr Buch und schreiben Sie einen Dialog in einem Café.

b Lesen Sie Ihren Dialog im Kurs vor.

> **HOW TO ...**
>
> ### order food in a café
>
> | Assistant | Customer |
> |---|---|
> | 1 *Can I help you?* | 2 *Can I have ____ , please?* |
> | 3 *Sure. Anything else?* | 4 *No, thank you./Yes. Can I have ____ , please?* |
> | 5 *Eat in or take away?* | 6 *Eat in/Take away, please.* |
> | 7 *That's ___ , please.* | |

9 Partnerarbeit: Sehen Sie sich die Speisekarte unten an.
Partner A: Kellner
Partner B: Gast. Bestellen Sie Speisen und Getränke.

Café Culture

Coffee	small	medium	large
Espresso	60c	–	90c
Black coffee	75c	€1.00	€1.25
White coffee	80c	€1.05	€1.30
Cappuccino	90c	€1.15	€1.40
Iced coffee	–	€1.50	€2.05
Drink			
Mineral water	79c	99c	€1.19
Orange juice	€1.09	€1.45	€1.99
Food			
Green salad	€1.99		
Chicken salad	€2.89		
Ham salad	€2.65		
Chicken sandwich	€2.05		
Ham sandwich	€1.95		

| Grammar | this, that, these, those |
| Can do | ask for and understand prices |

Reading

1 a Partnerarbeit: Schreiben Sie eine Liste mit Märkten in Ihrem Land/Ihrer Stadt.

b Lesen Sie den Text und ordnen Sie diese Fragen den Abschnitten 1–6 zu.

> Is it free?   Where is the market?
> When is it open?   Is it big?   What is it?
> What is on sale in the market?

Portobello Market

1. _____
It's in Notting Hill. Notting Hill is in west London.

2. _____
It's an antiques market.

3. _____
Yes, it is. It's very big. It's two kilometers from end to end. It's a market for Londoners and tourists.

4. _____
It's not open on weekdays. It's only open on Sundays.

5. _____
Yes, it is.

6. _____
Modern things, old things, beautiful things, ugly things … Antiques, old clothes and food are popular.

c Sind diese Sätze wahr (W) oder falsch (F)?

1 Portobello Market is in Notting Hill. ☒ W
2 It's not small. ☐
3 It's open on Fridays. ☐
4 Food is on sale in the market. ☐

2 a Wählen Sie einen bekannten Markt oder ein Geschäft aus und beantworten Sie dazu schriftlich die Fragen der Üb. 1b. Benutzen Sie ein Wörterbuch.

b Partnerarbeit: Berichten Sie über Ihren Markt/Ihr Geschäft.

A: *Where is it?* B: *It's in Berlin Mitte.*

B: *What kind of market is it?* A: *It's a book market.*

Vocabulary | clothes and colours

3 a [4.6] Hören Sie zu und ordnen Sie diese Farben den Kleidungsstücken zu:

1	green	a)	pair of shoes
2	white	b)	skirt
3	orange	c)	coat
4	red	d)	pair of trousers
5	yellow	e)	dress
6	black	f)	bag
7	blue	g)	hat
8	brown	h)	T-shirt

b Welche Beschreibung in Üb. 1a passt zu welchem Bild?

c Partnerarbeit: Beschreiben Sie die Kleidung der anderen Kursteilnehmer.

Listening and speaking

4 Lesen Sie den *How to*-Kasten. Zeigen Sie auf einen Gegenstand im Bild unten und nennen Sie den Preis.

HOW TO …

talk about prices

A: *How much is it?*   B: *It's …*

B: *How much are they?*   B: *They're …*

A: *How much is it?*

B: *It's four pounds fifty.*

5 **a** 4.7 Hören Sie zu. Einige der Preise im Bild sind falsch. Korrigieren Sie die Fehler.

b Hören Sie noch einmal zu und ergänzen Sie die Fragen. Überprüfen Sie diese mit Hilfe des Hörtextes auf Seite 138.

1 How much is _____ blue hat?

2 How much are _____ beautiful dresses?

3 How much is _____ yellow skirt?

4 How much are _____ white shirts?

£8.45 each
£12.85 each
£7.20 each
£22.00 each
£9.00 each
£16.99
£9.50 each
£3.50
£6.00 each

Grammar | *this, that, these, those*

6 Vervollständigen Sie den Kasten mit *that*, *these* oder *those*.

Active grammar

	this hat
	_____ bag
	_____ bracelets
	_____ jumpers

siehe Suchen und finden, Seite 51

7 Sehen Sie sich das Bild in Üb. 4 an. Ergänzen Sie hier mit *this*, *that*, *these* oder *those*.

1 How much are _____ white shirts?

2 How much is _____ orange T-shirt?

3 How much is _____ brown jumper?

4 How much are _____ dresses?

5 How much are _____ bags?

6 How much is _____ black hat?

7 How much is _____ yellow skirt?

8 How much are _____ red tops?

Speaking

8 Partnerarbeit: Fragen Sie nach dem Preis und beantworten Sie die Fragen Ihres Partners.

Partner A: Schlagen Sie Seite 127 auf.

Partner B: Schlagen Sie Seite 129 auf.

Writing

9 Schreiben Sie einen Abschnitt über den Markt/ das Geschäft, in dem Sie am liebsten einkaufen.

4.3 Around town

Grammar	possessive 's
Can do	ask about things and make simple transactions

Stefan

Shula

Mike

Andy

Vocabulary | irregular plurals

1   a Was sehen Sie auf den Fotos?

   1 *a supermarket, a woman ...*

   b Auf welchen Fotos können Sie diese Personen sehen?

	a	b	c	d	e
a person	✓	✓	✓	✓	✓
a man					
a woman					
a baby					
a child					
a wife					

2   a Unterstreichen Sie die richtige Pluralform.

   1 a two persons   **b** two people
   2 a two men   **b** two mans
   3 a two women   **b** two womans
   4 a two babys   **b** two babies
   5 a two children   **b** two childs
   6 a two wifes   **b** two wives

   b Finden Sie weitere Beispiele wie im Kasten unten.

REGULAR PLURALS	IRREGULAR PLURALS
bag – bags	man – men
salad – salads	baby – babies

siehe Suchen und finden, Seite 51

Reading and listening

3   a `4.8` Hören Sie zu und ordnen Sie jedem Dialog ein Foto zu.

Dialogue 1 – picture __
Dialogue 2 – picture __
Dialogue 3 – picture __
Dialogue 4 – picture __
Dialogue 5 – picture __

   b Hören Sie noch einmal zu und ergänzen Sie die Lücken.

   1   A: Can I have three (1) *tickets* to Bristol, please. Two adults and one child?
      B: Single or return?
      A: Return, please.
      B: That's forty-two thirty, please. ... Thank you. ... (2) _____ you are.

   2   A: Can I help you?
      B: Yes, please. Can I have a (3) _____ of aspirin, please?
      A: Twenty-four or forty-eight?
      B: Twenty-four, please.
      A: That's one forty-nine, (4) _____ . ... Thank you.

   3   A: Can I have (5) _____ _____ for *ChickenMan Returns*, please.
      B: That's fifteen pounds ninety, please.
      A: Can I pay by (6) _____ _____ ?
      B: Sure. ... Sign here, please. ... Thank you. Here you are.
      A: Thanks.

48

Jack

e

WILL CALL

PLEASE RETAIN YOUR TICKET STUBS

Grammar | possessive 's

6 a Ordnen Sie die Dinge unten den Personen auf den Fotos zu.

ASPIRIN

DUT £7.10

b Vervollständigen Sie Satz 3, 4 und 5 im Kasten.

> **Active grammar**
>
> Use 's to show possession.
>
> 1 They're Jack's cinema tickets.
> 2 She's Shula's baby.
> 3 She's _____ daughter.
> 4 They're _____ aspirin.
> 5 It's_____ train ticket.

siehe Suchen und finden, Seite 51

7 Schreiben Sie die Sätze um und benutzen Sie dabei den Namen + 's.

1 It's his passport. (Kevin)
   It's Kevin's passport.
2 They're her shoes. (Rosie)
   _____ .
3 This is his email address. (Takumi)
   _____ .
4 What is her address? (Adele)
   _____ .
5 Are you her brother? (Teresa)
   _____ .
6 That is his suitcase. (Janek)
   _____ .

Speaking

8 a Geben Sie dem Kursleiter einen Gegenstand, den Sie auf Englisch benennen können, z. B. eine Tasche, einen Stift.

b Raten Sie, welchem Teilnehmer was gehört.

A: *Is that Anna's bag?*
B: *No, it isn't. It's Helga's bag.*

4 A: (7) _____ can I get you?
B: Can I have a pint of LionBrew beer, please.
A: A pint or a half?
B: A pint please.
A: Anything else?
B: Yes. A dry (8) _____ wine, please.
A: That's four pounds and nine pence, please.

5 A: Thirty-one pounds and seven pence, please.
B: Here (9) _____ are.
A: Thank you. Enter your PIN (10) _____ , please. … Thank you.

4 a Partnerarbeit: Üben Sie die Dialoge mit verteilten Rollen.

b Lesen Sie die Dialoge noch einmal, aber ändern Sie jetzt einige Details.

A: *Can I have two tickets to London, please.*
B: *Single or return?*

5 a Tragen Sie nützliche Wendungen aus den Dialogen in den *How to*-Kasten ein.

HOW TO …

survive in town

Train station	*Single or return?*
	_____
Pub	*Can I have a pint/half of beer, please?*
	_____
Shop	_____
	_____

b Partnerarbeit: Schließen Sie Ihre Bücher. Schreiben Sie einen Dialog in einem Geschäft, Pub oder an einem Bahnschalter.

c Spielen Sie Ihren Dialog im Kurs vor.

Excuse me, where is the ...?

1 **a** Sehen Sie sich den Stadtplan an und benutzen Sie die Wörter im Kasten, um die Sätze zu ergänzen.

> opposite   next to   on   near

1   The car park is _____ King Street.
2   The bank is _____ the market.
3   The cinema is _____ the car park.
4   The chemist is _____ the bank.

b **4·9** Hören Sie zu und vervollständigen Sie den Stadtplan.

> gallery   train station   supermarket

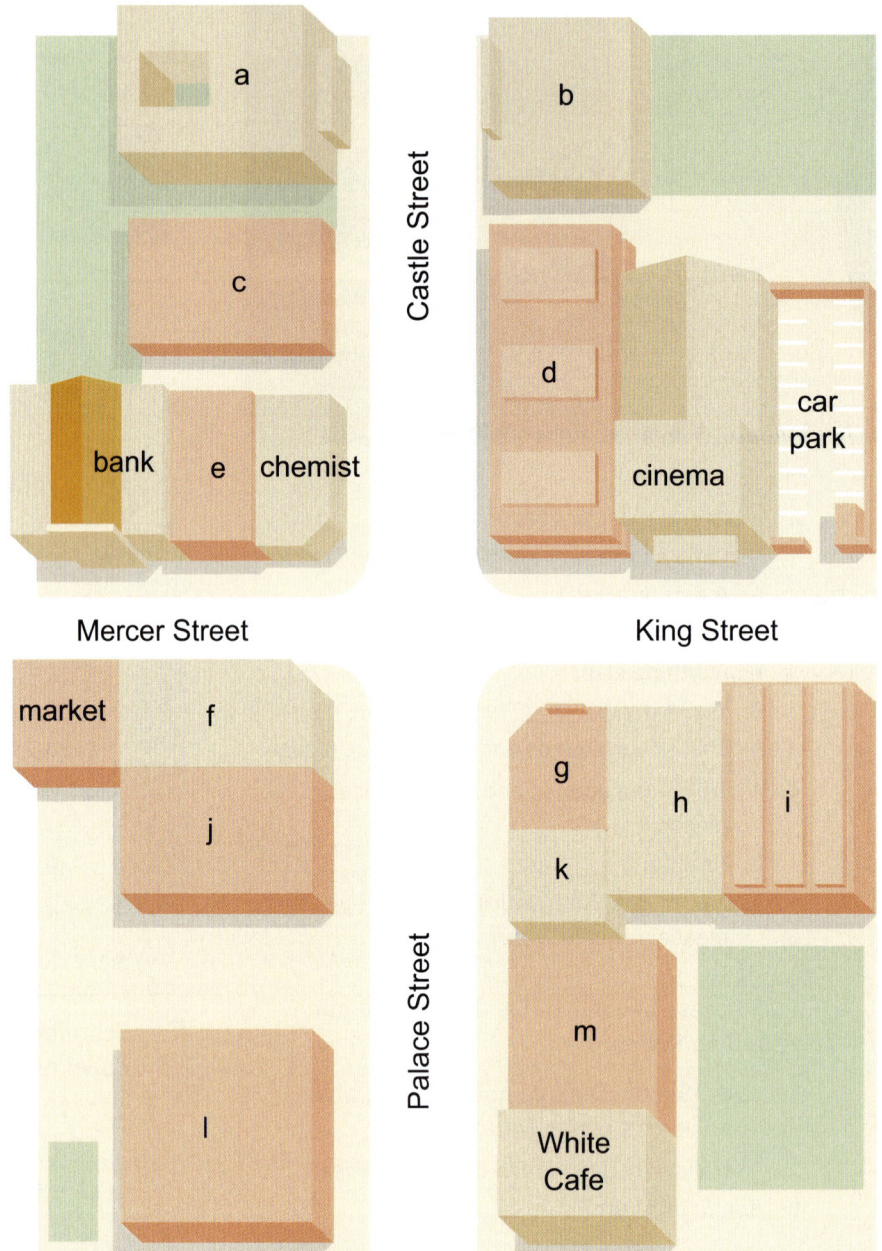

Castle Street

a

b

c

d

bank   e   chemist

car park

cinema

Mercer Street

King Street

market   f

g

h   i

j

k

m

l

White Cafe

Palace Street

2 **a** Sehen Sie sich den *How to*-Kasten an.

HOW TO …

ask where something is

A: *Excuse me, where's the ...?*
B: *It's ...*
A: *Thank you.*
B: *You're welcome.*

I'm sorry. I don't know.
OK. Never mind. Thank you.

b Partnerarbeit: Stellen Sie Fragen, um Ihren Stadtplan zu ergänzen. Ihr Partner kann Ihnen die fehlenden Informationen geben.

Partner A: Sie finden Ihren Stadtplan auf Seite 128.

Partner B: Sie finden Ihren Stadtplan auf Seite 127.

4 | Suchen und finden

Can I have?

Can I have	a cappuccino,	
	a piece of cake,	
	an espresso,	
	an orange juice,	please?
	a return ticket to Paris,	
	two mineral waters,	

Certainly./Sure.

Mit *Can I have* bestellt man etwas (im Café oder Laden) oder bittet um etwas.

this/that/these/those
Die Demonstrativpronomen

this

these

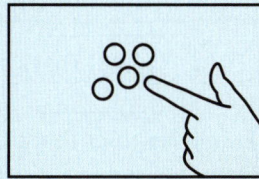

that

those

	nah	weit weg
Singular	*this*	*that*
Plural	*these*	*those*

How much are those shirts?

Are these books free?

That hat is great!

This jumper is beautiful.

Possessive 's
Besitzanzeigendes 's

Mit *'s* zeigt man Besitz oder Zugehörigkeit an. Es ist für Singular und Plural der Dinge gleich, die jemand besitzt.

It's Herbie's passport. (Singular)

She's Dylan's daughter. (Singular)

They're Jody's tickets. (Plural)

They're Damien's daughters. (Plural)

Irregular plurals
Unregelmäßige Pluralbildung

Der regelmäßige Plural wird mit *s* gebildet, das an das Wort angehängt wird:

ticket → tickets.

Bei Wörtern, die auf einen Zischlaut enden (-*s*, -*sh*, -*ch*), wird -*es* angehängt. Man spricht /ɪz/. (Zwei s-Laute hintereinander lassen sich nicht aussprechen.)

sandwich – sandwiches

address – addresses

wish – wishes

Wörter auf -*y* enden im Plural auf -*ies*. Diese Unregelmäßigkeit hört man nicht.

baby – babies

Wörter auf -*ife* enden im Plural auf -*ives*.

wife – wives

Einige Nomen haben besondere Pluralformen. Beachten Sie die Aussprache – einige Laute verändern sich:

child – children /aɪ/ – /ɪ/

woman – women /ʊ/ – /ɪ/

man – men /æ/ – /e/

wife – wives /f/ – /v/

person – people /ɜ:/ – /i:/

Prices
Preise, Kosten

Nach dem Preis erkundigen Sie sich so:

How much is/are ...?

So antworten Sie:

It's/They're ...

Beachten Sie Singular bzw. Plural!

How much is that computer?	*It's €799.*
How much are those books?	*They're €8.*

Normalerweise nennt man die Währung nicht dazu:

€1.99	*one euro ninety-nine/one ninety-nine*
£3.50	*three pounds fifty/three fifty*
$12.20	*twelve dollars twenty*

Wenn der Preis niedriger ist als 1 Euro/Pfund/Dollar, muss man *cents* oder *p* dazu sagen.

80c	*eighty cents*
39p	*thirty-nine p (= Mehrzahl von penny)*

Vocabulary | places in town

1 Welche Einrichtungen sehen Sie auf den
Bildern? Tragen Sie sie in das Kreuzworträtsel
ein. Wie heißt das Lösungswort?

Vocabulary | food and drink

2 Ergänzen Sie die Quittungen mit Speisen und
Getränken.

1

CAFE CULTURE RECEIPT
LONDON
★ ★ CUSTOMER COPY ★ ★

a CHICKEN SANDWICH............£2.99
b _____...................£1.09
c _____...................£0.99

TOTAL....................................£5.07

2

PAULO'S CAFE RECEIPT
LISBON
★ ★ CUSTOMER COPY ★ ★

a _____...................€0.99
b _____...................€1.35
c _____...................€0.70
TOTAL....................................€3.04

3

CAFE FRANCE RECEIPT
PARIS
★ ★ CUSTOMER COPY ★ ★

a _____...................€2.29
b _____...................€1.55
c _____...................€0.79

TOTAL....................................€4.63

Grammar | Can I have?

3 Ergänzen Sie die Sätze mit *Can I have + a, an*
oder *two*.

1 *Can I have an* espresso, please?
2 _____ cappuccino, please?
3 _____ ham salad, please?
4 _____ iced coffees, please?
5 _____ mineral water, please?
6 _____ pieces of cake, please?

Vocabulary | prices

4 Korrigieren Sie die Fehler.

1 (€1.90) That one euro ninety, please.
   That's one euro ninety, please.
2 ($2.45) That's two dollar forty-five, please.
   _____
3 ($0.50) That's fifty pence, please.
   _____
4 ($6.29) That's six euros twenty-nine, please.
   _____
5 (€3.60) That's three euros sixty cent, please.
   _____
6 ($0.99) That's ninety-nine dollars, please.
   _____

How to order food in a café

5 Schreiben Sie den Dialog in der richtigen
Reihenfolge auf und ergänzen Sie die Lücken.

a No, thank you.
b That's one euro, please.
c Eat in, please.
d Certainly. Anything _____ .
e Yes. Can I _____ a white coffee, please.
f Hello. Can I _____ you?
g Eat in or _____ away?

A: (1) *Hello. Can I help you?*
B: (2) _____
A: (3) _____
B: (4) _____
A: (5) _____
A: (6) _____
B: (7) _____

Vocabulary | *souvenirs and colours*

1 In diesem Rätsel sind acht Farbbezeichnungen versteckt. Finden Sie sie alle?

B	K	B	R	E	D
R	B	L	U	E	Y
O	R	A	N	G	E
W	P	C	D	R	L
N	Q	K	F	E	L
W	H	I	T	E	O
D	E	O	R	N	W

1	*b r o w n*	5	b _ _ _
2	w _ _ _ _	6	b l _ _ _
3	o _ _ _ _ _	7	y _ _ _ _ _
4	g _ _ _ _	8	r _ _

2 Welche Kleidungsstücke sehen Sie in diesem Bild?

1 *a hat*
2 _____
3 _____
4 _____
5 _____
6 _____
7 _____
8 _____

Grammar | *this, that, these, those*

3 Sehen Sie sich das Bild an. Welches Wort ist hier richtig?

€10.99 €15.99 €4.50 €4.99 €18.59 €77.99 €22.99 €5.99

1 *(this)/that/these/those* bags (€5.99)
2 *this/that/these/those* shirts (€10.99)
3 *this/that/these/those* T-shirts (€4.99)
4 *this/that/these/those* tops (€15.99)
5 *this/that/these/those* hat (€4.50)
6 *this/that/these/those* coats (€77.99)
7 *this/that/these/those* skirts (€22.99)
8 *this/that/these/those* pairs of trousers (€18.59)

How to talk about prices

4 Sehen Sie sich noch einmal das Bild in Üb. 3 an und schreiben Sie die fehlenden Fragen auf.

1 A: How much are those shirts?
   B: They're ten euros ninety-nine.

2 A: _____ ?
   B: They're four euros ninety-nine.

3 A: _____ ?
   B: It's four euros fifty.

4 A: _____ ?
   B: They're fifteen euros fifty.

5 A: _____ ?
   B: They're seventy-seven euros ninety-nine.

6 A: _____ ?
   B: They're twenty-two euros ninety-nine.

7 A: _____ ?
   B: They're eighteen euros fifty-nine.

8 A: _____ ?
   B: It's five euros ninety-nine.

Vocabulary | irregular plurals

1 **Wie lautet der Plural dieser Wörter?**

1 One child. Two _____ .

2 One woman. Two _____ .

3 One man. Two _____ .

4 One baby. Two _____ .

5 One person. Two _____ .

6 One wife. Two _____ .

Vocabulary | useful phrases

2 **Ergänzen Sie die Dialoge mit den Wörtern im Kasten.**

> or   pay by credit card   Sign   That's
> Single or return?   PIN number   Can I

A: Can I help you?

B: Yes. Can I have a ticket to Manchester, please?

A: (1) _____

B: Return please.

A: That's £12.90, please.

B: Can I (2) _____ ?

A: Yes. .... (3) _____ here, please. ... Thank you.

B: Thank you.

A: Can I help you?

B: Yes. Can I have a packet of aspirin, please?

A: Twelve (4) _____ twenty-four?

B: Twelve please.

A: (5) _____ €1.09, please.

B: (6) _____ pay by credit card?

A: Certainly. ... Enter your (7) _____ , please. ... Thank you.

B: Thank you.

Dimitri

Katarina

Arabella

Armand

Giacomo

Larisa

Grammar | possessive 's

3 **Beantworten Sie diese Fragen.**

1 Are they Dimitri's shoes?

   No, they aren' t. They' re Arabella' s shoes.

2 Is it Giacomo's coffee?

   _____ . _____ .

3 Are they Katarina's children?

   _____ . _____ .

4 Is it Larisa's hat?

   _____ . _____ .

5 Are they Armand's books?

   _____ . _____ .

6 Is it Arabella's orange juice?

   _____ . _____ .

4 **Lesen Sie diese Sätze. Was bedeutet 's? Schreiben Sie P (possessives 's) oder I (is).**

1 Amado's my brother. [*I*]

2 Blanca's brother is Claudio.

3 Where is Keiko's bag?

4 Johann's not here today.

5 Who is Hilda's friend?

6 Jake's camera is great.

7 Karla's my friend.

8 Is Suzanne's surname Webber?

5 | Places

Lead-in

1 **a** Ergänzen Sie die Sätze mit den Wörtern aus dem Kasten.

> south   north   west   east   centre

1 Darwin =   **4** Adelaide =

2 Perth =   **5** Alice Springs =

3 Brisbane =

b `5.1` Hören Sie zu und überprüfen Sie Ihre Antworten.

2 Berichten Sie über Städte in Ihrem Land. Verwenden Sie *in the north/south/east/west/centre of ...*
Hamburg is in the north of Germany.

3 **a** Welches Foto passt zu diesen Wörtern?

city _____   countryside _____   coast _____

b Ordnen Sie diese Wörter den Orten oben zu.

> buildings   trees   a river   a beach   roads   the sea

c `5.2` Hören Sie zu und überprüfen Sie Ihre Antworten.

4 **a** Finden Sie weitere Wörter für jeden Ort. Fragen Sie Ihren Kursleiter oder benutzen Sie ein Wörterbuch.

b Partnerarbeit: Sprechen Sie über die Fotos.

A: What's in photo B?   **B:** A hill, a river and ...

Grammar	*there is/are; some*
Can do	give a simple description of a place

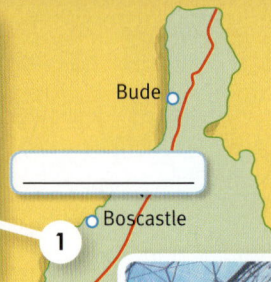

Bude

Boscastle
1

Bodmin

A39

Newquay

2

St Austell

A30

Truro

3

Redruth

Penzance

5

A30

A394

4

Reading

1 a Partnerarbeit: Erklären Sie, wo Sie am liebsten Ihren Urlaub verbringen.

My favourite place for a holiday is the south of France.

b Lesen Sie *My favourite place for a holiday*. Beschriften Sie die Karte mit den im Text unterstrichenen Orten.

My favourite place for a holiday is Cornwall. Cornwall is in the south-west of England. The coast and the countryside are very beautiful and the beaches are great.

There are two famous castles in Cornwall. Tintagel Castle is in the north of Cornwall and Pendennis Castle is in the south.

There's a great gallery in the west of Cornwall. It's called Tate St. Ives.

There is a new tourist attraction in south-east Cornwall. It's called The Eden Project. There are plants and trees from all over the world.

There's a beautiful outdoor theatre in the west of Cornwall. It's called the Minack Theatre.

2 a Beantworten Sie diese Fragen:

1 Where is Cornwall?
2 Where are the famous castles?
3 What is Tate St. Ives?
4 What is The Eden Project?
5 Where is the Minack theatre?

b [5.3] Schließen Sie Ihre Bücher und hören Sie zu. Wenn Sie den Signalton hören, ergänzen Sie laut das folgende Wort.

My favourite place for a holiday is Cornwall. Cornwall is in the south-west of

Students: ... *England.*

Speaking

3 a Sehen Sie sich die Liste an. Was gehört zu einem guten Urlaub? Wählen Sie drei Dinge.

> great beaches   beautiful countryside
> good food   great tourist attractions
> good theatres and museums
> good shops   beautiful buildings

b Lesen Sie den *How to*-Kasten.

HOW TO ...

give an opinion
I think ...

I think beautiful beaches are important (for a good holiday).

c Partnerarbeit: Was ist Ihrer Meinung nach wichtig für einen gelungenen Urlaub?

Grammar | *there is/are*

4 **a** Sehen Sie sich den Text noch einmal an. Markieren Sie alle Stellen mit *there's* und *there are*.

b Vervollständigen Sie den Kasten mit *is* oder *are*.

Active grammar

There	's	a great gallery.
There	(____)	a theatre.
There	_____	two famous castles. four great hotels.

siehe Suchen und finden, Seite 63

5 **a** Ergänzen Sie die Sätze mit *There's* oder *There are*.

1 *There's* a famous castle in Edinburgh.
2 _____ a beautiful beach in Barcelona.
3 _____ good restaurants in São Paolo.
4 _____ beautiful beaches in Greece.
5 _____ nice hotels in New York.
6 _____ a spice market in Istanbul.
7 _____ good museums in London.
8 _____ a famous mountain near Tokyo.

b Sehen Sie sich die Karte von Wien an. Welche Sehenswürdigkeiten gibt es dort?

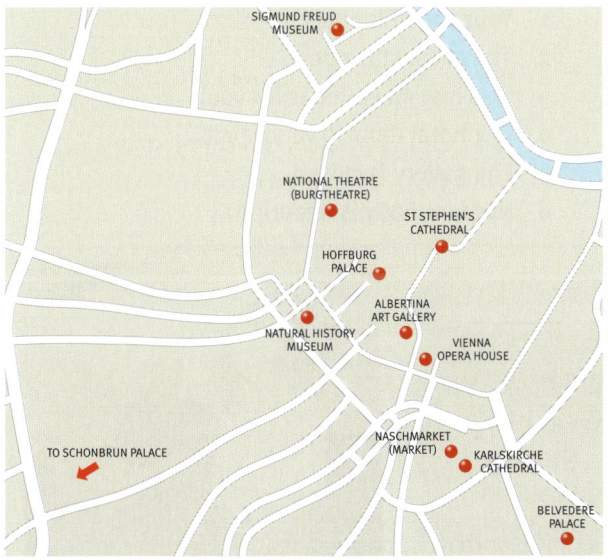

There are two famous cathedrals in Vienna. The Karlskirche Cathedral is in the south of Vienna. St. Stephen's Cathedral is ...

Vocabulary | *some, a lot of*

6 **a** Ordnen Sie diese Sätze den Bildern zu.

a There are *some* people in the theatre.
b There are *a lot of* people in the theatre.
c There's one person in the theatre.

b **5·4** Hören Sie zu und überprüfen Sie Ihre Antworten. Sprechen Sie nach.

7 **a** Sehen Sie sich die Tabelle an und ergänzen Sie die Sätze.

Newchester	
Cinemas	••••••••
Galleries	•••••••
Lakes	•
Shops	••••••••••••••••••
Restaurants	•••••••••••••••••
Rivers	•

1 *There are some* galleries in Newchester.
2 _____ restaurants in Newchester.
3 _____ river in Newchester.
4 _____ lake in Newchester.
5 _____ shops in Newchester.
6 _____ cinemas in Newchester.

b Fügen Sie in jeden Satz ein passendes Adjektiv an der richtigen Stelle ein.

> nice good beautiful big great modern

1 *There are some nice galleries in Newchester.*

Writing

8 Was ist Ihre Lieblingsreiseziel? Machen Sie sich Notizen. Berichten Sie dann Ihrem Partner.

There are a lot of good restaurants in the centre of town.

9 **a** Schlagen Sie nach unter *Texte verfassen* auf Seite 134 an.

b Beschreiben Sie Ihr bevorzugtes Reiseziel.

5.2 | In a new town

Grammar	Is/Are there; there isn't/aren't; some, any
Can do	ask for and understand basic information about a new town

Vocabulary | prepositions of place

1　**a** Orden Sie die Präpositionen im Kasten den Bildern a–h zu.

> under　opposite　in　on　in front of
> near　next to　behind

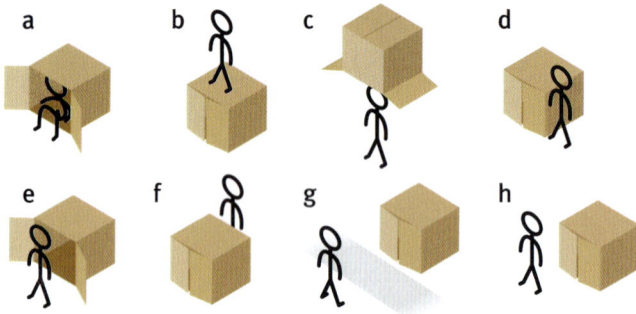

a　b　c　d

e　f　g　h

b Sehen Sie sich den Stadtplan unten an. Was können Sie dort entdecken?

c Ergänzen Sie die Sätze unten mit den Informationen aus dem Stadtplan.

1　The newsagent is *next to* the hotel.
2　The café is _____ the train station.
3　The chemist is _____ the Italian restaurant.
4　The cinema is _____ the town square.
5　The department store is _____ the chemist.

d `5·5` Hören Sie zu und überprüfen Sie Ihre Antworten. Decken Sie dann die Sätze ab und beschreiben Sie das Stadtzentrum.

Listening

2　**a** `5·6` Hören Sie zu und ergänzen Sie a–e auf dem Stadtplan.

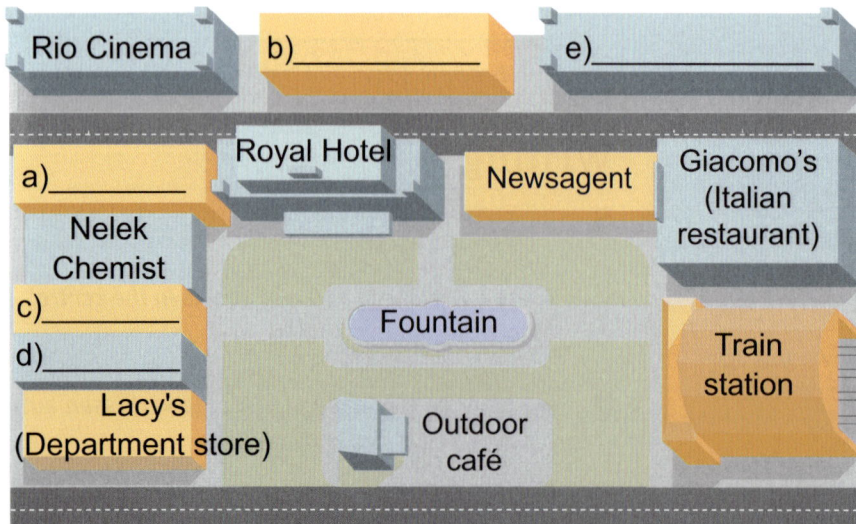

b Wahr oder falsch? Hören Sie noch einmal zu und korrigieren Sie die falschen Sätze.

1　There are two cafés near the hotel. `W`
2　There is a restaurant opposite the train station. ☐
3　There aren't any banks near the hotel. ☐
4　The department store is closed today. ☐
5　The cathedral and the museum are tourist attractions. ☐
6　There's a gallery in the square. ☐

3　**a** Partnerarbeit: Lesen Sie den *How to*-Kasten.

HOW TO …

receive good and bad news

Good news:
Good!　　　Great!

Bad news:
Never mind!　　　Oh no!

b Teilen Sie Ihrem Partner eine der folgenden guten oder schlechten Neuigkeiten mit. Dieser reagiert darauf entsprechend.

1　Your coffee is cold.
2　The chemist is open.
3　This instant coffee is for you.
4　Our hotel room is very small.
5　The gallery is closed.
6　Her new baby is beautiful.

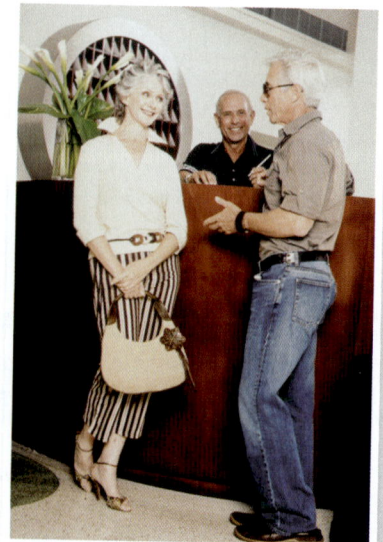

Rio Cinema　b)_____　e)_____

a)_____
Royal Hotel
Nelek Chemist
Newsagent
Giacomo's (Italian restaurant)
c)_____
d)_____
Fountain
Lacy's (Department store)
Outdoor café
Train station

Grammar | *There isn't/aren't any; Is/Are there any ...?*

4 a Vervollständigen Sie den Kasten mit *is*, *isn't*, *are* oder *aren't*.

Active grammar

⊖	There _____ (is not)	a bus stop near here.
⊖	There _____ (are not)	any galleries near here.
❓	_____ there	a bank near here?
Yes there is.		No, there _____ .
❓ Are	there any hotels near here?	
Yes, there _____ .		No, there _____ .

any: use *any* for plurals in negatives and questions with *there is/are*

b Sehen Sie sich noch einmal den Stadtplan auf Seite 58 an. Ergänzen Sie diese Sätze mit *There isn't/aren't*.

1 bus stops *There aren't any bus stops* in the square.
2 a supermarket _____ in the square.
3 car parks _____ in the square.
4 a market _____ in the square.
5 a cinema _____ in the square.
6 galleries _____ in the square

siehe Suchen und finden, Seite 63

5 a Was interessiert Sie an dem Wohnort Ihres Partners? Schreiben Sie dazu einige Fragen.

1 good cinemas
2 big museum
3 nice department stores
4 palace
5 modern supermarkets
6 popular galleries

A: *Are there any good cinemas in your home town?*

b Partnerarbeit: Stellen Sie sich gegenseitig Ihre Fragen.

A: *Are there any good cinemas in your home town?*
B: *Yes, there are. There are a lot of good cinemas.*

Vocabulary | nationalities

6 a Auf welche Länder beziehen sich die kursiv gedruckten Wörter?

1 a *French* restaurant 4 a *German* restaurant
2 an *Italian* restaurant 5 an *Indian* restaurant
3 an *English* restaurant 6 a *Chinese* restaurant

b Welche dieser Namen gehören zu den Restaurants 1–6?

Chez Pierre   WONG LI
King Henry's
    The Taj Mahal
LA SPIGA
    RATSKELLER

c 5·7 Hören Sie zu und überprüfen Sie Ihre Antworten.

7 a Finden Sie mit Hilfe eines Wörterbuchs weitere Ländernamen und Nationalitäten und schreiben Sie sie in eine Tabelle:

Country	Nationality
England	English
Scotland	_____
_____	Irish
Wales	_____

b Partnerarbeit: Diskutieren Sie diese Fragen. Beziehen Sie sich dabei auf verschiedene Nationalitäten.

What is your favourite kind of food/restaurant/music/language?
My favourite kind of food is Italian.

Speaking

8 a Partnerarbeit:

Partner A: Sie arbeiten an der Hotelrezeption. Schlagen Sie Seite 130 auf.
Partner B: Sie sind ein Hotelgast. Schlagen Sie Seite 129 auf. Stellen Sie Fragen wie *Is there a ... near here?* oder *Are there any ... near here?* und ergänzen Sie die Tabelle.

B: *Are there any cafés near here?*
A: *Yes, there are. There's a café next to the newsagent's and there's a café ...*

Grammar	can/can't
Can do	talk about general abilities

Harefield College

Welcome to Harefield College. We are Harefield's top language school. Our Language Plus! courses are very popular with students from all over the world.

Language Plus! Courses: A1 English

Course 171:	A1 English + 09:00 – 11:00
Course 172:	A1 English + 14:00 – 17:00
Course 173:	A1 English + 19:00 – 21:00
Course 174:	A1 English + 09:00 – 12:00
Course 175:	A1 English + 18:00 – 20:00
Course 176:	A1 English + 14:00 – 16:00
Course 177:	A1 English + 10:00 – 12:00
Course 178:	A1 English + 13:00 – 15:00

Vocabulary | abilities

1   **a** Sehen Sie sich die Broschüre an. Ordnen Sie die Symbole den Wörtern im Kasten zu.

> cook   play golf   drive   play the piano   swim
> use a computer   sing   dance

b Partnerarbeit: Zeigen Sie auf ein Symbol. Ihr Partner nennt die entsprechende Aktivität.

Listening

2   **a** `5.8` Hören Sie den Dialog zwischen Patricia und James und ergänzen Sie die Informationen über Vanda.

Name: *Vanda*   **From:** _____ in Germany

Relationship to James: _____   **English level:** _____

b `5.9` Hören Sie nun den 2. Teil des Dialogs. Schreiben Sie *Yes* oder *No* neben diese Aktivitäten für Vanda.

1	drive	*Yes*
2	swim	_____
3	play golf	_____
4	cook	_____
5	use a computer	_____
6	dance	_____
7	sing	_____
8	play the piano	_____

c Hören Sie noch einmal zu und überprüfen Sie Ihre Antworten. Welche Kurse sind für Vanda geeignet?

d Welche Kurse würden Sie gern belegen?

3   Lesen Sie den *How to-* Kasten. Begrüßen Sie Ihren Partner.

HOW TO …

greet a friend

A: *How are you?*

B: *Fine/OK/Not bad, thanks. And you?*

A: *Fine/OK/Not bad, thanks.*

Grammar | *can/can't*

4 **a** Ergänzen Sie den Kasten mit *can* oder *can't*.

Active grammar

⊕	I/you/ he/she/ we/they	can _____	swim. play golf.
❓	_____	I/you/he/she/we/they	cook? dance?

Yes, I/you/he/she/we/they can.
No, I/you/he/she/we/they can't.

b Schreiben Sie vollständige Sätze:

1 (They / ✗ / dance) *They can't dance.*
2 (you / swim?) _____ .
3 (He / ✓ / speak Italian) _____ .
4 (she / drive?) _____ .
5 (you / play golf?) _____ .
6 (I / ✗ / play the piano) _____ .
7 (We / ✓ / cook) _____ .
8 (they / use a computer?) _____ .

c Stellen Sie Ihrem Partner Fragen zu den Aktivitäten in Üb. 1a.

A: *Can you drive?*

B: *Yes, I can.*

siehe Suchen und finden, Seite 63

Pronunciation

5 **a** 5.10 Hören Sie zu und kreuzen Sie an, welches Wort Sie hören.

	can	can't		can	can't
1	☐	☐	4	☐	☐
2	☐	☐	5	☐	☐
3	☐	☐	6	☐	☐

b Hören Sie noch einmal zu. Schreiben Sie die Sätze.

c Welche Sprachen sprechen **a** Sie oder **b** Ihre Freunde/Familienmitglieder?

I can speak (a bit of / good) German and French. I can't speak Italian or Spanish. My brother can speak Spanish.

Vocabulary | telling the time

6 5.11 Hören Sie zu und sprechen Sie die Zeitangaben nach.

a **10:00** d **08:00**
b **15:00** e **13:00**
c **19:00** f **20:00**

7 **a** Nennen Sie eine Zeitangabe aus der Broschüre. Ihr Partner nennt den entsprechenden Kurs.

A: *From two o'clock in the afternoon to four o'clock in the afternoon.*

B: *Course 176.*

b Um welche Zeit findet Ihr Englischkurs statt?

Speaking

8 Sehen Sie sich die Stellenanzeigen an. Finden Sie im Kurs Teilnehmer, die für diese Stellen geeignet wären.

ENTERTAINER FOR CRUISE SHIP NEEDED Skills required:

A: *Can you dance?*
B: *Yes, I can.*
A: *Can you play the piano?*
B: *Yes, I can. But I can't sing.*
A: *Oh no!*

A: *Can you swim?*
B: *Yes, I can.*
A: *Can you drive?*
B: *Yes, I can. But I can't play golf.*
A: *Oh no!*

PERSONAL TRAINER NEEDED Skills required:

A B&B

1 **a** Was ist ein *B&B*?

b Partnerarbeit: Ordnen Sie diese Wörter den Buchstaben im Bild zu.

> blanket   shower   towels   tea bags   fridge
> kettle   television

c `5.12` Hören Sie sich dieses Gespräch an und überprüfen Sie Ihre Antworten.

d Schließen Sie Ihr Buch. An welche Dinge auf dem Bild können Sie sich erinnern?

There are some towels on the bed.

2 Hören Sie noch einmal zu und wählen Sie die richtige Antwort.

1 Breakfast is from
   a 07:15 **b** 07:30 ...

2 ... to
   a 09:30 **b** 10:30

3 Checkout time is
   a 11.45 **b** 12.15

3 **a** `5.13` Sehen Sie sich die Uhr an. Hören Sie zu und sprechen Sie nach.

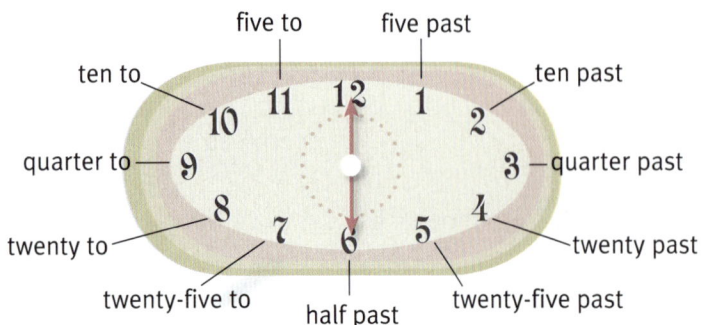

b Partnerarbeit: Wie lauten diese Zeitangaben?

a	03.30	**f**	19:45	**k**	14:25
b	17:15	**g**	06:20	**l**	04:55
c	20:45	**h**	13:05	**m**	10:10
d	11:30	**i**	09:35	**n**	21:40
e	19:10	**j**	08:15	**o**	12:15

4 **a** Sie besitzen ein *B&B*. Ergänzen Sie die Informationen über das Zimmer, das Sie vermieten. Schreiben Sie Y (*Yes*) oder N (*No*).

Room	(Y)	(N)	Where?
Double bed?			
En-suite?			
Television?			
Extra blanket?			
Towels?			
Kettle?			
Fridge?			
(other?)			

b Partnerarbeit: Begrüßen Sie Ihren Partner als Gast in Ihrem B&B. Zeigen Sie ihm sein Zimmer und informieren Sie ihn über die Zeiten für Frühstück und Abreise.

Lifelong learning

Im Wörterbuch wie zu Hause!

Beschriften Sie zu Hause und am Arbeitsplatz Alltagsgegenstände auf Englisch.

There is/There are
Es gibt

There is	a/an	pub near here.
There isn't		art gallery near here.
There are	two some a lot of	cafés near the bank. galleries in town.
There aren't	any	
Is there	a/an	restaurant/Irish pub near here?
Are there	any	tourist attractions near here?

Mit *there is/isn't/are/aren't* sagt man, ob es etwas gibt oder nicht gibt.

some/a lot of/any

Some und *a lot of* benutzt man im Plural, in positiven Aussagesätzen mit *there are*.

There are some cafés near the bank.

A lot of bedeutet *eine Menge* oder *viele*.

There are a lot of people in the bank.

Any benutzt man in verneinten Aussagen und in Fragesätzen mit *there are*.

Any ist eine unbestimmte Anzahl – der unbestimmte Artikel im Plural. Im Deutschen gibt es oft keine Entsprechung.

There aren't any hotels in this town. (not any = *keine*)

Are there any markets in this town? (keine deutsche Entsprechung)

can/can't

I			speak English.
You			say hello in Japanese.
He/She	⊕ can ⊖ can't		read a book in Russian.
We			write an email in Italian.
They			

?			
	I		speak English?
	you		say hello in Japanese?
Can	he/she		read a book in Russian?
	we		write an email in Italian?
	they		

Can und *can't* stehen vor dem Vollverb und haben bei allen Personen die gleiche Form.

I can speak Russian.

She can speak Russian.

Prepositions of place
Präpositionen des Ortes

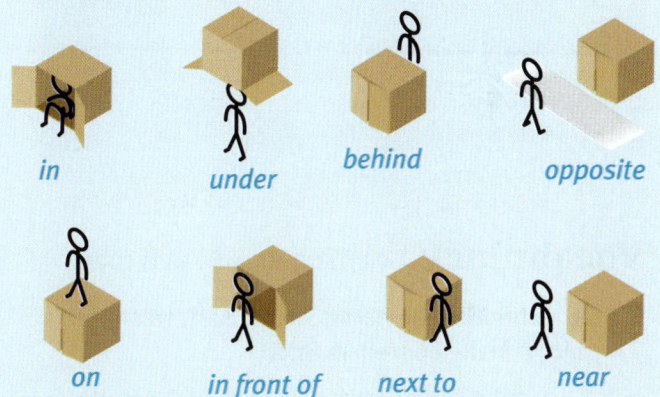

in *under* *behind* *opposite*

on *in front of* *next to* *near*

Telling the time
Die Uhrzeit

six o' clock
`06:00`

twenty to seven
`06:40`

ten past six
`06:10`

quarter to seven
`06:45`

quarter past six
`06:15`

five to seven
`06:55`

half past six
`06:30`

❗ Vorsicht: *halb sieben* = *half past six.*

Vocabulary | city, countryside and coast

1 **a** Schreiben Sie *north*, *south, east, west* und *centre* in die Lücken im Bild.

b Ergänzen Sie diese Sätze mit einem Wort aus dem Kasten.

> buildings   mountains   river   trees   beach

1 The _____ are in the centre of the city.
2 The _____ is in the south of the city.
3 The _____ is in the west of the city.
4 The _____ are in the north of the city.
5 The _____ are in the east of the city.

Grammar | there is/there are

2 Wie muss es hier richtig heißen?

My house is in the centre of town. (1) *There's/* *There are* a newsagent next to my house and (2) *there's/there are* two cafés on my road. (3) *There's/There* are a great restaurant near my house and (4) *there's/there* are two good cinemas near the restaurant. (5) *There's/There* are a train station opposite the restaurant. (6) *There's/There* are also a supermarket near my house and (7) *there's/there* are two good book shops next to the supermarket.

3 Sehen Sie das Bild von Noman Island an und ergänzen Sie die Sätze mit *There's/There are*.

1 *There are* good hotels on Noman Island.
2 _____ a big mountain on Noman Island.
3 _____ beautiful beaches on Noman Island.
4 _____ nice cafés on Noman Island.
5 _____ big market on Noman Island.
6 _____ great restaurants on Noman Island.

Vocabulary | some/a lot of

4 Ergänzen Sie die Sätze oben – wo möglich – mit *some* oder *a lot of*.

1 *There are a lot of good hotels on Noman Island.*
2 _____ .
3 _____ .
4 _____ .
5 _____ .
6 _____ .

Vocabulary | location

1 Sehen Sie sich das Bild an und ergänzen Sie die Sätze mit den Wörtern aus dem Kasten.

> behind   in   in front of   opposite   next to   near   under

1 The man is _in_ the café.
2 The café is _____ the book shop.
3 The bus stop is _____ the café.
4 The car park is _____ the bookshop.
5 The book shop is _____ the restaurant.
6 The bank is _____ the café.
7 The woman is _____ the bookshop.

Vocabulary | nationalities

2 Schreiben Sie zu jedem Land die entsprechende Nationalität.

1 Germany _____
2 India _____
3 Wales _____
4 Scotland _____
5 France _____
6 Italy _____
7 Ireland _____
8 England _____

Grammar | there isn't/aren't any; Is/are there any …

3 Sehen Sie sich den Plan des Einkaufszentrums an und vervollständigen Sie die Fragen und Antworten.

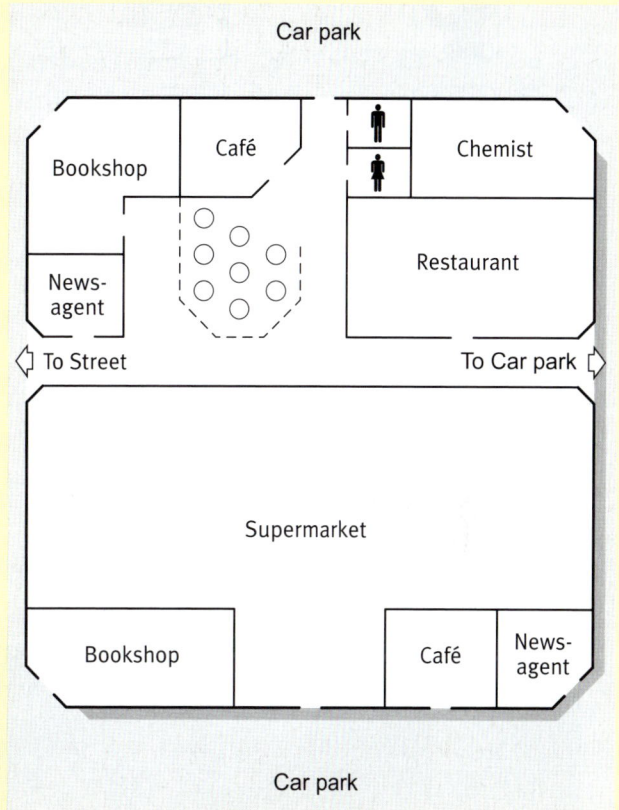

1 *Is there a chemist?*
  Yes, there is.
2 *Are there any banks?*
  No, there aren't.
3 _____ ?
  _____ .
4 _____ ?
  _____ .
5 _____ ?
  _____ .
6 _____ ?
  _____ .

4 Schreiben Sie bejahte und verneinte Sätze über das Einkaufszentrum.

1 *There's a car park.* car park
2 *There aren't any galleries.* galleries
3 _____ . pubs
4 _____ . supermarket
5 _____ . department stores
6 _____ . train station
7 _____ . bookshops
8 _____ . museums

Vocabulary | abilities

1 Schreiben Sie zu jedem Bild die entsprechende Tätigkeit.

1 *dance*

2 _____

3 _____

4 _____

5 _____

6 _____

7 _____

8 _____

Grammar | can/can't

2 Ergänzen Sie den Dialog mit den Wörtern aus dem Kasten.

> They can   I can   Can he   can
> Can you speak   I can't   ~~can you~~   He can

A: So, Mrs Redwood, (1) *can you* speak Italian?

B: (2) Yes, _____ . My mother and father are from Italy. (3) _____ speak Italian, English, French and German.

A: Great. (4) _____ French and German?

B: I (5) _____ speak German but (6) _____ speak French.

A: That's OK. Mr Ploton is the manager. (7) _____ speak French.

B: (8) _____ speak English?

A: No, he can't.

3 Sehen Sie sich die Tabelle an und vervollständigen Sie die Sätze.

	Jo	Simon	Leroy and Lena
sing	✔	✗	✗
play the piano	✗	✔	✔
use a computer	✗	✔	✔

1 (Leroy and Lena use a computer) Leroy and Lena *can use a computer*.

2 (Jo use a computer) Jo *can't use a computer*.

3 (Simon sing?)
   A: Can Simon sing?
   B: *No, he can't.*

4 (Leroy and Lena sing) _____ .

5 (Jo sing?)
   A: _____ ?
   B: _____ .

6 (Simon use a computer) _____ .

7 (Leroy and Lena play the piano?)
   A: _____ ?
   B: _____ .

8 (Jo play the piano) _____ .

9 (Simon play the piano) _____ .

Vocabulary | the time

4 Schreiben Sie die richtige Zeit unter jede Uhr.

a **05:00**

Five o' clock in the morning

b **15:00**

_____

c **20:00**

_____

d **09:00**

_____

e **13:00**

_____

f **22:00**

_____

6 | People

Lead-in

1 **a** Look at the adjectives in the box. Check the meaning in a dictionary.

> thin good-looking tall fat short happy young rich
> old   poor sad intelligent

b `6.1` Listen and repeat.

c Test your partner. Say a word. Your partner says the opposite.

A: *Short.*　　B: *Tall.*

2 **a** Put the sentences in the box in the correct place.

> He's not very rich.   He's rich.   He's very rich.   He's quite rich.

➕➕➕ _____　　➕➕ _____　　➕ _____　　➖ _____

b Talk about the people in the photos. Use the adjectives with *very*, *quite* or *not very*.

3 Talk about famous people with your partner.

A: *Jude Law is very good-looking.*

B: *Yes, he is.*

Grammar	Present Simple (1) *I/You; object pronouns*
Can do	say what you like/don't like

Listening

1 **a** The woman in the picture is called Cynthia. Write five questions for her.

Where are you from?

b 6.2 Listen. Can you answer any of your questions?

c Listen again. Draw 😊 or 🙁 for Cynthia next to each word/phrase below.

1 Dublin
2 Irish music
3 Brazilian music
4 half past nine in the morning
5 football
6 AC Milan football team
7 American food
8 Indian food
9 German cars
10 Italian fashion

Grammar 1 | Present Simple (1): *I like*

2 **a** Complete the Active grammar box with *do* or *don't*. Look at tapescript 6.2 on page 139 to help you.

Active grammar

➕ ➖	I		like	German cars.
	I		_____ like	Irish music.
❓	_____	you	like	football?

Yes, I _____ .   No, I _____ .

b Complete more sentences for Cynthia.
1 (😊 Rio) *I like Rio.*
2 (🙁 chicken) *I don't like chicken.*
3 (😊 London) _____ .
4 (😊 yellow and green) _____ .
5 (🙁 Mondays) _____ .
6 (😊 Spanish films) _____ .
7 (🙁 Manchester United) _____ .
8 (🙁 six o'clock in the morning) _____ .

c Make a question for each sentence above.
1 *Do you like Rio?*

siehe Suchen und finden, Seite 75

Pronunciation

3 **a** 6.3 Listen. Write the questions.
1 *Do you like Italian food?*

b Listen again. Repeat.

Speaking

4   **a**   Write one thing/person you like and one thing/person you don't like for each category below.

- food
- music
- famous people
- time of day
- football teams
- colours
- cars
- places

food: *like = Italian food   don't like = salad*

b   Tell your partner.

I like Italian food. I don't like salad.

c   Ask your partner questions with your things from Ex. 4a.

Do you like Italian food?

Grammar 2 | *me, you, him, her, it, us, them*

5   **a**   Write a sentence next to each picture.

a   I don't like *her*.
b   Do you like *me*?
c   I like *them*.
d   I don't like *him*.
e   I like *you*.
f   I like *it*.

Do you like me? _____

_____

_____   _____

_____

_____

b   **6.4**   Listen and check.

c   Complete the chart with the words in *italics* from Ex. 5a.

SUBJECT PRONOUN	OBJECT PRONOUN
I	_____
you	_____
he	_____
she	_____
it	_____
we	*us*
they	_____

6   **a**   Work in pairs.

Student A look at the list below.

Student B look at the list on page 130.

1   Tony Blair
2   Natassja Kinski
3   beautiful beaches
4   department stores
5   instant coffee
6   Bill and Hilary Clinton
7   golf

Read your list to your partner. Your partner says *I like/don't like* + object pronoun.

A: *Tony Blair.*

B: *I don't like him.*

b   Read the How to box.

say when you don't understand

A: *Salma Hayek?*
B: *Sorry?/Pardon?/Who's Salma Hayek?*
A: *She's an actor.*
B: *Oh, yes. I like her.*

c   Say more people and things to your partner. Your partner says *I like/don't like* + object pronoun.

Speaking

7   **a**   Write eight new questions. Use:

Do you like …?

Who's/What's your favourite …?

b   Do a 60-second interview with your partner. Use your questions from Ex. 7a.

6.2 Making friends

| Grammar | Present Simple (2) we/they; Wh- questions |
| Can do | start and continue a conversation with someone you don't know |

Anthony

Catherine

Vocabulary | jobs and activities

1   a Match the pictures a–f to the jobs in the box.

a

b

c

d

e

f

> architect   sales rep.   designer   reporter
> chef   builder

a = *designer*

b Write a verb from the box below in each gap.

> sell   write   build   cook   design (x2)

1   What do architects do?
    They *design* buildings, for example houses and shops.

2   What do sales reps. do?
    They _____ things, for example computers and books.

3   What do designers do?
    They _____ things, for example clothes and shoes.

4   What do reporters do?
    They _____ articles, for example newspaper articles.

5   What do chefs do?
    They _____ food, for example Chinese food and Italian food.

6   What do builders do?
    They _____ buildings, for example houses and shops.

c **6.5** Listen and check.

2   a Add another example for each answer above.
Architects design restaurants, too.

b Ask a question from Ex. 1b. Your partner gives the answer.

Listening

3   a **6.6** Listen. Match jobs from Ex. 1a to the people in the photo.

b Listen again. Mark the sentences True (T) or False (F).

Sharon and Pat

1   They live in Ireland.
2   They are on business.
3   They design shops and office buildings.

Catherine and Anthony

4   They are on holiday.
5   They live in Canada.
6   They are sales reps.

Grammar 1 | Present Simple + we/they

4   a Complete the Active grammar box with *do* or *don't*.

Active grammar

⊕	We/They	design	houses.
⊖	We/They	____ live	in Canada.
❓	Do	we/they	sell	computers?

Yes, we/they ____ . / No, we/they ____ .

b Are the sentences below true for you? Write Yes (Y) or No (N) next to the sentences.

1   I like American films.
2   I like Italian food.
3   I like British music.
4   I live near this school.
5   I like football.
6   I live in Berlin.

c Work in pairs. Make sentences about you and your partner.

We don't like American films.

siehe Suchen und finden, Seite 75

Sharon

Pat

Grammar 2 | Wh- questions

5 Complete the Active grammar box with *Who*, *What* or *Where*.

Active grammar

What	do	you	do?
_____	do	you	work/live?
_____	do	you	cook/write?
_____	do	you	work for?

siehe Suchen und finden, Seite 75

6 Write questions from the Active grammar box for each answer below.

1 A: *What do you do?* B: I'm a sales rep.
2 A: _____ ? B: I write articles.
3 A: _____ ? B: I work in Bremen.
4 A: _____ ? B: I work for GT Designs.
5 A: _____ ? B: I design cars.
6 A: _____ ? B: I'm a chef.
7 A: _____ ? B: I live in Zurich.
8 A: _____ ? B: I sell books.

7 Work in pairs. Read the How to box. Ask your partner questions.

HOW TO …

show interest

A: *What do you do?*
B: *I'm a builder/designer/sales rep, etc.*
A: *Oh really?/Great! What do you build/design/sell, etc?*

Reading

8 **a** Read the magazine article. Complete the details.

Name: Martin _____	Name: Clarissa _____
Job: _____	Job: _____
Age: _____	Age: _____

We're best friends!

Clarissa Hanson and Martin Dolan are best friends. Our reporter, Janice Hicks, talks to them.

How old are you?
Clarissa: He's 23 and I'm … over sixty.

What do you do?
Martin: I'm an accountant and she's an actor. We're best friends.

How are you the same?
Clarissa: We're the same in a lot of ways. We like good conversation, good food, good films. We're not rich but we're not poor.
Martin: We're quite intelligent. We like galleries, museums, that kind of thing.

How are you different?
Martin: I'm young and Clarissa is …
Clarissa: … I'm young-at-heart!

b Read the article again. Write Clarissa (C), Martin (M) or not Clarissa/Martin (N) next to each adjective.

1 rich *N* 4 poor
2 young 5 young-at-heart
3 intelligent

Speaking

9 Work in groups of four.
Students A and B: look at page 128.
Students C and D: look at page 130.
You are in a restaurant. You are next to the other pair. Read the details. Start and continue a conversation with the other pair.

6.3 Daily routines

Grammar	Present Simple (3) *he/she/it*
Can do	talk about the routines of people you know

a

b

Vocabulary | Verbs of routine

1 a Read the sentences. Write the correct underlined verb phrases under the pictures.

1 I <u>get up</u> at eleven o'clock.
2 I don't <u>have a shower</u> every day.
3 I <u>eat salad</u> every day.
4 I <u>start work</u> at half past seven in the morning.
5 I don't <u>watch TV</u>.
6 I <u>eat fast food</u> for breakfast.
7 I <u>finish work</u> at nine o'clock.
8 I don't <u>go to bed</u> early.

get up

b Change the sentences in Ex. 1a to make them true for you.

1 *I get up at half past seven every day.*

c Read your sentences to your partner.

Reading

2 a Work in pairs. Look at the photos above. Guess who says the sentences in Ex. 1a.

I think the person in photo b says sentence 1.

b Read the text. Check your answers.

Elaine is my best friend. She's a yoga teacher. She's poor but she's happy. She eats salad every day. She doesn't eat fast food and she doesn't watch TV.

Frank is my brother and he's a biker. He's quite short and very intelligent. He eats fast food for breakfast every day. He doesn't have a shower every day.

Roberta is my aunt. She's a sales rep. She starts work at half past seven in the morning and she finishes work at nine o'clock in the evening. She's not a happy person.

Adam is a musician. He gets up at eleven o'clock in the morning and he goes to bed at two o'clock in the morning. He's not very intelligent – but it's OK – he's good-looking and he's my husband. I love him!

c Answer the questions with *Yes, he/she does* or *No, he/she doesn't*.

1 Does Frank have a shower every day?
   No, he doesn't.
2 Does Adam get up at eight o'clock?
3 Does Elaine eat fast food?
4 Does Roberta start work at half past seven?
5 Does Frank eat fast food for breakfast?
6 Does Elaine watch TV?

c

d

Grammar | Present Simple (3) *he/she/it*

3 Look at the text again and complete the Active grammar box.

Active grammar

➕	He/She/It		start ____ finish ____	work at nine o' clock. work at half past seven.
➖	He/She/It		____ eat ____ like	fast food. salad.
❓	____	he she	get up have breakfast early?	at nine?
	Yes, he/she/it does.		No, he/she/it doesn't.	
➕	He/She/It	has		a shower every day.

siehe Suchen und finden, Seite 75

4 **a** Complete the text with a verb in the correct form.

> have   start   get   like   ~~work~~   finish   watch   eat

My best friend is Yasmin. She's a chef in a Spanish restaurant. She (1) *works* in the evening so she (2) _____ up around ten or eleven o'clock in the morning. She (3) _____ breakfast and lunch together – it's called 'brunch'. She (4) _____ TV in the afternoon and she (5) _____ work around four o'clock. She (6) _____ dinner at work. She (7) _____ work around midnight. She (8) _____ her job but we don't meet – she's always at work!

b Complete the sentences with the correct form of the words in **bold**.

1 He _____ _____ this music. **not like**
2 _____ they _____ here? **work**
3 What _____ he _____ ? **do**
4 Sarah _____ _____ a lot of emails. **not write**
5 What time _____ Mo _____ work? **finish**
6 _____ you _____ work early? **start**
7 Paul and Jo _____ _____ to bed early. **not go**
8 What _____ she _____ ? **write**
9 He _____ clothes. **design**
10 Which company _____ Amy _____ for? **work**

Speaking

5 **a** Complete each sentence below with the name of a friend/family member.

1 _____ is my best friend.
2 _____ is very intelligent.
3 _____ is very good-looking.
4 I love _____ .

b Make notes about each person above.

- What does he/she do? (e.g. *he's a teacher*)
- What adjectives describe him/her (e.g. *she's young, happy*)
- What are his/her routines? (e.g. *he gets up at eight o' clock*)

c Tell your partner about these people.

A: *Who's Erik?*

B: *He's my father. He's very intelligent. He's a sales rep. He's quite short. He gets up at …*

Listening

6 **a** **6.7** Listen to Adam's song. Write all the verbs you hear.

b Listen again and check.

c Work in pairs. Do you like the song? Write more lines for the song.

Writing

7 **a** Look at the *Texte verfassen* on page 135.

b Write a letter to a friend. Tell him/her about your life now.

1 **a** Look at the words in the box. Tick (✓) the words you know.

> book   DVD   MP3 player   tie   bag   flowers   suitcase   travel iron
> saucepans   wallet   CD   cookery book   candles   pen

b Match seven words in the box to the pictures on the website.

---

http://www.findanicepresent.com

my account | track order | quick order | help

Find a nice present

Search [_____] GO!

Information

Present Ideas

Name?	Nisha
Age?	29
Occupation?	Reporter
Company?	Newstime Magazine
Work long hours?	_____
Married?	_____
Have children?	_____
Travel a lot?	_____
Can cook?	_____
Watch a lot of films?	_____
Listen to a lot of music?	_____

1

4

7

2

5

8

3

6

9

---

2 **6.8** Listen to part 1 of the conversation. What is the problem?

3 **a** Look at the words in Ex. 1a. Check the new words in a dictionary.

b **6.9** Listen to part 2 of the conversation. Complete the website for Josef's friend, Nisha. Write Yes (Y) or No (N).

c Look at the findanicepresent chart on page 131. What are the three presents for Nisha?

4 **a** Work in pairs. Add two questions and four presents to the chart.

b Find a new partner.

Student A: close your book. Think of a friend.

Student B: ask questions from your chart. Find a good present for student A's friend. Look at the findanicepresent chart on page 131.

Lifelong learning

Kein Schnee von Gestern!

Spielen Sie Vokabelmemory – auch mit den Wörtern von letzter und vorletzter Woche.

The Present Simple
Die einfache Gegenwart

⊕		
I You	live work	
He She It	lives works	in Munich. near my brother. next to a cinema.
We They	live work	

Bei Vollverben gilt: *He, she, it* – das *s* muss mit!
Have wird mit *he, she, it* zu *has*.

⊖		
I You	don't	like eat
He She It	doesn't	like eat
We They	don't	like eat

chicken.
coffee.
salad.

Bei Vollverben steht mit *he, she, it* '*doesn't*'.

❓			
Do	I you	design write	
Does	he she it	design write	books? magazines?
Do	we they	design write	

Yes, *I/you/we/they do.*   Yes, *he/she/it does.*
No, *I/you/we/they don't.*   No, *he/she/it doesn't.*

Bei Fragen in der 3. Person Singular wird *-es* an *do* angehängt: *does* mit *he, she* und *it*.

❗ Antworten Sie nicht einfach *Yes* oder *No*, das klingt für englische Ohren sehr unhöflich. Benutzen Sie die Kurzantwort, z.B. *Yes, I do* oder *No, I don't*.

Statt *-s* wird bei Verben, die auf *-ch, -sh, -ss*, enden, *-es* angehängt (/ɪz/ ausgesprochen), z.B. *watches, washes, kisses*.

Bei Verben auf *-o* wird *-es* angehängt (/z/ gesprochen), z.B. *goes, does*.

I You We They	have go to finish	breakfast. work. work early.
He She It	has watches does	breakfast. TV. yoga.

Object pronouns
Personalpronomen im Akkusativ

Personalpronomen im Akkusativ sind grammatische Objekte des Verbs (wen oder was?). Sie folgen dem Verb.

SUBJECT PRONOUNS	OBJECT PRONOUNS
I / you / he / she / it / we / they	*me / you / him / her / it / us / them*

Do you like me?   *I like you.*   *We like him.*
He likes her.   *She likes it.*   *They like us.*
I like them.

Verbs of routine
Der Tagesablauf: Verben

1   get up

2   have a shower

3   have breakfast

4   start work

5   finish work

6   have supper

7   watch TV

8   go to bed

Vocabulary | adjectives to describe people

1 **a** Finden Sie in diesem Rätsel fünf Adjektive, die Menschen beschreiben.

s	h	o	r	t
b	s	a	i	h
o	l	d	c	i
m	l	u	h	n
h	a	p	p	y

1 s _ _ _ _   4 h _ _ _ _

2 r _ _ _   5 t _ _ _

3 o _ _

b Bilden Sie Gegensatzpaare, indem Sie die Adjektive aus Üb. 1a diesen Wörtern zuordnen:

1 tall _____   4 poor _____

2 unhappy _____   5 young _____

3 fat _____

Grammar 1 | Present Simple (1)

2 **a** Bilden Sie Sätze mit *I like/I don't like*.

1 (☺ / cappuccino) *I like cappuccino.*

2 (☹ / museums) *I don't like museums.*

3 (☺ / French music) _____ .

4 (☹ / Arsenal Football Club) _____ .

5 (☺ / Leipzig) _____ .

6 (☹ / Indian food) _____ .

7 (☹ / espresso) _____ .

8 (☺ / children) _____ .

b Ergänzen Sie jeweils eine Frage und eine Kurzantwort.

1 A: *Do you like black coffee?* black coffee

B: Yes, *I do.*

2 A: *Do you like the countryside?* the countryside

B: No, *I don't.*

3 A: _____ ? Chinese food

B: Yes, _____ .

4 A: _____ ? modern buildings

B: No, _____ .

5 A: _____ ? salad

B: Yes, _____ .

6 A: _____ ? supermarkets

B: No, _____ .

7 A: _____ ? department stores

B: Yes, _____ .

8 A: _____ ? American cars

B: Yes, _____ .

Grammar 2 | object pronouns

3 **a** Ersetzen Sie die unterstrichenen Wörter durch die richtigen Pronomen: *me, you, him, her, it, us* oder *them*.

Now that I'm seventy …

by Harold Parks

Now that I'm 70, I am happy. A lot of people are my best friends. My children are my best friends. I like (1) my children. My sister is my best friend – I like (2) my sister. My brother is my best friend. I like (3) my brother. The television is my best friend. We are together every evening. I like (4) the television. And you are my best friend. I like (5) you. Do you like (6) Harold Parks?

b Ersetzen Sie die unterstrichenen Wörter durch die richtigen Pronomen.

1 You and I are rich.   *We*

2 They like you and I.   ____

3 Kevin and Callum are builders.   ____

4 Do you like Kevin and Callum?   ____

5 Ella Fitzgerald is my favourite singer. ____

6 I like Ella Fitzgerald.   ____

7 Richard is my best friend.   ____

8 I like Richard.   ____

Vocabulary | jobs and activities

1 Ergänzen Sie die Sätze mit den richtigen Berufen.

1 _Designers_ design things.

2 _____ cook food.

3 _____ build buildings.

4 _____ sell things.

5 _____ write articles.

6 _____ design buildings.

Grammar | Present Simple (2) _we/they_

2 Sehen Sie sich die Tabelle an. Schreiben Sie Sätze mit _we_ und _they_.

	GRACE AND MARLON	STEVE AND SHENA
(1) like their job	YES	NO
(2) work in an office	YES	NO
(3) sell cars	NO	YES
(4) design cars	YES	NO

1 Grace: _We like our jobs. They don' t like their jobs._

2 Grace: _____ . _____ .

3 Grace: _____ . _____ .

4 Grace: _____ . _____ .

Grammar | _Wh-_ questions

3 **a** Ergänzen Sie jede Frage mit einem Wort.

1 What _do_ you design?

2 _____ do you do?

3 Where _____ you live?

4 _____ do you work for?

5 _____ do you work?

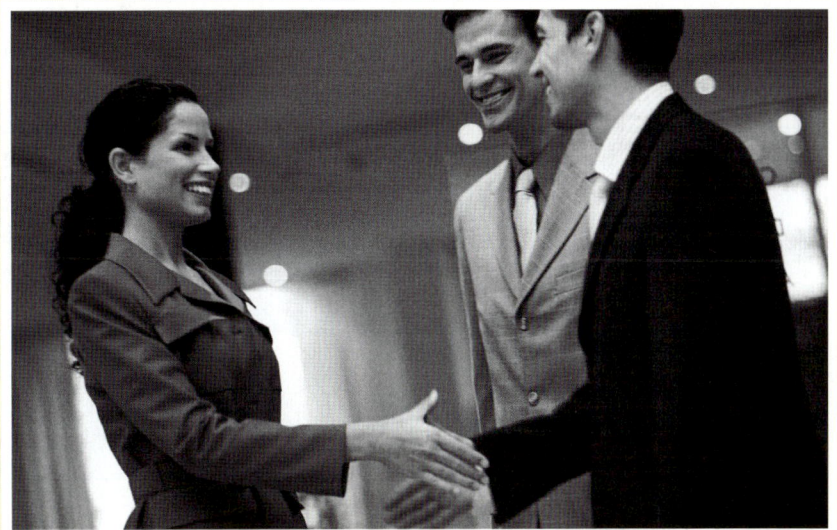

b Ergänzen Sie hier mit den Fragen 1–5 aus Üb. 3a.

Neil: Excuse me. Kate, this is Lance.

Kate: Hello Lance. Nice to meet you.

Lance: Nice to meet you, too.

Kate: (1) _What do you do?_

Lance: I'm a designer.

Kate: Oh really? (2) _____ ?

Lance: It's a company called Confident Designs.

Kate: (3) _____ ?

Lance: I design shoes and clothes.

Kate: Great! (4) _____ ?

Lance: In a small office in Manchester.

Kate: (5) _____ ?

Lance: In a house in a village near Manchester. What do you do?

Vocabulary | verbs of routine

1 a Ordnen Sie die Wörter in der linken und rechten Spalte einander zu.

1	watch	a)	to bed
2	start	b)	up
3	eat	c)	work
4	finish	d)	TV
5	go	e)	shower
6	get	f)	a sandwich
7	have a		

b Ordnen Sie die Wendungen aus Üb. 1a den Bildern oben zu.

1 *get up*   5 _____
2 _____   6 _____
3 _____   7 _____
4 _____

Grammar Present Simple (3) |
he / she / it

2 Sehen Sie sich die Bilder in Üb. 1b an und schreiben Sie Sätze.

1 *She gets up at 10.30.*
2 _____ .
3 _____ .
4 _____ .
5 _____ .
6 _____ .
7 _____ .

3 Verneinen Sie diese Sätze:

1 He eats chocolate.   *He doesn't eat chocolate.*
2 She likes chicken.
3 William starts work early.
4 Teresa gets up at seven-thirty.
5 He goes to bed late.
6 She finishes work at five o'clock.
7 He watches TV every day.

4 Lesen Sie diesen Text und beantworten Sie die Fragen.

1 Does Mrs Moody start work early? *Yes, she does.*
2 Does she have breakfast? _____ .
3 Does she drink coffee? _____ .
4 Does she go to the restaurant for lunch? _____ .
5 Does she finish work late? _____ .
6 Does she have any friends? _____ .

My manager is called Mrs Moody. She starts work at seven o'clock every morning. She doesn't have breakfast. She has a coffee at eleven o'clock. She has salad for lunch. She doesn't go to the restaurant - she eats her salad at her desk. She finishes work at about eight o'clock. She doesn't have any friends.

A

7 | Work

B

C

D

Lead-in

1 **a** What can you see in the photos?

b Match a word in the box to one of the photos/pictures A–H.

> office   factory   shop   hospital   university   school   restaurant
> call centre

E    F   G    H

2 **a** Match a person below to a place above.

1	a waiter	5	a sales assistant
2	a PA	6	a lecturer
3	a factory worker	7	a call centre worker
4	a nurse	8	a teacher

b **7·1** Listen and check.

c **7·2** Listen. Who is he/she? Where does he/she work?

1 She's a *sales assistant*. She works *in a shop*.

2 She's a _____ . She works _____ .

3 He's a _____ . He works _____ .

4 He's a _____ . He works _____ .

5 She's a _____ . She works _____ .

6 He's a _____ . He works _____ .

7 He's a _____ . He works _____ .

8 She's a _____ . She works _____ .

Listening and vocabulary

1 **a** Look at the pictures above. Who are the people? Where are they?

b [7.3] Listen. Answer the questions.

1 What is the man's name?
2 What is the woman's name?
3 What is the boy's name?

c Listen again. Write a conversation number next to each phrase below.

Phrase	Conversation
a Please sit down.	_2_
b Hold the line, please.	___
c Be quiet.	___
d Turn off your mobile phone.	___
e Listen to the conversation.	___
f Look at page 32.	___
g Come in.	___

d Write a phrase from Ex. 1c next to each picture below.

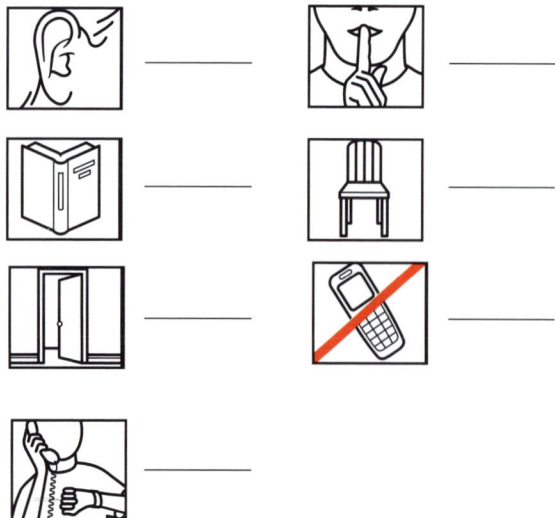

Grammar | imperatives

2 **a** Write a verb from Ex. 1c in the Active grammar box.

Active grammar

⊕ Be quiet.
_____ at page 45.

⊖ Don't _____ in.
Don't _____ down.

Use *please* to make an imperative polite.
***Please** be quiet. **Please** don't look at my emails.*

b Put a word/phrase from each box into the correct gap.

Turn off   ~~Don't be~~   Speak   Use

Our English class
(1) *Don't be* late.
(2) _____ English in class.
(3) _____ your mobile phone.
(4) _____ a good dictionary.

don't get up   eat   don't eat   don't watch

Hi David
Please (5) _____ late and (6) _____ TV all day.
And please (7) _____ a sandwich or salad for lunch. (8) _____ chocolate!
Thanks!
Jenny

siehe Suchen und finden, Seite 87

3 a [7.4] Work in pairs. Listen. Match an announcement/imperative to a place a–e below.

a hospital **b** shop **c** airport **d** restaurant **e** school

b Listen again. Write the imperative.

4 Write imperatives for **a** How to learn English and **b** How to succeed at work.

Learn English

1 *Speak English every day.*

Speaking

5 a Read the How to box.

> **HOW TO …**
>
> ### make a business phonecall
>
> B: *Hello. Parkside School.*
> A: **Can I speak to** *Mrs. Fischer, please?*
> B: **Hold the line, please.**
> C: *Hello. Alice Fischer.*
> A: *Hello, Mrs. Fischer.* **My name's …/It's …**
>
> Use *My name's* for people you don't know.
> Use *It's* for people you know.

b Work in groups of three. Practise phone calls. Use the names below.

1 Company = JK Designs
   A = Paul Walker   B = PA
   C = John Keen

2 Company = Bodgit Builders
   A = Angelo Romano   B = PA
   C = Sally Wood

3 Company = Renzo Rogers Architects
   A = Helen Davis   B = PA
   C = Hans-Martin Hoffmann

Lifelong learning

Vom Klassenraum ins richtige Leben!

Wenn Sie das nächste Mal etwas im Internet suchen oder buchen, versuchen Sie einmal, die englische Version der Website zu benutzen! Wo und wie können Sie noch "den Ernstfall proben"?

Reading

6 Read the text. Answer the questions.

1 What time does Tim start work?
2 What does Tim do between 8.00a.m. and 9.00a.m?
3 Where does Tim have lunch?
4 What does Tim do between 3.30p.m. and 6.00p.m?
5 What time does Tim finish work?
6 When does Tim have a long holiday?

Tim Clarke - a teacher in the UK

I get up at 6.45a.m. in the morning. I have a shower, I have breakfast and I go to school. I start work at 8.00a.m. I look at students' books and prepare lessons. I teach from 9.00a.m. to 12.30p.m. I have lunch in my classroom – a sandwich or a salad.

In the afternoon I teach from 1.30p.m. to 3.30p.m. After school I teach football or I work in my classroom. I go home at 6.00p.m. and I have dinner. After dinner I look at students' books and prepare lessons. I finish work at 9.30p.m. in the evening. Teachers work a lot but we have a long holiday in July* and August.

* for help with months look at Ex. 8a

Vocabulary | months

7 a [7.5] Read the months and listen. Mark the stress.

January	February	March	April
May	June	July	August
September	October	November	December

b Listen again and repeat.

c Look at the calendar pictures of the UK on page 130. Guess the month.

d Work in pairs. Complete the sentences with months. Explain your reasons.

1 My favourite month is …
2 I don't like …

My favourite month is June. It's not cold and it's not very hot.

Grammar	adverbs of frequency
Can do	say how often you do something

Vocabulary | work phrases

1 **a** Look at the phrases on the *What's your job?* board. Match each phrase to a picture 1–9.

b Think of one job for each work phrase.

work from home – artist

2 **a** **7.6** Listen. Write Yes (Y) or No (N) on the *What's your job?* board.

WHAT'S YOUR JOB?

	YES OR NO?	
work from home	____	*never*
have meetings	____	____
give presentations	____	____
call customers	____	____
write reports	____	____
take work home	____	____
travel abroad	____	____
answer the phone	____	____
work outdoors	____	____

b Work in pairs. Remember the questions.

c What is John's job?

   a sales rep. **b** reporter **c** police officer

Grammar | adverbs of frequency

3 **a** Listen again and look at the Active grammar box. Write a word/phrase from the box in each gap on the *What's your job?* board.

b Look at tapescript 7.6 on page 140. Complete the Active grammar box with the correct words.

Active grammar

100% ⬉ always
　　　usually
　　　　often
　　　　　sometimes
　　　　　　not often/not usually
　　0%　⬊ never

1) verb *be* + **adverb of frequency**

   I'm _____ _____ ! I love this game.

2) **adverb of frequency** + verb

   I _____ _____ three of four reports a week.

---

siehe Suchen und finden, Seite 87

4 **a** Correct the mistakes.

1 I work never from home.

   I never work from home.

2 She often doesn't travel abroad.

3 I take usually work home.

4 Always we call customers.

5 We write sometimes reports in the evening.

6 Never he works outdoors.

7 I don't give often presentations.

8 Always they call their customers in the evening.

b Write sentences about your daily routines. Use a phrase in the box and an adverb of frequency.

> get up   go to bed   start work   finish work
> watch TV   have a shower
> have (something for) breakfast/lunch/dinner

I usually get up at seven o' clock.

I always have a salad for lunch.

Pronunciation

5 **a** 〔7.7〕 Listen. Write the sentences.

b Listen again. How do you pronounce *often* and *usually*? Repeat the sentences.

Writing

6 **a** Read the notes 1–3 below. Match each one to a picture a–c.

1

Hi Uma
Can you answer my phone this afternoon? I have a meeting at two o'clock. Thanks,
Guy

2

Warren
I'm at home today. Can you call me? I have some questions for you.
Many thanks,
Piotr

3

Hello Livvy
Can you come to my office at 3 o'clock?
Thanks,
Ivan

 a

 b

 c

b Read the How to box. Then look at the list below and write a request note to Benita.

HOW TO …

write a request note

Start: *Hello / Hi, Jay.*

Request: *Can + request?*

Finish: *Thanks, / Many thanks, + your name.*

To do

~~call Mrs. Santiago~~

~~write report on visit to China~~

email to Benita — come to my office at 7 o'clock tomorrow morning?

Grammar	*would like*
Can do	welcome a visitor to your place of work

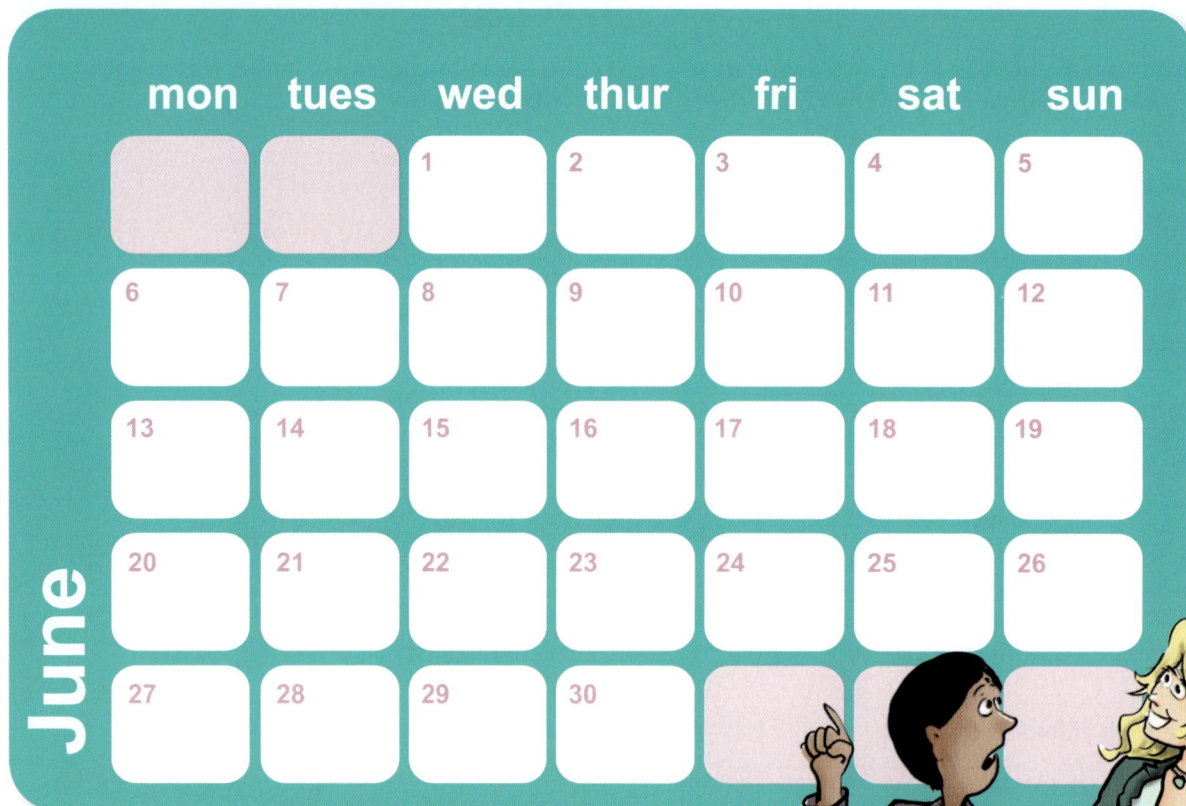

	mon	tues	wed	thur	fri	sat	sun
June			1	2	3	4	5
	6	7	8	9	10	11	12
	13	14	15	16	17	18	19
	20	21	22	23	24	25	26
	27	28	29	30			

Listening

1 **a** 〔7.8〕 Listen. What's the date?

    a 6th June   **b** 14th June   **c** 24th June

    b Listen again. What dates are the visits below.

    1   Mrs King: **a** 4th June   **b** 14th June
    2   Miss Brown: **a** 24th June   **b** 25th June
    3   Mr Wu: **a** 8th June   **b** 18th June

2 Michelle welcomes Mr Rogers and his colleague to the office. Work in groups of three. Act out the conversation.

    Michelle: *Hello, Mr Rogers. My name's ...*

Vocabulary | ordinal numbers

3 **a** 〔7.9〕 Look at the calendar again. Listen and repeat the ordinal numbers.

    b Work in pairs. Look at the chart on page 132. Say the ordinal numbers.

4 Read the How to box.

<table>
<tr><td rowspan="6" style="writing-mode: vertical-lr">HOW TO ...</td><td colspan="2">write and say dates</td></tr>
<tr><td colspan="2">Write -th after the number (but remember 1st, 2nd and 3rd!)</td></tr>
<tr><td>Write</td><td>Say</td></tr>
<tr><td>1st September</td><td>the first of September</td></tr>
<tr><td>2nd July</td><td>the second of July</td></tr>
<tr><td>3rd April</td><td>the third of April</td></tr>
<tr><td>15th January</td><td>the fifteenth of January</td></tr>
</table>

siehe Suchen und finden, Seite 87

5 **a** Write a date in numbers. Your partner says the date.

    20/09

    'the twentieth of September'

    b Ask and answer.

    A: *When is your birthday?*

    B: *It's ...*

Grammar | *would like*

6 a [7.10] Read and listen to the conversation. Complete the gaps.

Michelle: Please, come in. Sit down. What would you like (1) *to* drink? Tea? Coffee?

Mr Rogers: I'd like a coffee, please.

Ms. Khan: I'd (2) _____ a cup of tea, please.

Michelle: Would you like milk and sugar?

Mr Rogers: No thank you.

Ms. Khan: Milk, no sugar, please.

Michelle: (3) _____ you like a biscuit?

Mr Rogers: Yes, please.

Ms. Khan: No, (4) _____ you.

b Listen again and check.

c Read the conversation aloud in groups of three.

7 Complete the Active grammar box with *would* or *'d*.

Active grammar

would like + noun

? What *would* you like (to drink/to eat)?
_____ you like a coffee/a biscuit?
Yes, please.   No, thank you.

+ I _____ like   a cup of tea.
(*'d = would*)   an orange juice.

Would you like …? and *I'd like …* are polite.
Do you want …? and *I want …* are informal.

---

siehe Suchen und finden, Seite 87

8 a Complete the conversations with phrases from the Active grammar box.

1 **A:** *What would you like to drink?*
   B: _____ a coffee, please.

2 **A:** _____ a cup of tea?
   B: _____ (Yes)

3 **A:** _____ to eat?
   B: _____ a sandwich, please.

4 **A:** _____ biscuit
   B: _____ (No)

5 **A:** _____ a coffee?
   B: _____ (No)

6 **A:** _____ to drink?
   B: _____ an orange   juice, please.

Listening and vocabulary

9 a Match the words below to the pictures.

> soup fruit vegetables main courses
> desserts starters salad drinks snacks

b [7.11] Listen to Michelle, Mr Rogers and Ms Khan. Complete a–d on the map of the staff canteen.

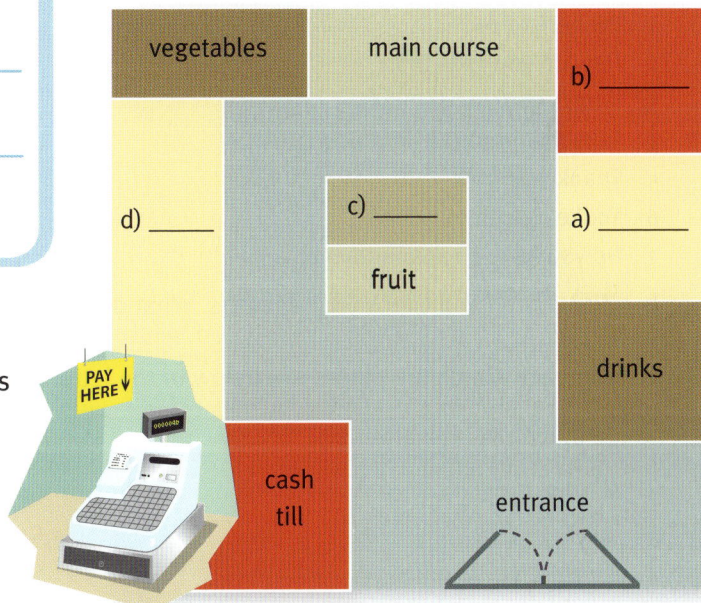

Speaking

10 a Work in pairs.

Student A: you are a visitor.

Student B: welcome Students A to your office. Offer drinks/snacks.

A: *Hello Mrs Capriati. My name is Uri Osman.*

B: *Nice to meet you, Mr Osman. This is my colleague, Miss …*

7 Communication

Take the lift to the third floor

5th Floor	PAs
4th Floor	Managers
3rd Floor	Sales reps.
2nd Floor	Accountants
1st Floor	Canteen
Ground Floor	Reception

3rd Floor

b   d

a

↑
LIFT

c

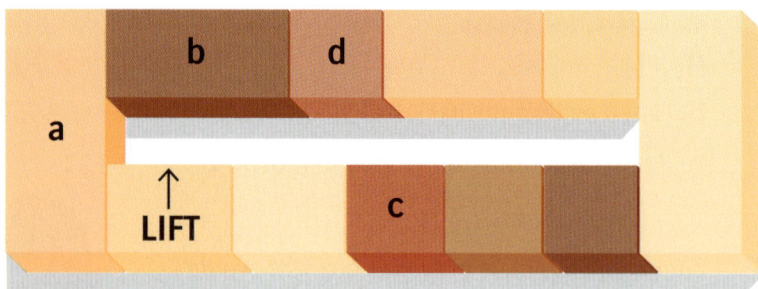

1 Work in pairs. Talk about the different floors of the building.

A: *What floor are the sales reps. on?*

B: *They're on the third floor.*

2 a Who says the phrases below the receptionist (r) or the visitor (v)?

1 I'm here to see …
2 How do you spell that?
3 What's your name, please?
4 Take the lift to the third floor.
5 Thank you.
6 You're welcome.
7 Do you have an appointment?

b 7.12 Listen and check your answers. What do *left* and *right* mean?

3 Listen again. Match the places 1–4 below to the letters a–d on the floor plan.

1 Patrick Swinton's office
2 Martina Hafner's office
3 toilet
4 Lorda Romero's office

4 a Work in pairs.

Student A: you are the receptionist. Think of a name of someone who works in the building. Write it on the floor plan. Tell your partner the name.

Student B: you are a visitor. Listen to the name Student A tells you. You have a meeting with this person. Act out the conversation.

A: *Good morning.*

B: *Good morning. I have a meeting with …*

b Find a new partner and repeat.

Imperatives
Die Befehlsform

sit down.

hold the line.

be quiet.

(Please) *turn off your mobile phone.*

listen to the conversation.

look at page 32.

come in.

Verneinte Befehle können Verbote sein!

don't sit down.

don't turn off your mobile phone.

(Please) *don't look at page 32.*

don't come in.

Verwenden Sie bitte immer *please*, um aus dem Befehl eine höfliche Bitte zu machen.

Adverbs of frequency
Adverbien der Häufigkeit (*wie oft?*)

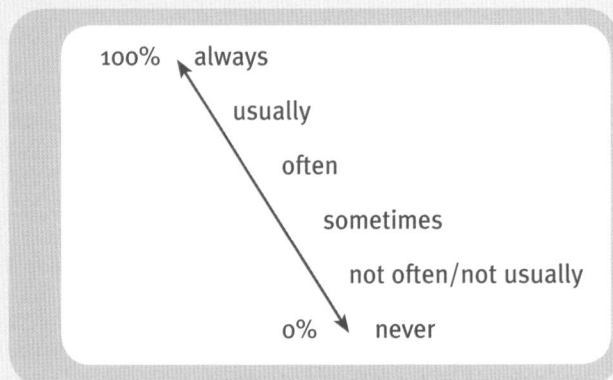

100% — always
usually
often
sometimes
not often/not usually
0% — never

Adverbien der Häufigkeit stehen nach dem Verb *be*.

She's <u>always</u> late.

They're <u>never</u> happy.

I'm <u>sometimes</u> at work at half past six.

Adverbien der Häufigkeit stehen vor dem Vollverb, d.h. auch: zwischen Hilfsverb und Vollverb.

I <u>never</u> answer the phone.

He doesn't <u>often</u> give presentations.

We don't <u>usually</u> eat desserts.

Would you like ...? I'd like ...

Mit der Frage *Would you like ...?* bietet man etwas an, z.B. ein Getränk.

Fragen

What would you like?

What would you like to drink?

Would you like a coffee? Yes, please/No, thank you.

Mit *I'd like ...* bittet man um etwas, bestellt etwas oder nimmt ein Angebot an.

Aussage oder Bitte

I'd like a cup of tea, please.

I'd like a starter, please.

Making requests
Aufforderungen

Mit *Can you* + Verb fordern Sie jemanden auf, etwas zu tun.

Can you call me, please?

Can you come to my office, please?

Can you look at this, please?

So antworten Sie:

⊕ *Yes, OK. /Sure./Of course.*

⊖ *I'm sorry, I can't./I can't, I'm afraid.*

Ordnungszahlen

1st first	11th eleventh
2nd second	12th twelfth
3rd third	13th thirteenth
4th fourth	14th fourteenth
5th fifth	15th fifteenth
6th sixth	16th sixteenth
7th seventh	17th seventeenth
8th eighth	18th eighteenth
9th ninth	19th nineteenth
10th tenth	20th twentieth

Datumsangaben – Britisch

Sie schreiben: *the meeting is on 12th July / 12/07, my holiday is from 21st May to 1st June*

Sie sagen: *the meeting is on the twelfth of July, my holiday is from the twenty-first of May to the first of June*

Datumsangaben – Amerikanisch:

Der Monat steht vor dem Tag!

Sie schreiben: *the meeting is on July 12th / 07/12*

Sie sagen: *the meeting is on July the twelfth*

Vocabulary | people and places

1 Ordnen Sie jeder Person links einen Arbeitsplatz rechts zu.

1 shop assistant   **a)** school
2 factory work   **b)** call centre
3 nurse   **c)** restaurant
4 waiter   **d)** shop
5 teacher   **e)** office
6 PA   **f)** university
7 call centre worker   **g)** factory
8 lecturer   **h)** hospital

Grammar | imperatives

2 Schreiben Sie einen Imperativ neben jedes Bild. Tipp: Benutzen Sie die Wörter in Klammern.

1 (quiet) _____

2 (down) _____

3 (watch) _____

4 (line) _____

5 (look) _____

6 (in) _____

How to make a business phone call

3 Ordnen Sie diese Sätze neu, so dass sich ein Telefongespräch ergibt.

Hold the line, please.   [   ]
Hello, Ms. Price.   [   ]
Good morning. Rordon Engineering.   [1]
Jurgen Schmitt.   [   ]
Hello Mr Schmitt. This is Vanessa Price.   [   ]
Good morning. Can I speak to Jurgen Schmitt, please?   [   ]

Vocabulary | months

4 **a** Ergänzen Sie die Monatsnamen unten und bringen Sie sie in die richtige Reihenfolge.

J _ l y   [   ]
_ c t _ b _ r   [   ]
J _ n _ _ r y   [1]
D _ c _ m b _ r   [   ]
_ _ g _ s t   [   ]
M _ y   [   ]
_ p r _ l   [   ]
F _ b r _ _ r _   [   ]
N _ v _ m b _ r   [   ]
J _ n _   [   ]
S _ p t _ m b _ r   [   ]
M _ r c h   [   ]

b In welchem Monat wurden diese Prominenten geboren?

1 Andre Previn (06/04/1929) *April*
2 Giorgio Armani (11/07/1934) _____
3 Stephen Hawking (08/01/1942) _____
4 Roger Federer (08/08/1981) _____
5 John Travolta (18/02/1954) _____
6 Bruce Springsteen (23/09/1949) _____
7 Woody Allen (1/12/1935) _____
8 Bono (10/05/1960) _____
9 Angelina Jolie (04/06/1975) _____
10 Sting (02/10/1951) _____
11 Brooklyn Beckham (04/03/1999) _____
12 Condoleezza Rice (14/11/1954) _____

Vocabulary | work phrases

1 **a** <u>Unterstreichen</u> Sie das richtige Verb.

1 *work/call/write* customers
2 *answer/have/write* the phone
3 *work/travel/write* reports
4 *call/work/take* work home
5 *give/work/travel* from home
6 *work/give/have* outdoors
7 *call/give/answer* presentations
8 *answer/travel/have* abroad
9 *have/write/work* meetings

b Ordnen Sie die Wendungen oben den Bildern unten zu.

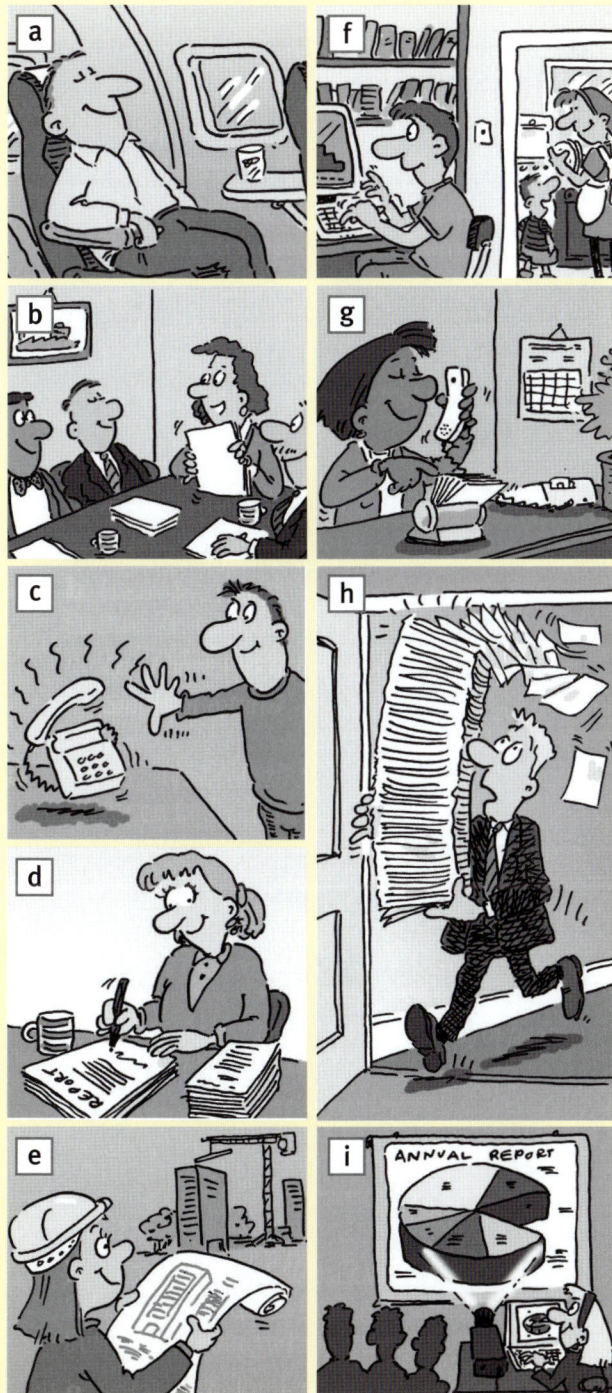

Grammar | adverbs of frequency

2 **a** Schreiben Sie die Adverbien der Häufigkeit im Kasten in die Lücken a–f.

> ~~often~~   never   sometimes   usually
> not often/not usually   always

100%   a _____
         b _____
         c *often*
         d _____
         e _____
0%   f _____

b Ordnen Sie diese Wörter neu und bilden Sie Sätze oder Fragen.

1 afternoon. watch TV never I in the

_____ .

2 work Maggie usually home. doesn't take

_____ .

3 We outdoors. work sometimes

_____ .

4 to always go Do bed you at 11 o'clock?

_____ .

5 golf He Sundays. often plays on

_____ .

6 abroad. They travel don't often

_____ .

3 Schreiben Sie die Adverbien der Häufigkeit an die richtige Stelle.

1 I swim in the sea. (not often)
I don't often swim in the sea.

2 I'm late for work. (sometimes)

_____ .

3 I drive. (never)

_____ .

4 I sing and play the piano at family parties. (usually)

_____ .

5 My manager answers the phone at work. (not usually)

_____ .

6 He is happy on Friday afternoons. (always)

_____ .

Vocabulary | ordinal numbers and dates

1 **a** Schreiben Sie die Wörter aus dem Kasten neben die richtigen Ordnangszahlen.

> fourth   fifth   sixth   second   eighth
> first   ninth   third   tenth   seventh

1st _____

2nd _____

3rd _____

4th _____

5th _____

6th _____

7th _____

8th _____

9th _____

10th _____

b Schreiben Sie die Datumsangaben aus.

1   the twenty-first of January   *21st January*

2   the eleventh of March   _____

3   the first of May   _____

4   the twelfth of December   _____

5   the twentieth of June   _____

6   the sixteenth of November   _____

7   the second of September   _____

8   the third of February   _____

Grammar | would like

2 **a** Ergänzen Sie das Gespräch mit den Wörtern aus dem Kasten.

> What would you like   I'd like a
> thank you   ~~What would you like to~~
> Would you like   I'd like

A: Hello, Mr Wallace. My name's Orla Birch.

B: Hello, Ms. Birch. This is Mrs Trenter.

A: Nice to meet you, Mrs Trenter.

C: Nice to meet you, too.

A: Please, come into my office. (1) *What would you like to drink?*

B: (2) _____ coffee, please.

C: And I'd like a cup of tea, please.

A: (3) _____ milk and sugar?

B: No, (4) _____ . Just black.

C: Yes, please.

A: (5) _____ to eat? A piece of cake?

B: I'd like some fruit, please.

C: (6) _____ a piece of cake. Thank you.

b Schreiben Sie Fragen und Antworten mit Hilfe der **fettgedruckten** Wörter.

1   A: *Would you like a black coffee?* **black coffee**

   B: *No, thank you.* **No**

2   A: _____ ? **piece of cake**

   B: _____ . **Yes**

3   A: _____ ? **mineral water**

   B: _____ . **No**

4   A: _____ ? **orange juice**

   B: _____ . **Yes**

5   A: _____ ? **ham sandwich**

   B: _____ . **No**

Vocabulary | food

3   Sehen Sie sich die Bilder an und ergänzen Sie die Speisekarte.

(1) *Starters*

Chicken (2) _____
Salad

(3) *Main* _____
Fish and chips

Spaghetti Bolognese
+ selection of
(4) _____

(5) *Desserts*

Ice cream
(6) _____

A

8 Leisure

B

C

D

Lead-in

1 a Match an activity in the box to a picture below.

> go cycling   eat out   play chess   play tennis   go sightseeing
> go for a walk   read a book   play football   go to the theatre
> do exercise   go swimming   watch TV

1 ____   5 ____   9 ____

2 ____   6 ____   10 ____

3 ____   7 ____   11 ____

4 ____   8 ____   12 ____

b 8.1 Listen and check. Repeat.

c Which activities can you see in the photos?

2 Work in pairs. Say an activity from Ex. 1a without the verb. Your partner says the verb.

A: *swimming*   **B:** *go swimming*

3 a How often do you do these leisure activities? Tell your partner.
I usually watch TV in the evening.   I never go to the theatre.

b Find a new partner. Tell him/her about your old partner.
He always goes swimming on Saturdays.

Grammar	*like* + *ing*; *want* + infinitive
Can do	explain why you want to do something

Speaking

1 a Look at the hotels. Say the phone numbers and email addresses.

b What can you see in the photos?

c Read the How to box. What leisure activities can you do at each hotel?

<table>
<tr><td rowspan="6" style="writing-mode:vertical-lr">HOW TO ...</td><td>

talk about things to do

Use *You can ...* or *we can ...* to talk about things to do in a place (e.g. hotel/city/country).

You can play golf at the Langstone Hotel.

We can go sightseeing in Paris.
</td></tr>
</table>

2 Do you know any good hotels? What can you do there?

I like The Palace Hotel in Vienna. You can swim. You can play tennis.

Listening

3 a [8.2] Listen. What is Gary and Annie's problem?

b [8.3] Listen. Complete the sentences with a hotel.

1 Gary wants to go to _____ .

2 Annie wants to go to _____ .

3 They both want to go to _____ .

c Listen again. Make a list of the leisure activities that you hear.

play golf

THE LANGSTON HOTEL

Tel: 0331 449 218
langstonhotel@newmail.co.uk

New Metro Hotel

Tel: 0991 722 3781
newmetrohotel@metromail.com

Blue Sea Hotel

TEL: 0649 559 221
blueseahotel@netmail.co.uk

Grammar | *like + ing; want + infinitive*

4 Complete the Active grammar box with *want* or *like*.

> ### Active grammar
>
> I _____ to go sightseeing.
> I don't _____ to play golf.
>
> I _____ playing golf.
> I don't _____ going sightseeing.

siehe Suchen und Finden, Seite 99

5 a Choose the correct form of the verb to complete the sentences.

1 I like *going out with friends/to go out with friends*.
2 Gary doesn't like *watching TV/to watch TV*.
3 Do you want *playing tennis/to play tennis*?
4 We like *going sightseeing/to go sightseeing*.
5 She doesn't want e*ating out/to eat out*.
6 Do they like *playing chess/to play chess*?
7 I don't like *swimming/to go swimming*.
8 Martin wants *reading/to read* now.

b Complete the conversation. Put the verb in brackets into the correct form.

A: Can you swim?
B: Yes, I can, but I don't like (1) *swimming* (swim). I like football.
A: Football? Can you play football?
B: No, but I like (2) _____ (watch) it on TV.
A: Do you want (3) _____ (play) golf?
B: No, thanks. I don't like (4) _____ (play) golf. I like (5) _____ (go) for a walk.
A: Where do you want (6) _____ (go)?
B: To the beach. I want (7) _____ (go) swimming. Where's your bicycle?
A: It's at home. But I don't want (8) _____ (go) swimming. I don't like (9) _____ (go) swimming. I want (10) _____ (go) for a walk.

6 Work in pairs. Look at the leisure activities on page 91. Answer these questions.

1 What do you like doing?
2 What don't you like doing?
3 What do you want to do this evening?
4 What do you want to do this Saturday and Sunday?

Vocabulary | adjectives

7 a Match a word in the box to a situation below.

> boring ~~exciting~~ difficult interesting fun easy

1 This is really *exciting*.

2 This is very _____.

3 This is _____.

4 This is _____.

5 This is very _____.

6 This is really _____.

b What do you think of the leisure activities on page 91. Tell your partner.
I think playing golf is difficult.

Speaking

8 a Choose a hotel from Ex. 1 for next weekend. Find other students to go with you.

A: *I want to go to the New Metro Hotel. I like going sightseeing. It's exciting.*
B: *I don't like going sightseeing. It's boring. I want to go to the Blue Sea Hotel ...*

Writing

9 a Look at the *Texte verfassen* on page 135.

b Write an email to one of the hotels in Ex. 1. Ask for more information.

How much is a double room?

Is a double room available for Saturday 29th and Sunday 30th next month?

Grammar	have got/has got
Can do	say what things you possess

labels in picture: p, garden, bedroom, c, a, b, bathroom, e, f, d, garage, kitchen, h, living room, n, o, g, j, i, k, l, m

Vocabulary | rooms and furniture

1 a Look at the house. Where do you:

a cook   **b** watch TV   **c** have a shower
d go to bed   **e** park your car   **f** play football

You cook in the kitchen.

b Match the words below to the letters a–p in the picture.

washing machine   basin   coffee table   sofa   bicycle   bed
fridge   bath   armchair   lamp   cooker   wardrobe   toilet
sink   car   mirror

c `8.4` Listen and check. Repeat.

2 a Make lists.

1 Which things do you find in a hotel room?
2 You buy a new house. Which seven things do you buy first?

b Compare with your partner.

c Work in pairs. What things in your house do you like? What things don't you like?

I like my bath. It's big.

I don't like my television. It's old.

Listening

3 a `8.5` Listen. Which things from Ex. 1b do you hear?

b Listen again. Answer the questions.

1 When is Paul's sister's wedding?
2 What does Paul's sister like doing?
3 What things from Ex. 1b has she got?
4 What things from Ex. 1b hasn't she got?

c Look at Jo's suggestion for a wedding present on page 131. Do you think it's a good idea?

d What is a good wedding present in your country?

Grammar | *have got/has got*

4 **a** Look at tapescript 8.5 on page 141. Underline examples of *have got* and *has got*.

b Complete the Active grammar box with *have* or *has*.

Active grammar

⊕ I		
⊖ You We They	_____ got ('ve got) haven't got	a bicycle. a sofa. a garden. a garage.
⊕ He ⊖ She It	_____ got ('s got) hasn't got	
❓ ____	I/you/we/they got	a bicycle?
❓ ____	he/she/it got	an armchair?

Yes, I/you/we/they ____ . Yes, he/she/it ____ .
No, I/you/we/they ___n't. No, he/she/it ___n't.

siehe Suchen und Finden, Seite 99

5 **a** Ask your partner questions with the words in Ex. 1b.

A: *Have you got an armchair?*
B: *Yes, I have. I've got two armchairs in my living room and I've got one armchair in my bedroom.*

b Complete the texts with *'ve*, *'s*, *haven't* or *hasn't*.

I live with my wife in a small house. We (1) **'ve** got a bedroom, a living room, a kitchen and a bathroom. We (2) ____ got a small garden – it's beautiful. But we (3) ____ got a garage.
My wife (4) ____ got a car. She drives to work every day. I (5) ____ got a car. I can't drive. But I (6) ____ got a bicycle.

I live in my sister's house. She (7) ____ got four bedrooms and two living rooms. She (8) ____ got a TV in her bedroom. She watches TV in bed. But she (9) ____ got a TV in the living room. She (10) ____ got a sofa and a big armchair in the living room.
She (11) ____ got a big cooker in the kitchen – it's great. We like cooking. She (12) ____ got a microwave oven. She doesn't like them.

Pronunciation

6 **a** **8.6** Listen and check your answers.

b How do you pronounce *I've*, *we've* and *she's*?

c Read the texts in Ex. 5b aloud.

Speaking

7 Find a new partner. Talk about your house, flat or bedroom.
My family has got a house. It's quite big. I've got a small bedroom. I've got a TV and a computer in my bedroom but I haven't got ...

Reading

8 **a** Do the *Technology* quiz on page 131.

b Complete the quiz for your partner.
A: *Have you got a camera-phone?*
B: *No, I haven't, but I want one.*

9 **a** What is your score and what is your partner's score?
A = 2 points   B = 1 point   C = 0 points

b Read your profile below.

0–6 points: you don't like new technology, you like old things. Your photographs are on paper, not on your computer. You've haven't got any DVDs or MP3s (but you've got some CDs). You use a map – you don't use a GPS device. Your television is quite old.

7–12 points: you like new technology and you sometimes buy new things. You've got some DVDs and you've got some MP3s. You sometimes read about new technology in newspapers and magazines. You take a digital camera on holiday.

13–18 points: you really like new technology. You've got a digital camera and you've got a lot of photos and MP3s on your computer. You've got a modern mobile phone. You often read about new technology in newspapers and magazines. You take a digital camera, an MP3 player and a camcorder on holiday.

c Work in pairs. Is your profile true for you and your partner?

d Write a true profile for you.

8.3 Eating out

Grammar	*question words*
Can do	suggest a restaurant; book a restaurant; order food in a restaurant

El Bulli

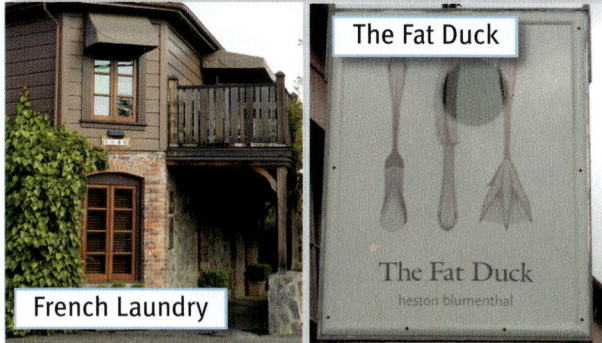

The Fat Duck

The Fat Duck
heston blumenthal

French Laundry

Reading

1 Work in pairs. Discuss.

1 Do you eat out a lot?

2 What is your favourite restaurant?

2 **a** Work in groups of three. Read about the top three restaurants in the world.

Student A: look at page 132. Read about *The Fat Duck*.

Student B: look at page 133. Read about *El Bulli*.

Student C: look at page 131. Read about *French Laundry*.

b Tell your partners about your restaurant.

c Discuss. Which restaurant in the article do you want to go to?

Listening

3 **a** **8.7** Listen to Mark and Alda. Which restaurant do they want to go to?

a *Sinatra's*   b *Wasabi*   c *Carlitto's*

b Listen again. Put the phrases in order.

Where's that? ☐

What food do they serve at *Wasabi*? ☐

How about dinner next Friday? ☐

How big is it? ☐

What about *Carlitto's*? ☐

Which restaurant do you want to go to? ☐

4 **a** Read the How to box.

HOW TO …

make suggestions

What about	:	dinnner next week?
How about	:	*Luciano's* Restaurant?

Good idea!/Yes/OK.

No. I don't like that restaurant.

b Work in pairs. Suggest a local restaurant to go to this evening.

Grammar | question words

5 Match the questions in the Active grammar box to the answers below.

Active grammar

Where	1 Where is *Carlitto's*?
Who	2 Who is Gordon?
What	3 What does she do?
What + noun	4 What food does he like?
Which + noun	5 Which restaurant do you like?
How + adjective	6 How tall is he?

a) Spanish food.   b) It's near my house.
c) She's a chef.   d) He's one metre ninety cm.
e) I like *Taste of India*. f) He's my friend.

siehe Suchen und Finden, Seite 99

6 **a** Complete the sentences with a question word from the Active grammar box.

1 *How* rich is she?

2 _____ café do you want to go to?

3 _____ fruit do you like?

4 _____ do you live?

5 _____ is the waiter?

6 _____ 's your name?

7 _____ good-looking is he?

8 _____ sofa do you like? This one or that one?

b Say the conversations in pairs.

7 Ask your partner questions.

A: *How tall are you?*

B: *I'm one metre sixty centimetres.*

Listening

8 a **8.8** Listen. Alda books a table at Carlitto's restaurant. What time is her booking?

b Listen again. Complete the How to box.

HOW TO …

book a table at a restaurant

Customer: *I'd ___ to book a table for Friday lunch/Saturday evening.*

Waiter: *___ many people?*
Waiter: *___ time?*
Waiter: *___ name, please?*

c Work in pairs.

Student A: phone *Carlitto's* Restaurant. Book a table for Saturday evening.

Student B: you work at *Carlitto's* restaurant. Answer the phone.

Vocabulary | food

9 a Match the underlined words in the menu to the pictures.

Menu

CARLITOS

STARTERS
Seafood cocktail
Fish soup
Green salad

MAIN COURSES
Roast beef *
Lamb chops *
Pork chops*
Vegetable pasta
* with potatoes or rice

DESSERTS
Ice cream
Chocolate cake
Cheese and biscuits

b **8.9** Listen and check.

c Work in pairs. Say what food you like/don't like from the menu.

d Choose your favourite starter, main course and dessert from the menu. Tell the class.

Writing

10 a **8.10** Listen. What do Mark and Alda choose from the menu?

b Listen and write the phrases. Who says each phrase?

Do you have a reservation? Waiter

c Work in groups of three. Look at tapescript 8.10 on page 142. Read the conversation aloud but change the food.

Waiter: *Are you ready to order?*

Mark: *Yes. I'd like a green salad, please.*

Speaking

11 Work in groups of three.

Student A: you are the waiter at *Salt and Pepper* Restaurant.

Students B and C: you are customers at *Salt and Pepper* Restaurant. Look at the menu on page 132. Enter the restaurant and order your meal.

A: *Good evening. Do you have a reservation?*

B: *Yes, we do. My name is …*

8 Communication
Addresses

1 a Work in pairs. Look at the people and their flats. What have they got in their flats?

He's got a lot of books in his flat.

b What does each person like doing? Tell your partner.

He likes playing golf.

2 Work in pairs.

Student A: look at page 129. Complete five of the addresses below. Don't show your partner.

Student B: look at page 132. Complete five of the addresses below. Don't show your partner.

3 Ask your partner questions to complete the other five addresses.

Student A: *Has Mr J. Coe got a lot of books in his flat?*

Student B: *No, he hasn't. Has Mrs A. Walker got ...*

IMPORTANT!

- Ask Yes/No questions. *Has X got ...? Does X like ...?*

- Ask one question. Then your partner asks one question. Then you ask another question, and so on.

Mr O. Pamuk	Mrs A. Walker	Mr G. Dyer	Miss T. Morrison	Mr J. Heller
_____	_____	_____	_____	_____

Miss Z. Smith	Mr J. Coe	Mr M. Haddon	Mrs M. Atwood	Mrs A. Levy
_____	_____	_____	_____	_____

like + verb + *-ing*

So sagen Sie, was Sie (nicht) gerne tun.

➕ *I like eating out.*

➕ *He likes travelling abroad.*

➖ *They don't like watching TV.*

want + *to* + verb (infinitive)

So sagen Sie, was Sie (nicht) tun möchten.

➕ *I want to go home.*

➕ *We want to see your new designs.*

➖ *She doesn't want to buy that car.*

have got

Have got bedeutet *haben* im Sinne von Zugehörigkeit oder Besitz (Kind, Katze, Computer).

I You We They	have got ('ve got) haven't got	a CD player. a television. a brother. two sisters.	
He She It	has got ('s got) hasn't got		
Have	I/you/we/they	got	any cousins? a cat?
Has	he/she/it		

Yes, I/you/we/they have.
Yes, he/she/it has.
No, I/you/we/they haven't.
No, he/she/it hasn't.

Im Amerikanischen wird *have got* selten benutzt. *Have* wird dann regelmäßig mit *do* benutzt.

I have two sisters but I don't have any brothers. Do you have a brother?

Question words
Fragewörter

- *Where* fragt nach dem Ort.

Where are you from? (*where ... from? = woher*)

Where do you live? (*where? = wo*)

- *Who* fragt nach Personen.

Who are you? (*wer?*)

- *What* und *which* fragen nach Dingen und Ideen.

What is your favourite song? (*Was ...?*)

What do you eat for breakfast? (*Was ...?*)

What film would you like to see? (*Welchen Film allgemein?*)

Which film would you like to see, Million Dollar Baby or Sideways? (*Welchen Film von diesen beiden?*)

What music do you like? (*Was für Musik allgemein?*)

Which John Lennon song is your favourite? (*Welches Lied aus einer begrenzten Auswahl – John Lennon?*)

- *How* + Adjektiv fragt nach Umfang, Anzahl oder Häufigkeit.

How tall is he? (*Wie groß ...?*)

How old are you? (*Wie alt ...?*)

How many cars have you got? (*Wie viele ...?*)

How often do you go out? (*Wie oft ...?*)

❗ *How much is it?* fragt nach dem Preis.

> **Tipp**
> *What do you do?* fragt nicht nach irgendeiner Tätigkeit oder Beschäftigung, sondern nach dem Beruf/Job!

Making suggestions:
What about ...?/How about ...?
Vorschläge machen

What about the new restaurant on Clerk Street?

How about a holiday in Cornwall this summer?

Vocabulary | leisure activities

1 **a** Welche Freizeitbeschäftigungen zeigen die Bilder?

1 *chess*   7 _____

2 _____   8 _____

3 _____   9 _____

4 _____   10 _____

5 _____   11 _____

6 _____   12 _____

b Welche Freizeitbeschäftigungen zeigen die Bilder oben?

1 *play chess*   7 _____
2 _____   8 _____
3 _____   9 _____
4 _____   10 _____
5 _____   11 _____
6 _____   12 _____

Grammar | like + -ing; want + infinitive

2 **a** Ergänzen Sie die Sätze mit *want* oder *like*.

1 Marcus and Pete *want* to play football.
2 Do you _____ eating out?
3 Which restaurant do you _____ to go to?
4 They don't _____ watching TV.
5 Does she _____ playing tennis?
6 Do you _____ to go for a walk?
7 I don't _____ playing chess.
8 We _____ to go to the theatre.

b Ergänzen Sie die Texte mit der richtigen Form der Verben in Klammern.

My name is Kate Watson. I'm a chef. I work for a small restaurant called The Happy Chicken. I like (1) *being* (be) a chef and I like (2) _____ (work) with food but I don't like (3) _____ (finish) work at one o'clock in the morning. I want (4) _____ (work) from nine to five and I want (5) _____ (go) out with my friends in the evening. I never see my friends – I'm always at work!

My name is Johan Holland. I'm a call centre worker. I like (6) _____ (work) with lots of people but I don't like my job. It's not exciting. I want (7) _____ (be) a sales rep. I like (8) _____ (travel) abroad and I like (9) _____ (sell) things. I don't want (10) _____ (call) customers for eight hours a day.

Vocabulary | adjectives

3 **a** Bilden Sie sechs Adjektive, indem Sie die Buchstaben in die richtige Reihenfolge bringen.

1 yase   e _____   4 iiucfdftl   d _____
2 igrobn   b _____   5 netgixic   e _____
3 nuf   f _____   6 sirtintegne   i _____

b Ergänzen Sie die Sätze mit den oben gefundenen Adjektiven.

1 I don't like having meetings at work. I want to sleep in meetings. They're _____ .

   Uri Anderson, 42, sales manager

2 I can speak Russian, English and Spanish. Languages are very _____ for me.

   Asenka Chazov, 14, student

3 I read two or three books every week. Books are very _____ .

   Armina Lang, 49, lecturer

4 I got 3 out of 20 in my maths test. Maths is very _____ for me.

   Edel Möller, 16, student

5 I like travelling abroad and meeting new people. It's _____ .

   Vashti Adamski, 26, reporter

Vocabulary | rooms and furniture

1 **a** Ordnen Sie die Wörter im Kasten den Bildern zu.

> washing machine ~~sofa~~ fridge
> coffee table car wardrobe bed
> mirror basin bath armchair cooker
> toilet sink

1 *sofa*

2 _____

3 _____

4 _____

5 _____

6 _____

7 _____

8 _____

9 _____

10 _____

11 _____

12 _____

13 _____

14 _____

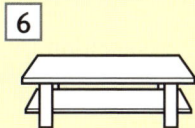

b Welche Möbel/Dinge gehören in welchen Raum?

Bathroom: _____ _____ _____

Bedroom: _____ _____ _____

Kitchen: *washing machine* _____ _____

_____

Living room: _____ _____ _____

Garage: _____

Grammar | *have got*

2 **a** Sehen Sie sich die Tabelle an und ergänzen Sie den Text aus Jamies Sicht.

	Jamie	Patricia
bedrooms	1	2
garage	✗	✓
garden	✗	✗
washing machine	✓	✗
bath	✗	✓
sofa	✓	✓
car	✓	✗

(1) *I've got* a small flat in Notting Hill in the UK.
(2) It _____ one bedroom and a living room. It
(3) _____ a garage or a garden. I (4) _____ a
washing machine in the kitchen and a sofa in the
living room. I (5) _____ a bath – just a shower. I
(6) _____ a car – it's a small, red sports car.

b Sehen Sie sich die Tabelle noch einmal an und ergänzen Sie nun den Text über Patricia.

(1) *She's got* a house in Auckland in New Zealand.
It (2) _____ two bedrooms and a garage but
(3) it _____ a garden. She (4) _____ a bath in the
bathroom and a sofa in the living room. She
(5) _____ a washing machine and she (6) _____ a
car.

3 Vervollständigen Sie diesen Dialog.

A: Hello. Can I help you?

C: No, thank you. I'm just looking.

A: Our televisions are on special offer today.
(1) _____ you _____ a television?

C: Yes, I (2) _____ .

A: (3) _____ you _____ a television in your bedroom?

C: No, I (4) _____ . But I don't want a television. I want a washing machine for my mother.

A: (5) _____ your mother _____ a television in her bedroom?

C: Yes, she (6) _____ . Now, how much is this washing machine.

A: It's £399. The television is only £299 ...

Grammar | question words

1 Ergänzen Sie hier jeweils mit dem richtigen Fragewort.

1 A: _What_ do you teach?
   B: I teach English.

2 A: _____ is your favourite actor?
   B: Jean Claude Van Damme.

3 A: _____ far is your school?
   B: It's about 2km from here.

4 A: _____ is Jackie?
   B: She's in the bathroom.

5 A: _____ Elvis song is this?
   B: It's _You Are Always on my Mind_.

6 A: _____ old is she?
   B: She's eighty-two.

7 A: _____ is your teacher?
   B: Mrs Malkmus.

8 A: _____ coffee table do you like?
   B: This one. It's very nice.

Vocabulary | food

2 Tragen Sie die Lebensmittel auf den Bildern in das Rätsel ein. Wie lautet das Lösungswort?

Book a restaurant

3 Ergänzen Sie den Dialog mit einem Wort aus dem Kasten.

See   How   like   time

Waiter: Hello. _Pasta Plate_ restaurant.
Sam: Hello. I'd (1) _____ to book a table for Saturday evening.
Waiter: Certainly, madam. (2) _____ many people?
Sam: Two.
Waiter: What (3) _____ ?
Sam: Nine o'clock, please.
Waiter: And what's the name, please?
Sam: Sam Allman.
Waiter: OK, that's fine Ms Allman. (4) _____ you on Saturday.
Sam: Thank you. Goodbye.

Order food in a restaurant

4 Ergänzen Sie den Dialog mit einem Wort aus dem Kasten.

have   ready   bill   table   reservation   like   drink   Come   Still

Waiter: Hello, madam. Do you have a (1) _____ ?
Sam: Yes, I do. My name's Sam Allman.
Waiter: Ms Allman. A (2) _____ for two?
Sam: Yes, that's right.
Waiter: (3) _____ with me, please.

Waiter: Are you (4) _____ to order?
Sam: Yes. I'd (5) _____ chicken soup, please, and pork chops.
Waiter: Certainly, madam. And for you, sir?
Tony: Can I (6) _____ fish rolls, please, and lamb steak?
Waiter: Certainly. What would you like to (7) _____ ?
Sam: Can I have an orange juice, please?
Tony: And I'd like a mineral water, please.
Waiter: (8) _____ or sparkling?
Tony: Sparkling, please.

Sam: Excuse me. Can I have the (9) _____ , please?
Waiter: Of course.

Sydney Harbour Bridge: Millennium Celebrations

9 The past

Wall Street Crash

Fall of the Berlin Wall

Mandela: New President of South Africa

Lead in

1 **a** Look at the photos. Match each one to a year below.

1989   1994   2000   1929

2 **a** [9.1] Look at the years in the box. Listen and repeat.

> 1963   1946   1981   1977   1957   1912   2002   1990

b Match a year in the box to a headline below.

a Sputnik in Space   e Nelson Mandela Free

b Charles and Di Royal   f Martin Luther King: 'I have a dream'
   Wedding   g Juan Peron: President of Argentina

c First ipod in Shops   h Elvis Presley is Dead

d Titanic Disaster

c Work in pairs. Tell your partner what you think.

A: *I think 'Sputnik in Space' is 1957.*

B: *I think it's 1963.*

d [9.2] Listen and check.

3 Write headlines from your life. Your partner guesses the year.

Dieter: Dieter's first day at university.

Paola: Is that 1995?

Dieter: No, it's 1999.

Bruce Lee

| Grammar | past of *be* affirmative |
| Can do | make simple statements about people from history |

Diana, Princess of Wales

Princess Grace

Elvis Presley

Reading

1 **a** Look at the underlined words in the texts. Check their meanings in a dictionary.

b Read the texts. Match a text to a photo.

1 He was a singer and an actor. He was born on 8th January, 1935, in Mississippi. His parents were very poor. He was a factory-worker, then a driver. His first song was *That's All Right*. He was 'The King of Rock and Roll'.
Famous quote: 'When I was a child, ladies and gentlemen, I was a dreamer'.

2 She was an actor and a princess. She was born on 12th November, 1929, in Philadelphia. Her parents were very rich. She was a model and then an actor. Her first film was *Fourteen Hours* in 1951. Her husband was Prince Rainier III of Monaco.
Famous quote: (about flowers) 'I talk to them and they talk to me'.

3 He was an actor and fighter. He was born on 27th November, 1940, in San Francisco. His parents were from Hong Kong. They weren't rich. His father was a singer. His last film was *Enter the Dragon*. He was short and thin but he was very strong and very fast.
Famous quote: 'Don't think. Feel'.

4 She was a princess and a fashion icon. She was born on 1st July, 1961, in Sandringham. Her parents were rich. She wasn't a good student at school but she was a good pianist. Her wedding was in St Pauls' Cathedral in London. Her husband was Prince Charles. Their life together was not happy.
Famous quote: 'There were three of us in this marriage'.

c Complete the sentences with names from the photos.

1 *Diana* and *Grace* were princesses.
2 _____ , _____ and _____ were born in the US.
3 _____ , _____ and _____ were actors.
4 _____ and _____ were poor as children.
5 _____ and _____ were the wives/husbands of famous people.

d Close your books. Work in pairs. What can you remember about the people in the texts?

Bruce Lee was born in San Francisco. His parents ...

Grammar | past of *be* (affirmative)

2 **a** Complete the Active grammar box with *was* or *were*.

Active grammar

I You	*was* _____	an actor. a singer.
He She It	_____ _____ _____	happy. born in 1982. great.
We They	_____ _____	singers. rich.

b **9·3** Listen and check.

siehe Suchen und finden, Seite 111

3 **a** Complete the sentences with *was* or *were*.

1 Coco Chanel *was* a fashion designer.
2 My husband and I _____ call centre workers from 2001 to 2004.
3 Colonel Tom Parker _____ Elvis Presley's manager.
4 Jackie Chan and Oprah Winfrey _____ born in 1954.
5 Prince William and I _____ born in 1982.
6 We _____ good football players in 1990. I can't play football now.
7 I _____ a good pianist at school.

b Who is your favourite 20th-century icon? Tell your partner.

4 **a** Read the How to box.

HOW TO …

talk about childhood

When I was a child, I was a good singer.
When they were young, they were very poor.

b Write two true sentences and one false sentence about you and your family

c Read your sentences to your partner. Your partner guesses true or false.

A: *When he was young, my father was an actor.*
B: *False.*
A: *No, it's true!*

Listening and vocabulary

5 **a** **9·4** Listen to the radio game show. Guess the person.

b Look at page 128. Check your answer.

c Listen again. Write true (T) or false (F).

1 He was born in 1950.
2 His parents were Julia and Alfred.
3 He was famous for his music.
4 He was from London.
5 He was married to Yoko Ono in his 20s.

6 **a** Read the texts below. Check any new words in your dictionary. Then complete the texts with a preposition from the box.

on   for   with   ~~in~~   to   of   to   at

She was born (1) *in* 1929 in New York. She was **good** (2) ____ horse-riding and painting. She was **married** (3) ____ John F Kennedy, the **President** (4) ____ the US, and then to Aristotle Onassis, a Greek businessman.

Billie Holiday was **born** (5) ____ the 7th of April, 1915, in Philadelphia. She was **famous** (6) ____ her music. She was **friends** (7) ____ the jazz musician Lester Young. Her second husband was **similar** (8) ____ her first husband. They were bad men and Billie Holiday was unhappy.

b Say a word in **bold** from the texts. Your partner says the preposition.

7 **a** Think of a famous person from history. Write sentences about him/her.

b Read your sentences to your partner. Your partner guesses the person.

9.2 | My first, my last ...

Grammar	past of *be*: negatives and questions
Can do	give a short description of a past experience

Speaking

1 Talk about the games. Use the phrases below.

I know how to play ...

I don't know how to play ...

It's difficult/easy/boring/ exciting/fun/ interesting.

Listening

2 **a** **9.5** Listen to Cristof, Isabella and Jasmine playing a game called *My first, my last*. How do you play *My first, my last*?

b Listen again. Write Cristof's answers and Jasmine's answers below.

MY FIRST TEACHER

1	What was his/her name?	*Mrs Lloyd*
2	How old was she?	____
3	Was she a good teacher?	____
4	Were you a good student?	____
5	Were you his/her favourite student?	____

MY LAST HOLIDAY

1	When was it?	_____
2	Where was it?	_____
3	Who were you with?	_____
4	Was it a good holiday?	_____
5	Was the hotel nice?	_____
6	Were there any tourist attractions?	_____
7	Was the weather nice?	_____

Grammar | past of *be* (negatives and questions)

3 **a** Complete the dialogue from the Ex.2.

Jasmine: (1) *Was* she a good teacher?

Cristof: She (2) _____ a good teacher but I (3) _____ a good student.

Isabella: _____ you her favourite student?

b Complete the Active grammar box with *was*, *wasn't*, *were* or *weren't*.

Active grammar

⊖	I *wasn't* (was not)	a good student.
	You *weren't* (were not)	happy at school.
	He/She/It _____	
	We *weren't*	good students.
	They _____	happy at school.

❓	*Was* I	a good student?
	_____ you	happy at school?
	Was he/she/it	
	_____ we	good students?
	Were they	happy?
	What _____ her name?	Jennifer.
	Where _____ your shoes?	In the kitchen.

siehe Suchen und finden, Seite 111

4 a Complete the sentences with *was*, *wasn't*, *were* or *weren't*.

1 I *was* very quiet at school. (✓)
2 My first car _____ very big but it was fun. (✗)
3 Who _____ your friends at school?
4 What _____ your favourite subject at school?
5 My first computer games _____ easy but they were exciting. (✓)
6 You _____ my English teacher at school. (✗)
7 _____ you late this morning?
8 Where _____ your last house?

b Work in pairs. Ask and answer the questions in *My first teacher* Ex. 2b.

Pronunciation

5 a [9.6] Listen. Mark the stress.

1 I was a good student.
2 I wasn't very intelligent.
3 Was she a good teacher?
4 Who was your best friend?

b How is *was/wasn't* pronounced in each sentence?

6 a [9.7] Listen. Write the sentences. Mark the stress.

b How is *were/weren't* pronounced in each sentence?

7 Work in pairs. Ask and answer the questions in *My last holiday* Ex. 2b.

Vocabulary | *yesterday, last, ago*

8 a Look at tapescript 9.6 on page 142. Underline the examples of *ago* and *last*.

b Complete the time expressions with *ago* or *last*.

1 today
2 yesterday
3 _____ night
4 yesterday morning/afternoon/evening
5 two days _____
6 _____ week
7 _____ month
8 six months _____
9 _____ year
10 ten years _____

Speaking

9 a When were these past experiences? Tell your partner.

- Your first day at school
- Your last meal in a restaurant
- Your last film at the cinema
- Your last flight
- Your first job

My first day at school was twenty-two years ago.

b Ask your partner questions with *Where were you ...?* and a time expression.

A: *Where were you yesterday afternoon?*
B: *I was at home.*

10 a Work in groups of three. Remember the rules for *My first, my last*.

b Play *My first, my last* on page 133.

Writing

11 Write a paragraph about your first teacher or your last holiday.

Vocabulary | housework

1 **a** Match a phrase in the box to a picture below.

> do the laundry
> vacuum the house
> cook dinner
> clean the bathroom
> wash the dishes
> iron a shirt

1
2
3
4
5
6

b **9.8** Listen and check. Mark the stress.

2 **a** Who does these things in your house? Tell your partner.

My wife does the laundry.
I iron my shirts.

b What housework do you like doing? What housework don't you like doing?

I don't like cooking dinner.

Reading

3 **a** Look at the text. Underline phrases from Ex. 1a.

Who does the housework now?

In the 1950s, life was simple. Women were housewives and men were factory workers, managers, sales reps., sales assistants, etc. But in the 21st century, life is different. Now there are over 21,000 househusbands in the UK. They don't have a job, they stay at home and look after the children. Are they crazy? We talk to one househusband, Jeff Timberland.

Do you like being a househusband?
Jeff: Yes, I do. Plus, childcare is £125 for one week, for one child. It's very expensive*.

What does your wife do?
Jeff: She's an architect.

Do you like doing housework?
Jeff: I don't like ironing my shirts – it's very boring. And I don't like washing the dishes. But I like vacuuming the house and cooking dinner.

Really?
Jeff: Yes, really.

What was your job before?
Jeff: I was a sales rep. I was a good sales rep. and I was happy. But my children are my job now.

Do you want to get another job?
Jeff: Yes, but not now. Billy and Harry are very young. They want their Dad, not a stranger.

* expensive = costs a lot of money

b Read the text again. Answer the questions below.

1 How many househusbands are there in the UK now?
2 Does Jeff like being a househusband?
3 What is Jeff's wife's job?
4 What housework does Jeff like doing?
5 What was Jeff's job before?
6 Does Jeff want to get a new job now?

c Work in small groups. Discuss.

1 Are there a lot of househusbands in your country?
2 Who usually looks after young children in your country?
3 Jeff says, 'They want their Dad, not a stranger'. Do you agree?

Listening

4 **a** `9.9` Listen to four events in Jeff's week. Match each conversation 1–4 to a picture a–d.

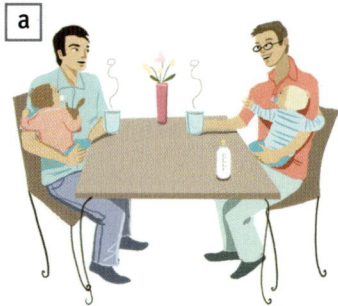

b Listen again. Who are the people in the pictures? Write the questions you hear beginning with *How ...?*

5 **a** Read the How to box.

HOW TO ...		
ask about an experience		
How was	:	your weekend?/your week?/your day?/ your flight?
It was great. ☺		It was ok. 😐
It wasn't very good. ☹		It was awful. 😠

b Work in small groups. Ask questions with *How was ...?*

A: *How was your weekend?*

B: *It was fine, thanks. I was at home on Sunday ...*

Grammar | *Can/Could you ...?; Can/Could I ...?*

6 **a** Complete these sentences from Ex. 4a.

Aunt Sally: Could you *carry* my suitcases?

Billy: Can I _____ chocolate for dinner?

Karen: Can I _____ on the TV?

Friend: Could you _____ the milk?

b Complete the Active grammar box with *I* or *you*.

Active grammar

Can Could	____	use your telephone? have a coffee?
Yes, ____ can.		No, ____ can't.
Can Could	____	carry my bags? iron my shirt?
Yes, of course.	Sorry, ____ can't.	

7 Ask your partner questions.

- use your pen
- spell your name
- use your mobile phone
- give me your email address
- give me €1
- open the window
- look at your book

A: *Could I use your pen?*

B: *Yes, of course.*

Speaking

8 Choose ONE thing you need from the box below. Look at the *To do list*. Find someone to help you. Write their name in the Who? column.

> a camera   an iron   a computer   a key
> a credit card

To do list

Who?

1 iron my shirt

2 open the door

3 buy a present for Jo

4 send an email to Tim

5 take a photo of Ella

A: *Hello. Can you buy a present for Jo?*

B: *Sorry, I can't. I haven't got a credit card.*

A: *Hi. Can I use your iron? I want to iron my shirt.*

B: *Yes, of course.*

9 | Communication

School days

1 **a** Match a subject in the box to a picture 1–6.

> maths languages science music art sport

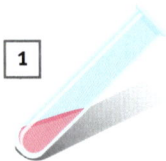

1

2

3

5 $2(3x-11)=8$ $y=?$

4 FOOTBALL

6 Hello **Bonjour** Hola Guten Tag

b **9.10** Listen and repeat.

c Complete the sentences with a subject above.

1 When I was at school, I was good at …

2 When I was at school, I was bad at …

2 **a** **9.11** Listen and complete the chart for Louise.

My school days

School name: *William Morris High School*

Where: _____

Years: _____

Good/bad school: _____

Good/bad student: _____

Good at: _____

Bad at: _____

Favourite lessons: _____

Best friend: _____

b Listen again. Check your answers.

Lifelong learning

Ohren spitzen, Augen auf!

Konzentrieren Sie sich beim Zuhören auf das Wesentliche – das wird meist betont und/oder wiederholt. Wissen Sie noch, wie Sie jemanden höflich unterbrechen und bitten, das Gesagte zu wiederholen?

3 **a** Complete the chart in Ex.2a for you.

b Make sentences. Tell your partner.

A: *I was very good at maths.*

B: *Really? I wasn't. I was good at music.*

4 Work in groups. Close your books and talk about your school days.

The past of *be*
Die Vergangenheitsform des Verbs *to be* (sein)

⊕	I	was	
	You	were	a teacher.
	He		born in 1963.
	She	was	very good.
	It		
	We	were	teachers.
	They	were	born in 1963.

⊖	I	wasn't (was not)	
	You	were'nt (were not)	a teacher. born in 1963. very good.
	He		
	She	wasn't (was not)	
	It		
	We	weren't (were not)	teachers. born in 1963.
	They	weren't (were not)	

❓	Was	I	
	Were	you	a teacher? born in 1963? very good?
	Was	he she it	
	Were	we	teachers?
	Were	they	born in 1963?

Wh- questions
Fragen mit Fragewörtern: w-Fragen

Who was your manager?

What were their jobs?

Where was your school?

Which shop was your favourite one?

When was the interview?

How old were you in 1990?

Asking permission
Um Erlaubnis bitten

Can I Could I	call you this evening, please? speak to Mrs Walsh, please? use your computer, please? ask a question, please? go home early, please?
Yes, you can./Sure. No, you can't./I'm sorry. You can't.	

Mit *Can I* und *Could I* können Sie um Erlaubnis bitten. *Can I* kann fordernd klingen, die höfliche Form ist *Could I*. Wenn Sie nicht mit guten Freunden sprechen, benutzen Sie lieber *Could I* und vergessen Sie *please* nicht.

Making requests
Jemanden auffordern etwas zu tun

Can you Could you	call me this evening, please? buy some fruit at the shop? answer the phone, please? clean the kitchen? do the laundry, please?
Yes, of course./Sure. No, I can't./I can't, I'm afraid.	

Mit *Can you/Could you* fordern Sie jemanden auf, etwas zu tun.

! Vorsicht! Was als Bitte gemeint ist, klingt leicht wie ein Befehl – verwenden Sie *Could you ..., please*, wenn Sie nicht mit engen Freunden sprechen.

Time expressions
Zeitangaben

yesterday

yesterday morning/afternoon/evening

last night/week/month/year

*two days ago = **vor zwei Tagen***

*a week ago = **vor einer Woche***

Vocabulary | saying years

1 Korrigieren Sie die Fehler in der Spalte 'Say'.

	Write	Say
1	1982	nineteen and eighty-two *nineteen eighty-two*
2	2004	two hundred and four _____
3	1803	eighteen zero three _____
4	1909	nineteen hundred and nine _____
5	1970	nineteen seventeen _____

Grammar | past of *be* (affirmative)

2 Ergänzen Sie die Texte mit *was* oder *were*.

1

Peter Sellers is a British icon. He (1) *was* born on 8th September, 1925, in Hampshire, the UK. His parents (2) _____ Agnes and Bill Sellers. They (3) _____ actors and singers in the theatre. In the 1950s, Peter Sellers (4) _____ a star of the radio. In the 1960s and 1970s he (5) _____ a film star. *The Pink Panther* and *Dr Strangelove* (6) _____ Peter Sellers' films.

2

The Beatles (1) _____ John, Paul, George and Ringo. They (2) _____ from Liverpool. Their first name (3) _____ *The Quarrymen*. In 1961 they (4) _____ popular in Liverpool and Hamburg. Their first hit, in 1962, (5) _____ *Love Me Do*. Their next song, *Please Please Me*, (6)_____ number one in early 1963. *Revolver* and *Let It Be* (7)_____ Beatles albums.

3 Setzen Sie diese Sätze mit *was* oder *were* in die Vergangenheit.

1 Jeff and I are late for the party.
2 My son and daughter are at home.
3 I'm a computer engineer.
4 You're my best friend.
5 We're in the garage.
6 Franz is my sister's best friend.
7 This book is really exciting.
8 They're at school today.
9 She's a university lecturer in London.
10 It's my favourite restaurant.

Vocabulary | prepositions

4 Schreiben Sie volle Sätze.

1 (Einstein/born/14th March, 1879)
Einstein was born on 14th March, 1879.

2 (Alfred Hitchcock/famous/his films)
_____

3 (Margaret Thatcher/friends/Ronald Reagan)
_____

4 (Martin Luther King and Spike Lee/born/ Atlanta in Georgia)
_____

5 (Marilyn Monroe / married / Joe DiMaggio and Arthur Miller)
_____

6 (Lyndon Johnson/President/America/1963 to 1969)
_____

7 (Some of Nina Simone's music/similar/Billie Holiday's music)
_____

8 (Mikhail Glinka/good/singer)
_____

Grammar | past of be (negatives and questions)

1 Ergänzen Sie das Interview mit *was, wasn't, were* or *weren't*.

Interviewer: So, Melissa, when you (1) *were* a child, (2) _____ you a good singer?

Melissa: No, I (3) _____ . I (4) _____ a very bad singer.

Interviewer: Who (5) _____ your singing teacher?

Melissa: Her name (6) _____ Mrs Parsons. She (7) _____ great – really great!

Interviewer: Who (8) _____ your favourite singers?

Melissa: Aretha Franklin and Billie Holiday (9) _____ my favourite singers.

Interviewer: (10) _____ your parents singers?

Melissa: No, they (11) _____ . My mother (12) _____ a scientist and my father (13) _____ a househusband.

2 Korrigieren Sie die Fehler.

1 Was you a good singer when you were young?
   Were you a good singer when you were young?
2 Richard and Alex isn't at work yesterday.
3 I not a maths teacher. I was a science teacher.
4 Were Ronald Reagan a film star?
5 My father not a composer but he was a musician.
6 Was you at home last night?
7 When were your last holiday?
8 Who your best friend was at school?
9 What were Marlon Brando's last film?
10 Were your father a politician?

Vocabulary | *yesterday, ago, last*

3 **a** Lesen Sie den Text. Bringen Sie die Bilder in die richtige zeitliche Reihenfolge.

My name is Emily Barnes. I work for Trans-Global Software. I travel abroad a lot. For example, last week I was in Moscow. Three days ago I was in Athens. Fifteen days ago I was in New York. Yesterday I was in London. Last month I was in Paris.

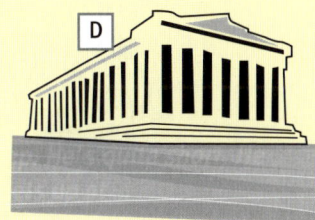

b Ergänzen Sie mit *yesterday, ago* oder *last.*
Today is Wednesday 24th March, 2006

1 23rd March, evening = *yesterday evening*
2 17th March = _____ _____ _____
3 2005 = _____ _____
4 23rd March/24th March, night = _____ night
5 Monday 15th March – Sunday 21st March =
   _____ _____
6 14th March = ten _____ _____
7 February 2006 = _____ _____
8 23rd March, morning = _____ _____

Vocabulary | housework

1 **a** Welches Wort ist hier richtig?

1 *cook/iron/wash* dinner
2 *wash/clean/do* the laundry
3 *iron/vacuum/cook* the house
4 *cook/wash/clean* the bathroom
5 *iron/cook/vacuum* a shirt
6 *cook/iron/wash* the dishes

b Schreiben Sie die Tätigkeiten aus Üb. 1a neben die Bilder unten.

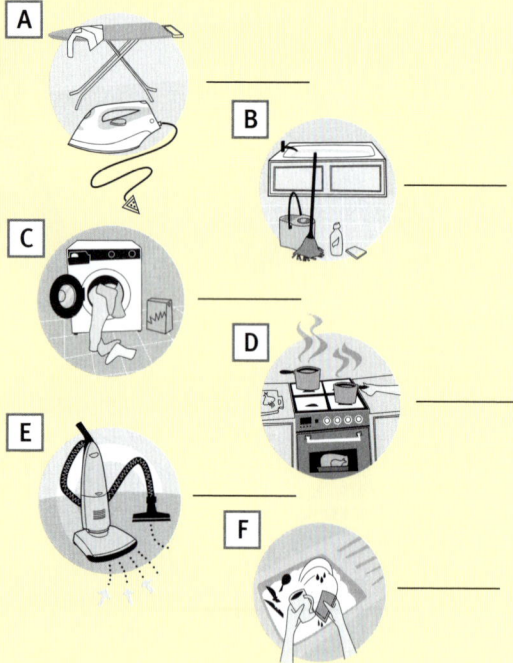

How to ask about an experience

2 Ordnen Sie die Fragen im Kasten den Antworten zu.

> How was the flight?   How was your weekend?
> How was your holiday?   How was school?
> How was the party?

1 **A:** _____
  B: It was OK, but the air stewards weren't very nice.
2 **A:** _____
  B: It was good. My teacher liked me!
3 **A:** _____
  B: It was great. There were fifty people there.
4 **A:** _____
  B: Fine thanks. I was in town on Saturday and I was at home on Sunday.
5 **A:** _____
  B: It was great. The weather was lovely and the food was very nice.

Grammar | ...? Can/Could you ...?; Can/Could;

3 **a** Bilden Sie Fragen, indem Sie die Wörter in die richtige Reihenfolge bringen.

1 you? I to Can talk
  Can I talk to you?
2 you dinner? Can cook
  _____
3 the Could open you window?
  _____
4 down? I Can sit
  _____
5 home at work I tomorrow? Could
  _____
6 on television? Could turn you the
  _____

b Ordnen Sie die Dialoge den Bildern zu.

1 **A:** Could you carry my suitcase?
  B: Of course.
2 **A:** Can I use your phone?
  B: Yes, you can.
3 **A:** Could I have a cup of tea?
  B: Yes, of course.
4 **A:** Could you take a photo of us?
  B: Yes, sure.
5 **A:** Could you answer the phone?
  B: Yes, OK.

a

b

c

d

e

A

10 Stories

B

C

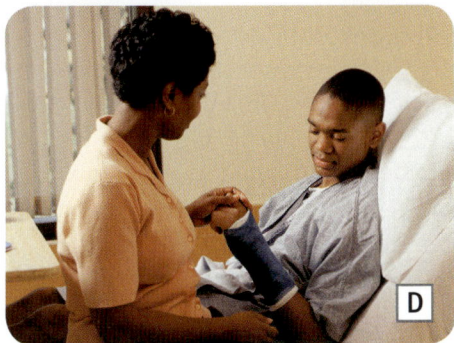

D

Lead-in

1   a   Complete each situation with a verb from the box.

> win   arrests   get   meet   ~~lose~~   steals   find   break   stay   move

1   You *lose* your wallet/purse.
2   A thief _____ your mobile phone.
3   You _____ in bed all day.
4   You _____ the lottery.
5   You _____ married.
6   You _____ €10 on the street.
7   A police officer _____ you.
8   You _____ to a new house.
9   You _____ your arm.
10 You _____ your favourite actor.

b   🔊 10.1 Listen and check.

c   Look at the pictures. Match a phrase to each picture.

2   a   Are the experiences in Ex. 1a good or bad? Complete the table.

GOOD EXPERIENCES	BAD EXPERIENCES
	You lose your wallet/purse.

b   Change the words in Ex. 1a for new words. Tell your partner. Your partner responds with an adjective.

A: *You move to a new city.*   B: *That's exciting.*

A: *You lose your camera.*   B: *That's bad.*

Grammar	Past Simple (regular verbs)
Can do	understand a simple narrative of past events

The Story of the Mona Lisa (PART 1)

Every day 15,000 people visit The Louvre Museum in Paris. Most of them want to see the *Mona Lisa*. But what is the story of this painting?

The artist was, of course, Leonardo da Vinci. He started the painting in 1503 and he finished it about four years later. Leonardo was Italian but in 1516 he moved to France with the painting. The King of France liked it and the *Mona Lisa* stayed in France.

Speaking

1 Work in pairs. Look at the paintings. Answer the questions.

1 Who is the artist?
2 Who are your favourite artists?
3 What are your favourite paintings?

Reading

2 **a** Look at *The Story of the Mona Lisa (Part 1)*. Read the text aloud.

b Read again. Complete the information below.

Place (now): *The Louvre, Paris*
Artist: _____
Start painting: _____
Finish painting: _____
Move to France: _____

Grammar 1 | Past Simple affirmative (regular verbs)

3 **a** Underline the verbs in *The Story of the Mona Lisa (Part 1)*.

b Which verbs are in the Past Simple?

c How do you make the Past Simple of regular verbs?

4 **a** Complete the Active grammar box with the correct form of the verb.

Active grammar

Present Simple	Past Simple
I like the painting.	I <u>liked</u> the painting.
She stays with her friends.	She _____ with her friends.
They start work early.	They _____ work early.

Add *-ed* to make the past simple of regular verbs.

b Complete the texts with a verb from the box in the Past Simple.

> finish   ~~want~~   start   ask

Pope Julius II (1) *wanted* a new ceiling in The Sistine Chapel. He (2) _____ Michelangelo to paint the ceiling of the Sistine Chapel. Michelangelo (3) _____ it in 1508. He (4) _____ it in 1512.

> live   work   play   move (x2)

Marcel Duchamp was an artist. He was born in 1887. He (5) _____ in Paris and he (6) _____ chess with his brothers. In 1914 he (7) _____ to New York. He (8) _____ in a library in New York. In 1918 he (9) _____ to Argentina.

siehe Suchen und finden, Seite 123

Pronunciation

5 **a** [10.2] Listen and repeat the Past Simple of the verbs in the box.

> want   ask   move   start
> finish   live   play   work
> cook   close   talk   arrest
> listen   walk

b How is the -ed ending of each verb pronounced? Copy the table and put the verbs in the correct column.

/t/	/d/	/ɪd/
ask<u>ed</u>	mov<u>ed</u>	want<u>ed</u>

6 **a** Read the texts in Ex. 4b aloud.

b [10.3] Listen and check your pronunciation.

Listening

7 [10.4] Listen to *The story of the Mona Lisa (Part 2)*. Mark these sentences True (T) or False (F).

a The *Mona Lisa* moved to the Louvre.

b It stayed in Napoleon's bedroom.

c The Louvre closed in 1910.

d The police talked to Picasso.

e The police talked to Vincenza Peruggia.

Grammar 2 | Past Simple negatives and questions

8 **a** Answer the questions.

1 Did Napoleon like the *Mona Lisa*?   *Yes, he did.*
2 Did the *Mona Lisa* stay in Napoleon's bedroom?
3 Did the police talk to Picasso?
4 Did the police talk to Vencenzo Peruggia?

b Complete the Active grammar box with *did* or *didn't*.

> ### Active grammar
>
> | ⊖ | I/You/He/She/ It/We/They | didn't stay _____ talk | in Italy. to the police. |
> |-----|-----|-----|-----|
> | ❓ | _____ | I/you/he/she/it/ we/they | stay \| in Italy? talk \| to the police? |
>
> Yes, I/you/he/she/we/they _____ .
> No, I/you/he/she/we/they _____ .

siehe Suchen und finden, Seite 123

9 **a** Make questions, answers and negatives.

1 (Picasso/not like/the *Mona Lisa*)
    Picasso didn't like the Mona Lisa.
2 (Marcel Duchamp/play chess?)
    A: *Did Marcel Duchamp play chess?*   B: Yes, he did.
3 (Leonardo da Vinci/not live/Spain)   _____ .
4 (the police/arrest/Picasso?)
    A: _____ ?   B: No, _____ .
5 (the *Mona Lisa*/not stay/Italy)   _____ .
6 (Andy Warhol/work for/Vogue?)
    A: _____ ?   B: Yes, _____ .
7 (Picasso/not move to/New York)   _____ .
8 (Van Gogh/move to/London?)
    A: _____ ?   B: Yes, _____ .

b Work in pairs. Write six questions about Leonardo da Vinci and the *Mona Lisa*.

Speaking

10 **a** Work in pairs. What do you think?

1 Who was the thief?
2 Where was the *Mona Lisa* for two years?
3 How did the thief steal the *Mona Lisa*?

b Read the last part of the story on page 132. Answer the questions above.

Reading

1 **a** Who or what is in the news? Write a list.

Jude Law

Real Madrid Football Club

b Was it a good week or a bad week for each person/thing in your list?

2 **a** Read the article below. Complete the gaps with *good* or *bad*.

b `10.5` Listen and check.

c Read again. Are these statements True (T) or False (F)?

1 Romero Cline got married last week. [T]
2 Monica Hawkins works in a restaurant. ☐
3 Emiliana Rotman doesn't have €14 million. ☐
4 Emiliana Rotman is very sad. ☐
5 *Gilt's* concert was on Saturday. ☐
6 Sia Kahn bought a T-shirt. ☐
7 Mr and Mrs Blatt found the coins under the fish. ☐
8 Mr and Mrs Blatt bought three fish. ☐

3 Close your books. What can you remember about the four stories?

MONDAY
12TH JUNE

Good week, bad week

It was a _____ week for ... actor Romero Cline, 43. He went to Las Vegas last week and he met Monica Hawkins, a waitress in a fast food restaurant. Three days later, they got married.

It was a _____ week for ... Mr and Mrs Blatt from the UK. They had fish for dinner and they found three gold coins inside the fish. 'The fish was £3.50,' said Mrs Blatt, 'but the gold coins are £1,000 each!'

It was a _____ week for ... Emiliana Rotman from Sweden. She won €14 million on the Euro lottery but she lost her ticket. 'Never mind,' said Emiliana, 'That's life!'

It was a _____ week for ... pop group Gilt. Gilt's concert was last Friday but the tickets said 'Saturday'. 'Only five people came and saw the concert,' said Sia Kahn, Gilt's singer. 'They took photos and bought a T-shirt, but it wasn't a good day.'

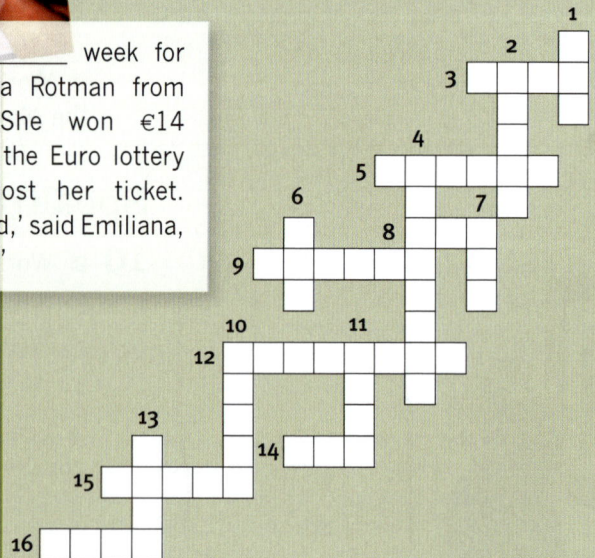

Grammar | Past Simple (irregular verbs)

4 **a** Look at the articles in Ex. 2a again. Underline all the verbs in the Past Simple.

b Complete the Active grammar box with *take* or *took*.

Active grammar

Some verbs are irregular in the Past Simple (but only in affirmative sentences).

⊕	I/You/He/She/We/They	went to Paris. _____ a lot of photos.
⊖	I/You/He/She/We/They	didn't go to Paris. didn't _____ a lot of photos.
❓	Did I/you/he/she/we/they	go to Paris? _____ a lot of photos?

Yes, I/you/he/she/we/they did.
No, I/you/he/she/we/they didn't.

---

5 **a** Complete the magazine crossword on page 118 with the Past Simple of the verbs below. Some are regular, some are irregular.

ACROSS   3 come   5 play   8 see   9 buy   12 finish   14 have   15 move   16 go

DOWN   1 meet   2 ask   4 listen   6 get   7 win   10 find   11 say   13 lose

b Complete the text with the verb in brackets.

Yesterday, Emiliana Rotman (1) *found* (find) her lottery ticket and (2) _____ (win) €14 million. 'I (3) _____ (not find) the ticket,' Emiliana (4) _____ (say). 'My brother (5) _____ (come) to my house for dinner and he (6) _____ (see) it under my sofa. So we (7) _____ (not have) dinner at home. I (8) _____ (take) him to a nice restaurant.'

6 **a** Look at the phrases below. What did/didn't you do last week? Write sentences.

---

buy some new clothes   go to a supermarket   take a photo   lose something   say 'I love you'   find some money   come to class late

---

I bought some new clothes last week.

b Work in pairs. Ask and answer questions.

A: *Did you go to a supermarket last week?*

B: *Yes, I did. I bought some food.*

Vocabulary | high numbers

7 **a** Read the How to box. When is *and* used?

HOW TO …

say high numbers

100	a/one hundred
915	nine hundred **and** fifteen
1,000	a/one thousand
2,690	two thousand, six hundred **and** ninety

b **10.6** Listen and write the prices.

Lovely ELECTRONICS

was €149 **sale** price ____

was €1399 **sale** price ____

was €625 **sale** price ____

was €2189 **sale** price ____

was €505 **sale** price ____

was €469 **sale** price ____

8 Write new prices in the advert. Tell your partner the prices.

The DVD player was €179. Now it's €105.

Speaking

9 **a** Ask five people 'How was last week for you?' Make notes.

b Tell your partner about the people you talked to.

A: *It was a good week for Dario and Rikka. Dario started a new job and Rikka went to Paris.*

Writing

10 **a** Look at your list from Ex. 1a. Choose one person or thing. Write a short good week/ bad week news story.

Vocabulary | adjectives of character

1 **a** Match a word 1–6 in the table to a picture a–f.

	me	brother/sister/friend
1 competitive		
2 confident		
3 shy		
4 funny		
5 friendly		
6 cool		

b **10.7** Listen and check your answers. Mark the stress of each word.

2 **a** Look at the table in Ex. 1a. Give yourself a score out of 10 for each word.

1 competitive: 9/10 (I'm very competitive.)

b Write the name of a brother, sister or good friend in the table. Give him/her a score out of ten for each word.

c Show your table to your partner. Explain your scores.

I'm very competitive. My score is nine out of ten. My brother isn't very competitive. His score is four out of ten.

Listening

3 **a** **10.8** Listen to *The Fisherman*. Correct the sentences below.

1 Mishima lived in a house on the beach and he was rich.
2 Nobu and Akio worked in the city. They were not competitive.
3 Mishima wanted his sons to be fishermen.

b Listen again. Tick (✓) all the adjectives you hear.

- [ ] old
- [ ] small
- [ ] happy
- [ ] funny
- [ ] modern
- [ ] shy
- [ ] easy
- [ ] good
- [ ] great
- [ ] friendly
- [ ] bad
- [ ] poor
- [ ] little
- [ ] famous
- [ ] competitive

c Work in pairs. Try to remember the story.

Mishima was an old man. He lived …

4 **a** Find an example of *why* and *because* in tapescript 10.8 on page 143. Then read the How to box.

> **HOW TO …**
>
> ### ask for and give reasons
>
> Use *Why? …* to ask for reasons.
> Use *Because …* to give reasons.
>
> A: *Why are you late?*
> B: *Because there was a lot of traffic*
>
> A: *Why do you like her?*
> B: *Because she's intelligent and confident*

b Tick the sentences that are true for you.

I liked *The Fisherman* story. ☐
I am happy. ☐
I want to learn English. ☐
I play the lottery. ☐

c Work in pairs. Ask questions with *Why …?* about the sentences above. Answer with *Because …*.

A: *Why did you like The Fisherman story?*
B: *Because it was interesting.*

Grammar | comparatives and superlatives

5 **a** Look at tapescript 10.8 on page 143. Complete each sentence below.

1 My company is _____ than your company.
2 My job is _____ than your job.
3 I am _____ than you.
4 I am _____ _____ than you.
5 My job is _____ _____ job.
6 I am _____ _____ person in the world.

b Look at the Active grammar box and answer the questions.

1 Match an adjective to a–c below:
   a long adjective
   b short adjective
   c 2 syllables, ends in -y
2 How do you make the comparative and superlative for each kind of adjective?
3 What word comes after comparatives?
4 What word comes before superlatives?

Active grammar

Adjective	Comparative	Superlative
big	bigger than	the biggest
happy	happier than	the happiest
intelligent	more intelligent than	the most intelligent

Note: *good – better – best*
       bad – worse – worst

6 **a** Make the comparative and superlative of the adjectives in Ex. 3b.

b Write sentences to compare you and your brother/sister/friend from Ex. 2. Then tell your partner.

I'm more competitive than my brother.

c Work in groups of three. Write superlative sentences using the adjectives in Ex. 1a.

I'm the most competitive. Giuseppe is the coolest.

Speaking

7 **a** Which type of child were you?

1 an only child (no brothers or sisters)
2 a youngest child
3 a middle child
4 an oldest child

b Find two partners (who were different types of children to you). Make a list of the differences between the types of children.

Youngest children are usually the most confident.

c Think of reasons for the differences. Give examples.

Youngest children are usually the most confident because their brothers and sisters look after them. For example, Jim Carrey is the youngest child in his family.

8 Present your ideas to the class.

Who killed Sir Rufus Montgomery?

Sir Rufus Montgomery is **dead**. Sir Rufus was a famous politician and businessman. Sir Rufus <u>died</u> at home between 10.00p.m. and 11.00p.m. last night. The <u>killer</u> took a famous painting from the house. Sir Rufus's house is in Eastbridge, ten miles from Craxton.

There are four <u>suspects</u>: Julia Montgomery (his wife), Cecil Watson (his butler), Emily Topps (his maid) and Rachel West (his secretary).

1 a Read the news story. Check the underlined words in a dictionary.

b Complete Inspector Legg's notes.

> *Who died?* *Sir Rufus Montgomery*
> *Where?*
> *When?*
> *Who are the suspects?*

2 a **10.9** Listen. Inspector Legg talks to Julia, Cecil, Emily and Rachel. Complete the chart below for each of the suspects.

Name	Julia	Cecil	Emily	Rachel
1 Who do you think is the killer?				
2 Did you like Sir Rufus? Why/Why not?				
3 What did you do between 8.00p.m. and 10.00p.m. yesterday? Who did you see?				
4 What did you do between 10.00p.m. and 11.00p.m. yesterday? Who did you see?				

b Listen again. Check your information.

3 a Work in groups of four–five. Read your role.

Student A = You are Julia Montgomery. Go to page 129.

Student B = You are Cecil Watson. Go to page 128.

Student C = You are Emily Topps. Go to page 130.

Student D = You are Rachel West. Go to page 132.

Student E = You are Inspector Legg. Go to page 133.

b Make notes as Inspector Legg asks questions. Who is the killer?

The Past Simple
Die einfache Vergangenheit

⊕	I You He She It We They	lived worked stayed	in Berlin. with my sister. in a nice hotel.

Für die regelmäßige Vergangenheit hängen Sie -ed an das Verb.

⊖	I You He She It We They	saw bought had	a new camera. a nice car. a computer.

Viele häufige Verben haben eine unregelmäßige Vergangenheitsform:

have—had	do—did	go—went
come—came	see—saw	get—got
say—said	buy—bought	give—gave
make—made	find—found	win—won
speak—spoke	eat—ate	read /ri:d/—read /red/
write—wrote		

⊖	I You He She It We They	didn't talk didn't listen didn't go	to Cynthia. to the pop star.

Die verneinte Vergangenheit bilden Sie mit *didn't* (did not) und Infinitiv, nicht mit der Vergangenheitsform des Verbs.

She didn't went to the cinema.

She didn't go to the cinema.

❓	Did	I You He She It We They	move walk go come	to work? to school? to London?

Die Frage bilden Sie entsprechend der *Do*-Frage in der Gegenwart: Did + Subjekt + Infinitiv des Verbs. Wenn Sie ein Fragewort verwenden, steht es vor *did*. Auch hier verwenden Sie die Vergangenheitsform des Verbs nicht.

Did they moved to Munich?

Did they move to Munich?

Why ...? Because

Why fragt nach dem Grund oder der Ursache:

Why did you get up late?

Because gibt Grund oder Ursache an:

Because I went to bed late.

Because kann zwei Sätze verbinden (Konjunktion):

I went to bed late because I went to a party.

More + noun
More + Nomen

I want a job with more money.
I changed jobs. Now I've got more time.

High numbers
Zahlen über 100

Nach *hundred* steht *and* (/ənd/ ausgesprochen).

100—a/one hundred
101—a/one hundred and one
499—four hundred and ninety-nine
1000—a/one thousand
1001—a/one thousand and one
10,560—ten thousand, five hundred and sixty
1,000,000—a/one million

Vocabulary | good and bad experiences

1 Lesen Sie die Sätze. Schreiben Sie die fehlenden Wörter in das Rätsel. Wie lautet das Lösungswort?

1 You *meet* a famous person.
2 You _____ to a new house.
3 You _____ the lottery.
4 A police officer _____ you.
5 You _____ your wallet or purse.
6 You _____ some money on the street.
7 A thief _____ your mobile phone.
8 You _____ your arm.

Hidden phrase

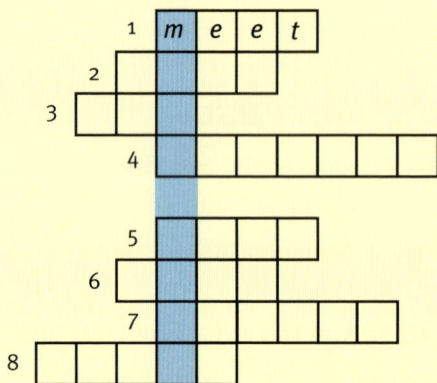

	1	m	e	e	t
	2				
3						
	4						
	5				
6					
	7				
8					

Grammar | Past Simple (affirmative)

2 Ergänzen Sie die Sätze mit den Verben im Kasten im *Past Simple*.

> cook   arrest   ask   want   walk   ~~start~~
> listen   work

1 My lesson *started* at nine o'clock.
2 They _____ a lot of questions.
3 She _____ dinner at the weekend.
4 I _____ to eat out tonight.
5 He always _____ to you.
6 You _____ to school every day.
7 The police officer _____ Spike.
8 Patrick _____ for MC Software.

Grammar | Past Simple negatives and questions (regular verbs)

3 **a** Ergänzen Sie den Text mit der richtigen Form der Verben in Klammern.

Van Gogh's early life

Van Gogh (1) _____ (be) born in Holland in 1853. In 1869 he (2) _____ (start) work. His company, Goupil & Cie, was from Paris. Van Gogh (3) _____ (not move) to Paris but he (4) _____ (not stay) in The Hague. In 1873 he (5) _____ (move) to London. He (6) _____ (love) a woman called Eugenie Loyer but she (7) _____ (not love) him. Van Gogh was very unhappy. He (8) _____ (not like) his job and in 1874 he moved to Paris. But Van Gogh (9) _____ (not stay) in Paris ...

b Schreiben Sie Fragen und Antworten zu Van Gogh.

1 (Van Gogh/stay/Paris?)
   A: *Did Van Gogh stay in Paris?* **B:** *No, he didn't.*
2 (Van Gogh/move/London?)
   A: _____ ? **B:** Yes, _____ .
3 (Van Gogh/love/Eugenie Loyer?)
   A: _____ ? **B:** Yes, _____ .
4 (Eugenie Loyer/love/Van Gogh?)
   A: _____ ? **B:** No, _____ .
5 (Van Gogh/like/his job?)
   A: _____ ? **B:** No, _____ .

Pronunciation | /t/, /d/ and /ɪd/

4 Wie spricht man diese Verben aus? Schreiben Sie /t/, /d/ oder /ɪd/ neben die Endung *-ed*.

1 wanted /ɪd/   5 walked ___   9 asked ___
2 liked /t/   6 closed ___   10 finished ___
3 moved /d/   7 arrested ___ 11 played ___
4 talked ___   8 listened ___ 12 cooked ___

Grammar | Past Simple (irregular verbs)

1 **a** Ergänzen Sie die Sätze mit der Vergangenheitsform der Verben in Klammern.

1 My brother _____ (get married) last year.

2 Oliver and Emma _____ (buy) a house in Spain.

3 We _____ (go) to the cinema last night.

4 You _____ (see) her. She was at the party.

5 Rachel _____ (say) no.

6 My manager and my wife _____ (meet) your daughter yesterday.

7 He _____ (give) an awful presentation yesterday.

8 Irena and I _____ (find) a beautiful hotel in the centre of Prague.

b Tragen Sie die Vergangenheitsformen der Verben unten in das Rätsel ein. **Tipp:** Einige Verben sind unregelmäßig. Wie lautet das Lösungswort?

1 give
2 come
3 take
4 meet
5 have
6 arrest
7 start
8 say
9 move
10 find

Hidden phrase

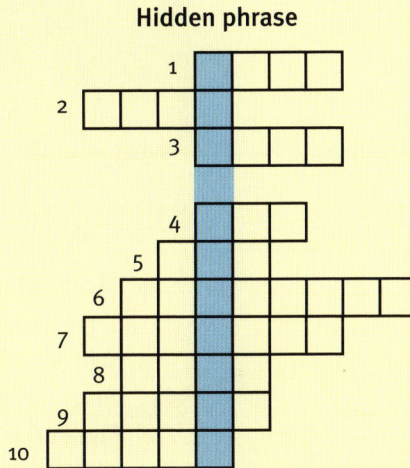

c Ergänzen Sie den Text mit der richtigen Form der Verben in Klammern.

Newly-weds win 15 million in Euro Lottery

· · · · · · · · · · · · · · · ·

Janice and Derek Parker from Cornwall (1) _____ (win) €15 million in the Euro Lottery last week. Janice and Derek (2) _____ (get married) on Saturday morning. 'We (3) _____ (not go) on holiday,' (4) _____ (say) Janice. 'We (5) _____ (not have) any money. But we (6) _____ (go) to a nice restaurant. In the evening I (7) _____ (look) at the lottery numbers and I (8) _____ (be) so happy.' And last Friday Derek (9) _____ (buy) a present for Janice. What (10) _____ (he/buy) for her? He (11) _____ (not buy) a new car or a new house. He (12) _____ (buy) a new washing machine for her!

d Bilden Sie Fragen, indem Sie die Wörter in die richtige Reihenfolge bringen.

1 find you your Did wallet?
Did you find your wallet?

2 Terry go out night? Did last

_____

3 car? they Did a buy new

_____

4 her? Did love you

_____

5 to Harry London? Did move

_____

6 say 'Yes'? Did you

_____

7 lose passport you on Did holiday? your

_____

8 Did lottery? win we the

_____

Vocabulary |

high numbers

2 Ergänzen Sie die Zahlen mit *thousand* und *hundred*.

1 2,150 – *two thousand, one hundred and fifty*

2 1,010 – one _____ and ten

3 980 – nine _____ and eighty

4 15,612 – fifteen _____ , six _____ and twelve

5 9,999 – nine _____ , nine _____ and ninety-nine

6 86,321 – eighty-six _____ , three _____ and twenty-one

7 115, 290 – one _____ and fifteen _____ , two _____ and ninety

8 200,109 – two _____ _____ , one _____ and nine

Vocabulary

1 **a** Ergänzen Sie die fehlenden Buchstaben.

1 f r _ _ n d l _
2 s h _
3 c _ m p _ t _ t _ v _
4 c _ n f _ d _ n t
5 c _ _ l
6 f _ n n _

b Ergänzen Sie diese Sätze mit den Worten aus Üb. 1a.

1 He always wants to win. He's very _____ .
2 I always laugh a lot when we talk. She's very _____ .
3 He's not very confident. He's quite _____ .
4 James Bond is good-looking, intelligent and popular. He's really _____ .
5 My manager always says 'Hello' and 'How are you?' in the morning. She's very _____ .
6 She's not shy. She's very _____ .

How to ask for and give reasons

2 **a** Schreiben Sie Fragen mit *Why*.

1 A: She's in bed.
   B: *Why is she in bed?*
2 A: He was at home yesterday.
   B: _____ ?
3 A: I ate out last night.
   B: _____ ?
4 A: She finishes work at one o'clock in the morning.
   B: _____ ?
5 A: They always take work home.
   B: _____ ?

b Ordnen Sie die Antworten a–e den Fragen 1–3 zu.

a) Because she's a chef.
b) Because they are very busy.
c) Because she went to bed late.
d) Because I didn't have any food in the house.
e) Because he's on holiday from work.

Grammar | comparatives and superlatives

3 **a** Vervollständigen Sie die Sätze über diese Sänger:

Placido Domingo
born: 1941
famous: tall:
1 2 3 4 5 6 7 8 9 10   1 2 3 4 5 6 7 8 9 10

Jose Carréras
born: 1946
famous: tall:
1 2 3 4 5 6 7 8 9 10   1 2 3 4 5 6 7 8 9 10

Luciano Pavarotti
born: 1935
famous: tall:
1 2 3 4 5 6 7 8 9 10   1 2 3 4 5 6 7 8 9 10

1 Pavarotti is *taller than* Carréras. (tall)
2 Domingo is *the tallest* of The Three Tenors. (tall)
3 Domingo is _____ Carréras. (old)
4 Pavarotti is _____ of The Three Tenors. (old)
5 Domingo is _____ Carréras. (famous)
6 Pavarotti is _____ of The Three Tenors. (famous)
7 Carréras is _____ Domingo. (young)
8 Carréras is _____ of The Three Tenors. (young)
9 Pavarotti is _____ Domingo. (short)
10 Carréras is _____ of The Three Tenors. (short)

b Korrigieren Sie die Fehler.

1 Tokyo is the bigger city in the world.
   Tokyo is the biggest city in the world.
2 France is bigger that the UK.
   _____ .
3 He's more confidenter than me.
   _____ .
4 Who's the most cool actor in the world?
   _____ .
5 This is Steve Martin's funnyest film.
   _____ .
6 The fisherman is the more intelligent than his sons.
   _____ .

Communication activities

Communication 1 | Ex. 3, page 14

Student A

Hotel: Hotel Miller.
Where: London, the UK.
Phone number: _____ .
Hotel: Hotel Calmia.
Where: Rio de Janeiro, Brazil.
Phone number: oo 55 21 476 293.
Hotel: Hotel Calmia.
Where: Madrid, Spain.
Phone number: oo 34 91 538 923.

Lesson 2.2 | Ex. 7b, page 23

You are Terri

Name: Terri Nielson
Age: 42
From: the UK
Address: 19 Filamore Street, London
Phone №: 020 3890 3124
Mobile №: 07933 348 672

Lesson 3.3 | Ex. 7, page 37

Student A

You are an assistant in a Tourist Information Office. Give information about The Louvre.

Harrods

What: _____
Open: _____
Where: _____
Free: _____

You are a tourist. Ask for information about Harrods.

LOUVRE

What: A museum and a gallery
Open: Monday—Sunday
Where: Paris
Free: No

Lesson 2.3 | Ex. 7, page 25

Student A

IDENTIFICATION

Name: Emma Koch
Age: 29
From: Munich, Germany
Job: Actress
Email address: koch@bluezone.de
Phone number: 089 488 711

Lesson 4.2 | Ex. 8, page 47

Student A

Communication 4 | Ex. 2b, page 50

Student B

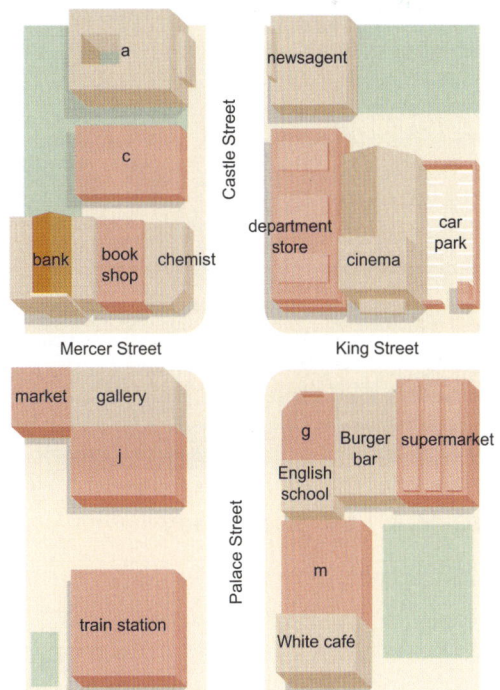

Ask for:
- the sports shop
- the bus stop
- the shoe shop
- the Blue Café
- the museum

Communication activities

Communication 4 | Ex. 2b, page 50

Student A

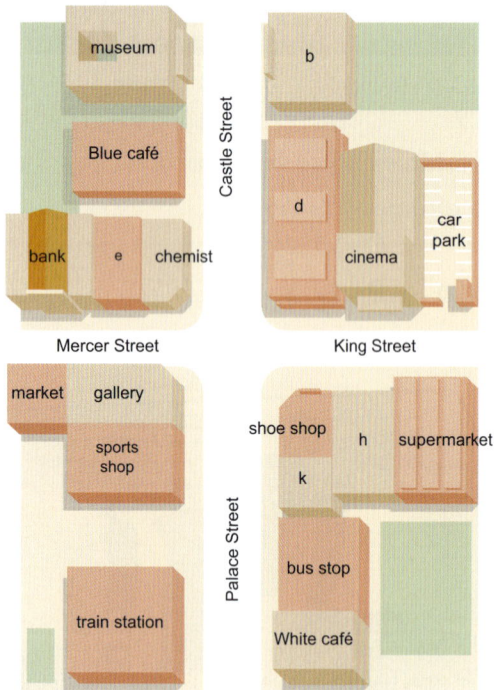

Ask for:
- the burger bar
- the department store
- the newsagent
- the English school
- the bookshop

Communication 10 | Ex. 3a, page 122

CECIL WATSON

You are Sir Rufus Montgomery's butler. You didn't like Sir Rufus. You wanted to change jobs and make more money.

Sir Rufus and Julia had dinner at 7.00p.m. Emily cooked dinner for you at 8.00p.m. You ironed Sir Rufus's shirts from 9.00p.m. to 10.00p.m.

You went for a walk in the garden at 10.00p.m. You saw Rachel in the garden. You came back at 10.30p.m. and you went to the kitchen. Julia was in the kitchen. You went to bed at 10.45p.m.

Extra information: Emily can't drive.

Lesson 9.1 | Ex. 5b, page 105

Answer: John Lennon

Communication 1 | Ex. 3, page 14

Student B

Hotel: Hotel Calmia.
Where: Rio de Janeiro in Brazil.
Phone number: _____
Hotel: Hotel Miller.
Where: London, the UK.
Phone number: 00 44 207 245 764.
Hotel: Hotel Miller.
Where: New York, the US.
Phone number: 00 1 212 987 110

Lesson 6.2 | Ex. 9, page 71

Student A

Name	William Young		From	Australia
Live in	Vancouver, Canada			
Holiday or business	business			
Job	Sales rep			
Do	sell tea and coffee to supermarkets			
Work for	Coffee Love			
Work where	in Vancouver			
Wife	Ingrid Young (Student B)			

Student B

Name	Ingrid Young		From	Scotland
Live in	Vancouver, Canada			
Holiday or business	business			
Job	Sales rep			
Do	sell suitcases and packpacks to shops			
Work for	The Big Bag Company			
Work where	near Vancouver			
Husband	William Young (Student A)			

Lesson 2.2 | Ex. 7a, page 23

You are Vittoria.

Name: Vittoria Lombardi
Age: 42
From: the UK
Address: 60 Bishop Road, Hampstead, London
Phone Nº: 020 8110 4455
Mobile Nº: 07146 993 381

Lesson 2.3 | Ex. 7, page 25

Student B

Name:	Miguel Fonseca
From:	São Paolo, Brazil
Age:	41
Job:	Manager
Email address:	m.fonseca@zilly.br
Phone number:	08122 781177

Lesson 3.3 | Ex. 7, page 37

Student B

You are an assistant in a Tourist Information Office. Give information about Harrods.

What: A shop
Open: Monday–Saturday
Where: London
Free: Yes

You are a tourist. Ask for information about The Louvre.

LOUVRE

What: _____
Open: _____
Where: _____
Free: _____

Lesson 4.2 | Ex. 8, page 47

Student B

Communication 10 | Ex. 3a, page 122

JULIA MONTGOMERY

You are Sir Rufus Montgomery's wife. You didn't love Sir Rufus because he wasn't a good husband. He didn't give you money for clothes.

You had dinner with Sir Rufus at 7.00p.m. After dinner you played chess with Sir Rufus. You talked to Rachel from 9.00p.m. to 10.00p.m. Then she had dinner. Emily cooked dinner for Rachel. You went to your bedroom.

You went to the kitchen at 10.30p.m. You saw Cecil. Then you went to bed.

Extra information: Rachel can't cook.

Lesson 5.2 | Ex. 8a, page 59

Student B

You are a hotel guest. Ask questions with *Is there a … near here?* or *Are there any … near here?* Complete the chart.

What?	Yes/No	Where?
Restaurant	Yes (2)	1= next to the gallery 2=behind the hotel
Market		
Bookshop		
Tourist information office		
Coffee shop		
Train staiton		
Bank		
Chemist		

Communication 8 | Ex. 2, page 98

Student A

Person	Address
Mr M. Haddon	14d Bookly Road
Mrs A. Walker	14c Bookly Road
Miss Z. Smith	16b Bookly Road
Mr J. Heller	14a Bookly Road
Mr G. Dyer	12a Bookly Road

Communication activities

Lesson 2.2 | Ex. 7a, page 23

You are Hans.

Name: Hans Melo

Age: 34

From: Germany

Address: 90 Clapton Road. Clapton, London

Phone Nº: 020 8169 7197

Mobile Nº: 07225 893223

Lesson 5.2 | Ex. 8a, page 59

Student A

You are hotel receptionist.

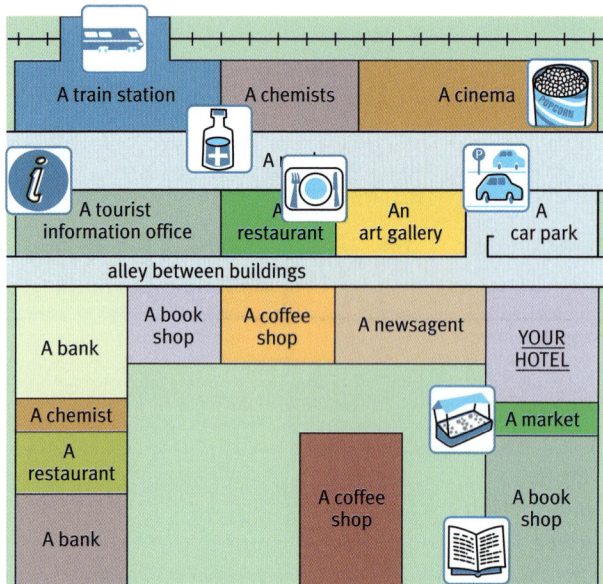

Communication 10 | Ex. 3a, page 122

EMILY TOPPS

You are Sir Rufus Montgomery's maid. You didn't like Sir Rufus. Sir Rufus never said thank you.

You cooked dinner for Sir Rufus and Julia. They had dinner at 7.00p.m. You washed the dishes after dinner. You cooked dinner for Cecil at 8.00p.m.

You went to your friend's house in Craxton at 9.00p.m. You came home at 11.00p.m. and you went to bed.

Extra information: Cecil can't play chess.

Lesson 6.2 | Ex. 9, page 71

Student C

Name	Ron Price		From	the UK
Live in	Liverpool, the UK			
Holiday or business		holiday		
Job	teacher			
Do	teach English			
Work for	an English school in Liverpool			
Work where	in Liverpool			
Wife	Pamela Young (Student D)			

Student D

Name	Pamela Price		From	the US
Live in	Liverpool, the UK			
Holiday or business		holiday		
Job	designer			
Do	bags			
Work for	Bag Designs			
Work where	in Liverpool			
Husband	Ron Price (Student C)			

Lesson 7.1 | Ex. 7c, page 81

See page 150 for answers

Lesson 6.1 | Ex. 6a, page 69

Student B

1 big cities
2 John Lennon's music
3 Prince Charles and Camilla Parker Bowles
4 museums
5 Julia Roberts
6 Bill Gates
7 the countryside

Communication 6 | Ex. 3c, page 74

findanicepresent chart

http://www.findanicepresent.com

| my account | track order | quick order | help |

Find a nice present

Search [   ] GO!

| for him | for her | for children | best sellers | special offers |

Who for?

- teenager?
- work long hours?
- married?
- have children?
- travel a lot?
- can cook?
- watch a lot of films?
- listen to a lot of music?

For him

- a wallet
- a tie
- a book
- an MP3 player
- a travel iron
- a set of saucepans
- a DVD
- a CD

For her

- a stylish bag
- a pen
- candles
- flowers
- a suitcase
- a cookery book
- a DVD
- a CD

Lesson 8.2 | Ex. 3c, page 94

A present for Paul's sister: money

Lesson 8.3 | Ex. 2a, page 96

Student C

The Top Restaurants in the World.

FRENCH LAUNDRY

French Laundry is in California in the US.

It is the number three restaurant in the world.
(Restaurant Magazine, 2005)

There are 17 tables but 400 people want to book a table every day!

Lesson 8.2 | Ex. 8a, page 95

Read the quiz questions. Tick (✓) A, B or C.

A = Yes, I have.   B = No, but I want one.

C = No, and I don't want one.

	A	B	C
1 Have you got a computer?			
2 Have you got an MP3 player?			
3 Have you got a digital camera?			
4 Have you got a camera-phone?			
5 Have you got a DVD player?			
6 Have you got a camcorder?			
7 Have you got a LCD TV?			
8 Have you got a GPS device?			
9 Have you got a CD player in your car?			

Communication activities

Lesson 7.3 | Ex. 3b, page 84

Ordinal numbers

- Add -*th* to make ordinal numbers.
- Some of the numbers are irregular.
  Yellow=irregular
- Some of the numbers have irregular spelling.
  Green=irregular spelling

1st first	11 eleventh	21 twenty-first
2nd second	12 twelfth	22 twenty-second
3rd third	13 thirteenth	23 twenty-third
4th fourth	14 fourteenth	24 twenty-fourth
5th fifth	15 fifteenth	25 twenty-fifth
6th sixth	16 sixteenth	26 twenty-sixth
7th seventh	17 seventeenth	27 twenty-seventh
8th eighth	8 eighteenth	28 twenty-eighth
9th ninth	19 nineteenth	29 twenty-ninth
10th tenth	20 twentieth	30 thirtieth

Lesson 8.3 | Ex. 2a, page 96

Student A

The Top Restaurants in the World

The Fat Duck is near London in the UK.

"It's the number one restaurant in the world"
Restaurant Magazine, 2005

It serves very unusual food, for example bacon and egg ice cream.

The Fat Duck
heston blumenthal

Lesson 10.1 | Ex. 10b, page 117

The Story of the Mona Lisa (PART 3)

Two years later the police arrested Vencenzo Peruggia. He was the thief. But how did he steal the Mona Lisa? Vencenzo was in the Louvre on August 21, 1911. The museum was very quiet. When Vencenzo walked out, the Mona Lisa was under his coat. The painting stayed in Vencenzo's apartment, near the Louvre, for two years. In 1913 Vencenzo wanted to sell the painting. He wanted to sell it in Italy. The police arrested him in Milan.

Communication 10 | Ex. 3a, page 122

RACHEL WEST

You are Sir Rufus Montgomery's secretary. You didn't like Sir Rufus. Six months ago you said 'Could I have more money?' Sir Rufus said 'No'.

You finished work at 8.00p.m. You had a bath from 8.00p.m. to 9.00p.m. You talked to Julia from 9.00p.m. to 10.00p.m. You went to the kitchen at 10.00p.m. Emily cooked dinner for you.

You went for a walk in the garden at 10.30p.m. You saw Cecil in the garden. You came back at 11.00p.m and went to bed.

Extra information: Julia can't cook.

Lesson 7.1 | Ex. 7c, page 81

Answers: April   July   October   January

Lesson 8.3 | Ex. 11, page 97

Students B and C

Salt and Pepper
Menu

STARTERS
Chicken salad
Vegetable soup
Fruit salad

MAIN COURSES
Beef and vegetables with rice
Lamb curry
Fruit salad

DESSERTS
Chocolate ice cream
Fruit cake
Cheese and buscuits

Communication 8 | Ex. 2, page 98

Student B

Mrs M. Atwood	16a Bookly Road
Mr J. Coe	14b Bookly Road
Miss T. Morrison	12b Bookly Road
Mr O. Pamuk	16c Bookly Road
Mrs A Levy	12c Bookly Road

Lesson 8.3 | Ex. 2a, page 96

Student B
The Top Restaurants in the World

elBulli

El Bulli is near Barcelona in Spain.

It is the number two best restaurant in the world.
(Restaurant Magazine 2005)

Normal restaurants have three courses: starter, main course and dessert… El Bulli has 27 courses!

Communication 10 | Ex. 3a, page 122

INSPECTOR LEGG

You are Inspector Legg. You want to find the killer. Ask the questions in the chart on page 122. Make notes.

Lesson 2.2 | Ex. 7a, page 23

You are Sanjay.

Name: Sanjay Naveen
Age: 28
From: India
Address: 16 Davis Street, Ealing, London
Phone №: 020 7440 1005
Mobile №: 07881 442901

Lesson 9.2 | Ex. 10b, page 107

The "my first my last" Phrase Game

Start

1. my first bicycle
2. my last visit to the cinema
3. my first best friend
4. my last night in a hotel
5. my first day at school
6. my last CD
7. my first CD
8. my last visit to a museum
9. my first computer
10. my first camera
11. my last book
12. my first mobile phone
13. my last visit to a tourist attraction
14. my first holiday

Finish.

133

Texte verfassen

A holiday email

Geben Sie einen Betreff an.

Verwenden Sie die Anrede *Hi* oder *Hello* + Name

Beenden Sie Ihre E-Mail mit *See you next week* oder *See you soon* oder *Hope to see you soon.*

Beginnen Sie mit *How are you?* oder *Thanks for your email.*

Beschreiben Sie Ihren Urlaubsort, Ihr Hotel usw.

Benutzen Sie Kurzformen: *we're, it's, ...*

Erklären Sie kurz, welche Anhänge Sie mitschicken.

Verwenden Sie bei Familienmitgliedern oder engen Freunden die Grußformel *Love*, + Name (Liebe Grüße).

From: louisebrown@umail.com
To: claudia2000@wowmail.com
Subject: we're on holiday!
Attachment: JPG (0.22 MB) JPG (0.16 MB)

Hi Claudia

How are you?

We're on holiday in switzerland. We're in Lausanne. Our hotel is The Atlantis Hotel. It's great. The Lausanne is small and beautiful. It's on Lake Geneva.

The two attachments are photos. Photo 1 is Jason and me. We're at Lake Geneva. Photo 2 is Jason in our hotel room.

See you next week!

Love,
Louise

A description | my favourite place for a holiday

Benutzen Sie ...'s, um auszudrücken, wem etwas gehört.

Machen Sie Ortsangaben: *in, near, next to, ...*

Erklären Sie, wo Sie am liebsten Ihren Urlaub verbringen: in the *north /south/east/west/centre* of + Land.

Denken Sie daran, dass man Orts- und Ländernamen groß schreibt: *London, Berlin, Austria, Poland* usw.

Verwenden Sie Adjektive, um Ihre Beschreibung anschaulicher zu machen: *popular, great, modern, beautiful, old, ...*

My favourite place for a holiday is London. It's the capital of the UK and it's in the south-east of England. There are a lot of museums, shops, restaurants and other tourist attractions.

London's parks are great. Hyde Park is in the centre of London. It's very big and in summer there are concerts in the park. Hampstead Heath is beautiful too. It's a big park in the north of London.

The British Museum is very popular. It's very big and the building is quite old. But I think The Science Museum is London's top attraction. It's in South Kensington, near the centre of London. The exhibitions are great!

The London Eye is a new tourist attraction. It's a big wheel. It's on the River Thames, near Big Ben. It's expensive but the views of London are amazing.

A letter to a friend

Geben Sie hier das Datum an.

Verwenden Sie die Anrede: *Dear* + Name

Verbinden Sie Sätze mit *and* oder *but*.

Stellen Sie persönliche Fragen.

Betonen Sie zum Schluss, dass Sie weiter Kontakt möchten.

15 Westbrook Road,
Lenton,
Nottingham,
NG7 2TD

24th September, 2006

Dear Fatima,

How are you? Long time, no see!

I live in Nottingham now. My new address is at the top of this letter. I'm a PA in a computer company and Jeremy is a sales assistant in a department store. Life is good and I'm very happy. I get up at 7 o'clock and have breakfast but Jeremy gets up at 9 o'clock. He starts work at 10 o'clock. We finish work at 6 o'clock and Jeremy cooks dinner. In the evening we watch TV or read a book.

How is your life? Are you still a builder?

Please write and tell me your news.

Love,
Fran

Geben Sie hier Ihre Adresse an.

Beginnen Sie mit *How are you?* oder *I hope you're well.*

Verwenden Sie die Grußformel *Best wishes* + Name (Viele Grüße). Bei engen Freunden können Sie auch *Love,* + Name (Liebe Grüße) schreiben.

A formal email

Geben Sie einen Betreff an.

Verwenden Sie die Anrede *Dear* + Name

Beenden Sie Ihre E-Mail mit *I look forward to your reply.*

From: amywatson@mymail.com
To: waterbridgehotel@wowmail.com
Subject: double room for June 3rd/4th

Dear Waterbridge Hotel,

I would like some more information about your hotel.

- Do you have a double room available on Saturday 3rd June and Sunday 4th June?
- How much is a double room for two nights?
- Is breakfast included?
- Has the hotel got a swimming pool?

I look forward to your reply.

Yours sincerely

Ralph Bingham

Benutzen Sie keine Kurzformen.

Verwenden Sie in formellen Briefen und E-Mails die Grußformel *Yours sincerely,* + Name

Tapescripts

Unit 1 Recording 1
R=Receptionist G=Guest
R: Good morning.
G: Good morning.
R: Welcome to Easton Hotel.
G: Thank you.
Photo A

A=Alonzo C=Camila
A: Hello. I'm Alonzo Moreno.
C: Hello. I'm Camila Diaz. Nice to meet you.
A: Nice to meet you, too.
Photo D

J=James N=Nina
J: Hi Nina.
N: Hi James.
Photo B

M=Maria H=Helga
M: Hello. I'm Maria Hofmann. What's your name?
H: I'm Helga Peters.
Photo C

Unit 1 Recording 2
1 Good morning.
2 Welcome to Leonard Hotel.
3 Hello.
4 Nice to meet you.
5 Hello. What's your name?

Unit 1 Recording 3
zero, one, two, three, four, five, six, seven, eight, nine

Unit 1 Recording 4
R=Receptionist C=Cristina
R: Hello.
C: Hello. I'm Cristina Branco.
R: Welcome to Bally Hotel, Miss Branco. You're in room 329.
C: Thank you.
Thank you.

Unit 1 Recording 5
1
A=Auguste B=Betty
A: Good morning.
B: Good morning.
2
A=Auguste C=Camilla
A: Good afternoon.
C: Good afternoon.
3
A=Auguste D=Daniel
A: Good evening.
D: Good evening.
4
A=Auguste P=People
A: Good night.
P: Good night.

Unit 1 Recording 6
a, b, c, d, e, f, g, h, i, j, k, l, m, n, o, p, q, r, s, t, u, v, w, x, y, z

Unit 1 Recording 7
a h j k / b c d e g p t v / f l m n s x z / i y / o / q u w / r

Unit 1 Recording 8
1 India 2 Australia 3 Argentina 4 Japan 5 the US 6 Brazil 7 the UK 8 Germany 9 Italy 10 Poland

Unit 1 Recording 9
1
M=Martin S=Sunny
M: Sunny Deva?

S: Yes.
M: Hello, Mr Deva. I'm Martin. Welcome to the UK.
S: Thank you.
2
R=Rachel A=Ana
R: Ana Goncalvez?
A: Yes.
R: Hello, Mrs Goncalvez. I'm Rachel. Welcome to Germany.
A: Thank you.
3
A=Abby N=Nicole
A: Nicole Redman?
N: Yes.
A: Hello, Ms Redman. I'm Abby. Welcome to the US.
N: Thank you.

Unit 1 Recording 10
1
A: Coffee?
B: Yes, please.
2
W=Waiter C=Customer
W: Black pepper?
C: No, thank you.
3
P=Peter D=David
P: Hello. I'm Peter.
D: I'm David. Nice to meet you.
4
Woman: Excuse me …
5
Man: Oh! Sorry!
6
A: He's Ronaldinho. He's from Brazil.
B: Pardon?
A: He's from Brazil.

Unit 1 Recording 11
1
Woman: You're in room 829.
2
T=Todd J=Janice
T: Hello. I'm Todd Williams.
J: I'm Janice Simpson …
3
K=Karen J=Janice
K: Hi Janice.
J: Hi Karen. Come in.
K: Thank you.
J: Coffee?

Unit 1 Recording 12
L=Luisa B=Boris A=Andy
A: Hi Boris.
B: Hi, Andy. This is Luisa.
A: Nice to meet you, Luisa.
L: Nice to meet you, too.

Unit 1 Recording 13
A=Andy L=Luisa
L: Where are you from, Andy?
A: I'm from the US.
L: Where are you from in the US?
A: I'm from New York. Where are you from?
L: I'm from Argentina.
A: Where are you from in Argentina?
L: I'm from Rosario.

Unit 1 Recording 14
1 Where are you from?
2 Where are you from in Germany?
3 I'm from Hamburg.

Unit 1 Recording 15
Australia: six, one.
Brazil: double five.
China: eight, six.

Japan: eight, one.
Mexico: five, two.
Russia: seven.
Spain: three, four.
Turkey: nine, o.
The UK: double four.
The US: one.

Unit 1 Recording 16
1
M=Man W=Woman
M: Directory enquiries.
W: The Lamden Hotel, please.
M: Where is it?
W: It's in Rome, in Italy.
M: Thank you.
Machine: The number is: double o – three – nine – six – eight – one – two – nine – four – one.
I repeat: double o – three – nine – six – eight – one – two – nine – four – one.
2
A: Directory enquiries.
B: Hotel Kelem, please.
A: Where is it, please?
B: It's in Istanbul, in Turkey.
A: Thank you.
Machine: The number is: double o – nine – o – two – one – two – nine – six – three – four – seven.
I repeat: double o – nine – o – two – one – two – nine – six – three – four – seven.

Unit 2 Recording 1
1 mother son 2 father daughter
3 sister brother 4 father son
5 wife husband 6 mother daughter

Unit 2 Recording 2
A mobile phone B phone
C phone number D email address
E computer F website G photo
H passport I first name J surname
K address

Unit 2 Recording 3
L=Liz S=Sabrina
L: Ooh! Who's he?
S: Carl? He's my brother. He's 26 years old.
L: Twenty-six? I'm twenty-six.
S: You're thirty-six!
L: Oh, yes.
S: She's my sister, Anna. She's thirty-two. And he's my father, Marek. He's from Poland. He's sixty.
L: Who's she?
S: She's my mother, Sofia. She's from Italy. She's fifty-seven. And my daughter, Sarah. She's one. And my son, Tom. He's three.
L: Ooh! Who's he?
S: He's my husband, James.
L: Oh! How old is he?
S: He's forty.

Unit 2 Recording 4
ten, eleven, twelve, thirteen, fourteen, fifteen, sixteen, seventeen, eighteen, nineteen, twenty.

Unit 2 Recording 5
twenty, twenty-one, thirty, thirty-three, forty, forty-nine, fifty, fifty-six, sixty, sixty-seven, seventy, seventy-four, eighty, eighty-eight, ninety, ninety-nine

Unit 2 Recording 6
1 Christina's my mother.
2 She's sixty-five. 3 Janet's my daughter.
4 David's my son. 5 He's fifteen.

6 Jeff's my brother.   7 Eric's my father.

8 Diana's my wife.

Unit 2 Recording 7

1 59 Princes Street, Edinburgh

2 31 Globe Road, London

3 80 Boulevard de Clichy, Paris

4 46 Lower Abbey Street, Dublin

5 70 Brook Street, Boston

Unit 2 Recording 8

B=Ben J1=Judge 1 J2=Judge 2

B: Hello.

J1/J2: Hello.

J1: What's your name?

B: Ben Gibson.

J1: How do you spell that?

B: Gibson. G – I – B – S – O – N

J1: Where are you from, Ben?

B: I'm from Australia.

J1: How old are you, Ben?

B: I'm twenty-nine.

J2: What's your address?

B: Seventeen, Kings Road, Angel, London

J1: What's your phone number?

B: My home number is 0 – two – 0 – eight, three – nine – one, double two – four. And my mobile number is 0 – seven – eight, seven – two – four, nine – one.

J1/J2: Thank you.

J2: OK, Mr Gibson!

B: Oh! OK! Yes …

B: Every morning, she's on my train, where is she from, and what's her name …

Unit 2 Recording 9

J1=Judge 1 J2=Judge 2 J3=Judge 3

J4=Judge 4 J5=Judge 5

T=Terri V=Vittoria H=Hans S=Sanjay

1

J1: Thank you. Ben. Goodbye. He's awful.

J2: Yes, awful.

2

J3: Thank you, Terri.

T: OK. Thank you. Goodbye.

J3: Goodbye. She's good.

J4: Yes, she's good.

3

J1: Thank you Vittoria.

V: Oh, thank you.

J1: Goodbye.

V: Goodbye.

J1: She's OK.

J5: Yes, she's OK.

4

J3: Thank you Hans. Thank you.

H: OK. Thank you. Goodbye.

J3: He's great!

J2: Yes, he's great.

5

J4: Thank you Sanjay.

S: OK, thank you.

J4: Goodbye.

S: Goodbye.

J4: He's bad.

J1: Yes, he's bad.

Unit 2 Recording 10

1

S=Simon

A: What's your name, please?

S: Simon Ambrose.

A: How do you spell that?

S: Ambrose. A – M – B – R – O – S – E.

2

A: What's your address, please?

B: 82 via Speranza, Rome.

A: How do you spell that, please?

B: Via: V – I – A. Speranza: S – P – E – R – A – N – Z – A.

Unit 2 Recording 11

A: What's the website?

B: www.emailfriends.net

A: Uh-huh. Who's she?

B: Her name's Frieda Lang.

A: What's her job?

B: She's a teacher.

A: What's her email address?

B: frieda@teachernet.de

A: What's his name?

B: Tom Mackinstosh.

A: What's his job?

B: err … He's an accountant.

A: What's his email address?

B: It's tom@mackintosh.com

A: Hmmm … What's her name?

B: Her name's Junko Nakamura. She's a student.

A: Oh! I'm a student. What's her email address?

B: junura@jmail.jp

A: How do you spell that?

B: Junura: J – U – N – U – R – A, at jmail: J – M – A – I – L dot J – P.

A: Thank you!

Unit 2 Recording 12

1 doctor   2 artist   3 teacher

4 student   5 actor   6 police officer

7 engineer   8 accountant   9 sales assistant   10 manager

Unit 2 Recording 13

1 He's a teacher   2 She's an actor

3 He's a student   4 She's an engineer

Unit 3 Recording 1

a castle, a cathedral, a palace, a museum, a gallery, a department store, a market, a mountain, a lake

Unit 3 Recording 2

1 They're from Spain.

2 Their mother is Tina.

3 Their hotel is in Vienna.

4 They're students.

5 They're in Istanbul.

6 Where is their camera?

Unit 3 Recording 3

1 a suitcase   2 a map   3 a top

4 a camera   5 a pair of shoes   6 a book

7 a pair of trousers   8 a skirt

9 a backpack   10 an MP3 player

Unit 3 Recording 4

R=Ravi D=Diane E=Eva

1

A: Hello, sir. What's in your suitcase, please?

R: What's in my suitcase? Um, a map, a camera, two books, a top and two pairs of trousers. Oh, and a pair of shoes.

2

A: Hello Madam. What's in your suitcase?

D: Oh, err. Let me see. A camera – no! Two cameras, an MP3 player, a pair of shoes, two skirts, three tops, three books and a backpack.

3

A: Hello Madam. What's in your suitcase, please?

E: What's in my suitcase? Umm, a camera, two maps, two books, three tops, an MP3 player, a pair of trousers and a skirt and … err … five pairs of shoes.

Unit 3 Recording 5

a two suitcases   b five maps

c seven tops   d three cameras

e two pairs of shoes   f four books

g eight pairs of trousers   h six skirts

Unit 3 Recording 6

MB=Mr Boyle J=Jane Miles

MB: Excuse me.

J: Yes?

MB: I'm Mr Boyle. What's your name?

J: Jane Miles.

MB: What's in your suitcase, Miss Miles.

J: I'm not Miss Miles. I'm Mrs Miles.

MB: Sorry. OK, a camera …

J: It isn't a camera. It's an MP3 player.

MB: Oh! Sorry. An MP3 player … and two books …

J: They aren't books. They're maps.

MB: Yes, of course. Sorry …

Unit 3 Recording 7

Monday, Tuesday, Wednesday, Thursday, Friday, Saturday, Sunday

Unit 3 Recording 8

1

A=Assistant B=Man

A: Good morning.

B: Good morning. Is [beep] near here?

A: No, it isn't. It isn't in London. Are you in a car?

B: Yes, I am.

A: It's about twelve kilometres from here. Here's a map. We are … here. And it is … there.

B: OK. Is it free?

A: No, it isn't.

B: And is it open today?

A: Yes, it is.

B: OK, great. Thank you. Goodbye.

A: Goodbye.

2

A=Assistant B=Woman

A: Good morning.

B: Good morning.

A: Can I help you?

B: Yes. Is [beep] open today?

A: Yes, it is.

B: Good. Is it near here?

A: Yes, it is. Here's a map. We are … here. And it is … there. It's near Oxford Street.

B: Great. Thank you. Are museums in London free?

A: Yes, they are.

B: OK, great. Thank you. Goodbye.

A: Goodbye.

3

A=Assistant B=Man

A: Good morning. Can I help you?

B: Yes. Is [beep] open today?

A: No, it isn't. It's closed on Mondays.

B: Oh.

A: Sorry.

B: OK. Goodbye.

A: Goodbye.

Unit 3 Recording 9

L=Louis S=Sara

L: Hello.

S: Hi, Louis. It's Sara.

L: Hi Sara. How are you and Paul?

S: Fine thanks. And you?

L: Fine thanks. Where are you?

S: We're in Morocco.

L: Are you in Casablanca?

S: No, we aren't. We're in Marakesh.

L: Is it beautiful?

S: Yes, it is. It's very beautiful.

L: Is it hot?

S: Yes, it is. It's very hot.

L: Is your hotel nice?

Tapescripts

S: No, it isn't. It's very small and very old.
L: Oh dear! Is the food nice?
S: Yes. It's very nice. Are Mum and Dad OK?
L: Yes, they are. They're fine.
S: OK – see you on Friday.
L: See you on Friday. Bye.
S: Bye.

Unit 4 Recording 1
A café B cashpoint C train station
D newsagent E cinema F car park
G pub H bookshop I bank
J chemist K restaurant L supermarket
M bus stop N market

Unit 4 Recording 2
1 This is an instant coffee. It's very popular in the UK with milk and sugar.
2 This is a black coffee or a filter coffee. It's very popular in the US.
3 This is a white coffee. It's a black coffee with milk.
4 This is an espresso. It's very popular in a lot of countries, for example Spain.
5 This is a cappuccino. It's an espresso with hot milk. It's very popular in a lot of countries, for example Italy.
6 This is an iced coffee. It's very popular in hot countries, for example Greece.

Unit 4 Recording 3
1
A: Yes, madam. Can I help you?
B: Yes. Can I have a chicken salad, please.
A: Certainly. Anything else?
B: Yes. Can I have a large cappuccino, please.
A: Of course.
2
A: Good afternoon.
B: Good afternoon.
A: So, a ham sandwich and a small orange juice. Anything else?
B: Yes. Can I have an espresso, please.
A: Sure. Eat in?
B: Pardon?
A: Eat in or take away?
B: Take away, please.
A: Espresso to go … That's …
3
A: Yes, sir. Can I help you?
B: Yes, can I have a cup of tea and a piece of chocolate cake, please.
A: Certainly. Anything else?
B: Err, can I have a medium black coffee, too, please.
A: Of course. So, a cup of tea, a piece of chocolate cake and a medium black coffee.
B: Yes, thank you.
A: No problem …

Unit 4 Recording 5
1
A: Can I help you?
B: Yes. Can I have an espresso please, to go.
A: Anything else?
B: No, thank you.
A: That's one pound ten please.
2
A: Can I help you?
B: Can I have a cappuccino and a mineral water, please.
A: Anything else?
B: No, thank you.
A: That's three eighty-nine, please.
3
A: Good morning. Can I help you?
B: Coffeeeeee!
A: Coffee. Err, black.
B: Coffeeeeee!

A: OK. One large black coffee. That's one dollar nineteen cents.
4
A: Bonjour.
B: Hello. Can I have a cappuccino, please?
A: With sugar?
B: No, thank you.
A: Anything else?
B: A piece of chocolate cake, please.
A: Certainly. That's four euros thirty-four.
5
A: Can I help you.
B: Can I have an iced coffee, please.
A: An iced coffee and … is that a chicken sandwich?
B: Yes.
A: That's three thirty-nine, please.

Unit 4 Recording 6
1 a green T-shirt   2 a white pairs of shoes
3 an orange dress   4 a red coat
5 a yellow hat   6 a black pair of trousers
7 a blue bag   8 a brown skirt

Unit 4 Recording 7
S=Seller C=Claudia A=Adam
S: Hello. Can I help you?
C: Yes, how much is this blue hat?
A: It isn't blue. It's green!
C: No it isn't! It's blue.
S: It's three pounds fifty.
C: Ooh! And how much are these beautiful dresses?
A: They aren't beautiful. They're ugly!
C: No they're not. They're …
S: They're twelve pounds eighty-five.
C: How much is that yellow skirt?
A: Yuk!
S: It's seventeen ninety-nine.
A: Seventeen ninety-nine? How much are those white shirts?
S: They're eight pounds forty-five. The orange shirts are nine pounds.
A: Hmm – it's my birthday on Wednesday, Claudia … Claudia? … Claudia? Where is she?

Unit 4 Recording 8
1
T=Tony W=Woman
T: Can I have three tickets to Bristol, please two adults and one child.
W: Single or return?
T: Return, please.
W: That's forty-two thirty, please. … Thank you. … Here you are.
2
M=Man S=Shula
M: Can I help you?
S: Yes, please. Can I have a packet of aspirin, please.
M: Twenty-four or forty-eight?
S: Twenty-four, please.
M: That's one forty-nine, please. … Thank you.
3
J=Jack M= Man
J: Can I have three tickets for *ChickenMan Returns*, please.
M: That's fifteen pounds ninety please.
J: Can I pay by credit card?
M: Sure. … Sign here, please … Thank you. Here you are.
J: Thanks.
4
M1=Man 1 M2=Man 2
M1: What can I get you?
M2: Can I have a Lion Brew beer, please.
M1: A pint or a half?
M2: A pint please.

M1: Anything else?
M2: Yes. A dry white wine, please.
M1: That's four pounds and nine pence, please.
5
W=Woman M=Man
W: Thirty-one pounds and seven pence, please.
M: Here you are.
W: Thank you. Enter your PIN number, please. … Thank you.

Unit 4 Recording 9
1
A: Excuse me. Where is the gallery?
B: Err … Ah yes, it's next to the market on Mercer Street.
A: Great. Thank you.
B: You're welcome.
2
A: Excuse me. Where's the train station?
B: I'm sorry, I don't know.
A: OK. Never mind. Thank you. *[Asking someone else]* Excuse me, where's the train station?
C: The train station? … It's on Palace Street, opposite the White Café.
A: Great. Thank you.
C: You're welcome.
3
A: Excuse me. Where's the nearest supermarket?
B: The nearest supermarket is opposite the car park, on King Street.
A: Great. Thank you.
B: You're welcome.

Unit 5 Recording 1
1 Darwin is in the north of Australia.
2 Perth is in the west of Australia.
3 Brisbane is in the east of Australia.
4 Adelaide is in the south of Australia.
5 Alice Springs is in the centre of Australia.

Unit 5 Recording 2
A: City
B: Buildings and roads
A: Countryside
B: Trees and a river
A: Coast
B: The sea and a beach

Unit 5 Recording 3
S=Speaker
S: My favourite place for a holiday is Cornwall. Cornwall is in the south-west of … England. The coast and the countryside are very beautiful and the beaches are … great. There are two famous castles in Cornwall. Tintagel Castle is in the north of Cornwall and Pendennis Castle is in the … south. There is a great gallery in the west of Cornwall. It's called Tate St. Ives. There is a new tourist attraction in south-east Cornwall. It's called … The Eden Project. There are plants and trees from all over the … world. There is a beautiful outdoor … theatre in the west of Cornwall. It's called the Minack Theatre.

Unit 5 Recording 4
Picture 1 There's one person in the theatre.
Picture 2 There are some people in the theatre.
Picture 3 There are a lot of people in the theatre.

Unit 5 Recording 5
1 The newsagent is next to the hotel.
2 The café is in front of the train station.
3 The chemist is opposite the Italian

restaurant.
4 The cinema is behind the town square.
5 The department store is near the chemist.

Unit 5 Recording 6
R=Receptionist M=Man W=Woman
R: Hello sir, madam. Can I help you?
M: Yes. Is there a café near this hotel?
R: Yes, sir, there is. There's a café next to this hotel and there's another café in front of the train station.
W: Are there any good restaurants near here?
R: There's a good Chinese restaurant next to the chemist. There's an Indian restaurant behind this hotel. That's very good. And there's an Italian restaurant next to the newsagent.
M: Great. And, is there a bank near here?
R: Yes, sir, there is. There's a bank next to the department store but it isn't open today. It's Saturday.
M: Oh no!
R: But there's a cashpoint in this hotel. It's over there.
M: Oh! Great!
W: Are there any tourist attractions near here?
R: Yes, madam, there are. There's a good museum behind the Italian restaurant and a there's a famous cathedral near here. Here's a map. We're here … the cathedral is here … and the museum is here.
W: Great. Thank you. And are there any galleries near here?
R: No, madam, there aren't.
W: Never mind. Come on George, let's go …

Unit 5 Recording 7
Chez Pierre is a French restaurant.
The Taj Mahal is an Indian restaurant.
La Spiga is an Italian restaurant.
Ratskeller is a German restaurant.
Wong Li is a Chinese restaurant.
King Henry's is an English restaurant.

Unit 5 Recording 8
P=Patricia J=James
P: Hi, James. How are you?
J: Fine, thanks, Patricia. And you?
P: I'm OK. What's that?
J: It's a brochure for Harefield College.
P: Harefield College? Is that the language school in the centre of town.
J: That's right. The *Language plus* courses are very popular.
P: *Language plus*? But your English is fine.
J: It's not for me. It's for my cousin, Vanda. She's from Augsburg in Germany.
P: Augsburg?
J: It's near Munich. Vanda's English level is A1.
P: Oh, I see. The course is for her!
J: Yes!

Unit 5 Recording 9
P: Can she drive?
J: Yes, she can.
P: OK. So course 175 is not good for Vanda. Can she swim?
J: No, she can't.
P: Aha! So, perhaps course 174. Can she play golf?
J: No, she can't. And she can't cook. But she can use a computer.
P: So course 178 is not good for Vanda. Can she dance?
J: Yes, she can. And she can sing. She's very good.
P: Oh … I can't dance and I can't sing.

J: Never mind.
P: But I can play the piano.
J: Vanda can't play the piano. So course 173 is OK. But it's not a morning course.
P: So?
J: She's a waitress in a restaurant in the afternoon and evening.
P: Oh, I see.

Unit 5 Recording 10
1 I can speak English. 2 I can't speak Italian. 3 Can you speak German? 4 He can speak Russian. 5 She can't speak Spanish. 6 Can they speak Portuguese?

Unit 5 Recording 11
A Ten o'clock in the morning.
B Three o'clock in the afternoon.
C Seven o'clock in the evening.
D Eight o'clock in the morning.
E One o'clock in the afternoon.
F Eight o'clock in the evening.

Unit 5 Recording 12
T=Teresa N=Nick B=Brenda
T: Welcome to my B&B. I'm Teresa. Nice to meet you.
N: Nice to meet you, too.
T: Where are you from?
N: Croydon. It's in south London.
T: Oh, yes. Great. OK. Come with me, please. This is your bedroom. There's an en suite bathroom with a shower. There's a double bed and there are some towels on the bed.
B: Is there an extra blanket?
T: Yes. There's a blanket on the bed, next to the towels.
B: Great.
T: There's a kettle on the table and there are some tea bags next to the kettle.
N: Is there a fridge?
T: Yes, there is. It's under the table.
B: What time is breakfast?
T: It's from half past seven to half past ten.
N: And what's the checkout time?
T: Checkout time is quarter to twelve.
N/B: Great.
B: It's very nice.
N: Yes, beautiful.
T: Any questions, just ask.
N: Thanks. Bye.
N: This room is awful!
B: I know – awful!

Unit 5 Recording 13
six o'clock, five past six, ten past six, quarter past six, twenty past six, twenty-five past six, half past six, twenty-five to seven, twenty to seven, quarter to seven, ten to seven, five to seven

Unit 6 Recording 1
thin good-looking tall fat short happy young rich old poor sad intelligent

Unit 6 Recording 2
DJ=Disk Jockey CC=Cynthia Castro
DJ: Now it's time for our 60-second interview. Today Cynthia Castro is in the studio. Welcome to *Radio Dublin* Cynthia.
CC: Thank you.
DJ: Cynthia … your 60-second interview starts … now.
DJ: What's your job?
CC: I'm a singer.
DJ: Where are you from?
CC: I'm from Rio but Dublin is my home now. My husband is Irish.

DJ: Do you like Dublin?
CC: Yes, I do.
DJ: Do you like me?
CC: Sorry?
DJ: It's a joke. Do you like Irish music?
CC: No, I don't. I like Brazilian music.
DJ: What's your favourite time of day?
CC: Half past nine in the morning. It's time for my first coffee.
DJ: Do you like football?
CC: Of course! I'm Brazilian.
DJ: What's your favourite football team?
CC: AC Milan.
DJ: Do you like American food?
CC: No, I don't. I like Indian food.
DJ: What are your favourite things in life?
CC: I like Brazilian music, German cars, Italian fashion …
DJ: Ah! Time is up. Thank you Cynthia Castro!
CC: You're welcome.
DJ: That was our 60-second interview!

Unit 6 Recording 3
1 Do you like Italian food?
2 Do you like coffee?
3 Are you from Brazil?
4 Are you a student?
5 Do you like London?
6 Do you like Paris?
7 Are you happy?
8 Do you like this film?

Unit 6 Recording 4
1 Do you like me? 2 I like you.
3 I don't like him. 4 I don't like her.
5 I like it. 6 I like them.

Unit 6 Recording 5
1
A: What do architects do?
B: They design buildings, for example houses and shops.
2
A: What do sales reps. do?
B: They sell things, for example computers and books.
3
A: What do designers do?
B: They design things, for example clothes and shoes.
4
A: What do reporters do?
B: They write articles, for example newspaper articles.
5
A: What do chefs do?
B: They cook food, for example Chinese food and Italian food.
6
A: What do builders do?
B: They build buildings, for example houses and shops.

Unit 6 Recording 6
S=Sharon C=Catherine
P=Pat A=Anthony
S: Excuse me. Your coat is on the floor.
C: Sorry?
S: You're coat. It's on the floor.
C: Oh! Thank you very much.
S: No problem! Are you on holiday?
C: Yes, I am. I'm here with my husband. He's in our room. We really like this city.
S: Yes, it's great. Where are you from?
C: I'm from South Africa and my husband is from Canada. We live in the UK. Where are you from?
S: We're from Ireland.
C: Are you on holiday?
S: No, we aren't. We're on business.

C: What do you do?
S: We're architects.
C: Great! What do you design?
S: We design houses and office buildings.
C: I'm a sales rep and my husband is a chef.
S: Oh really? What do you sell?
C: I sell towels and blankets to hotels.
P: And who do you work for?
C: It's a small company. It's called PDS HotelCare.
S: Great! My name's Sharon and this is my husband, Pat.
C: Nice to meet you. My name's Catherine. Ah! Here's my husband. Anthony, this is Sharon and Pat. They're from Ireland.
A: Nice to meet you.
P: Nice to meet you, too.
C: Sharon and Pat are architects. They design houses and office buildings.
A: Oh really? Where do you work?

Unit 6 Recording 7
A=Adam E=Emma
A: Hey, Emma. Listen. This song is for you.
E: What's it called?
A: It's called *She's my soulmate.*
E: Ahhh!
A: She gets up early – I get up late,
But that ok – she's my soulmate.
She eats a salad – I eat a pizza
But she's my soulmate – I love her, I need her
She finishes work – I watch TV
I don't do much – I just drink tea
But she still loves me – I love me too
We're a great team – yes it's true
Soulmate, soulmate,
I'm so happy we are together
Soulmate, soulmate,
My life with you, is so much better!
E: That's, err, yes, that's very … nice.
A: Thank you. Do you really like it?
E: I like the music – I don't like the words …

Unit 6 Recording 8
J=Josef N=Nadine
J: Oh dear. Oh dear! Oh dear, oh dear, oh dear.
N: What's the problem, Josef?
J: I can't find a present for Nisha.
N: Who's Nisha?
J: She's my friend. It's her birthday on Thursday.
N: Do you know www.findanicepresent.com
J: No. What is it?
N: It's a great website. It finds presents for you. Look. This is the website.
J: Is it free?
N: Yes, it is.

Unit 6 Recording 9
J=Josef N=Nadine
J: Is it free?
N: Yes, it is. OK, there are some questions about Nisha. How old is she?
J: She's twenty-nine.
N: What does she do?
J: She's a reporter.
N: Who does she work for?
J: *NewsTime* Magazine.
N: So does she work long hours?
J: Yes, she does.
N: Is she married?
J: No, she isn't.
N: Does she have any children?
J: No, she doesn't.
N: Does she travel a lot?
J: Yes, she does. She travels all over the world.
N: Can she cook?
J: No, she can't.

N: Does she watch a lot of films?
J: No, she doesn't.
N: Does she listen to a lot of music?
J: Yes, she does.
N: OK – there are three presents.

Unit 7 Recording 1
1 I'm a waiter. I work in a restaurant.
2 I'm a PA. I work in an office.
3 I'm a factory worker. I work in a factory.
4 I'm a nurse. I work in a hospital.
5 I'm a sales assistant. I work in a shop.
6 I'm a lecturer. I work in a university.
7 I'm a call centre worker. I work in a call centre.
8 I'm a teacher. I work in a school.

Unit 7 Recording 2
M=Man W=Woman
1
W: Yes, sir. Can I help you?
2
W: Good morning. Can I speak to Mr Jones, please?
M: This is Mr Jones.
W: Mr Jones, my name is Tina from The Great Mobile Phone Company. How are you today, Mr Jones? Oh!
3
M: OK children. Settle down, please. Kevin! Don't do that!
4
M: Here are your drinks. Are you ready to order?
5
W: Hello, TM Architects office. Can I help?
M: Can I speak to Mr Flynn, please?
W: I'm afraid he's in a meeting this morning. Can he call you back?
6
M: Good morning. This lecture is about Hamlet by Shakespeare. Hamlet is the Prince of Denmark. Hamlet's father, the king, is killed by …
7
M: Hello, Bill. Are you ok? How is your wife? Good. OK, time to start work …
8
W: Excuse me, doctor. That's his right leg. The problem is his left leg.
M: Oh yes, of course. Thank you nurse Taylor.

Unit 7 Recording 3
1
PA=Personal Assistant J=Jake A=Alice
PA: Hello. Parkside School.
J: Can I speak to Mrs Fischer, please?
PA: Hold the line, please …
A: Hello. Alice Fischer.
J: Hello Mrs Fischer. My name's Jake Parker. I'm interested in the advert for teachers. It's in today's newspaper …
A: Oh, yes. Great.
2
A=Alice J=Jake
A: Jake Parker?
J: Yes.
A: I'm Alice Fischer. nice to meet you.
J: Nice to meet you, too.
A: Come in Mr Parker. Please sit down.
J: Thank you.
3
J=Jake S=Steven
J: OK class, be quiet. Look at page 32 in your books. Page 32. OK? Now listen to the conversation.
J: Steven. please turn off your mobile phone.
S: Sorry, sir.

Unit 7 Recording 4
1
M: Please come with me. Your table is ready.
2
W: Taylor. Be QUIET.
3
W: This is a message for Dr. Morgan. Please go to A&E immediately.
4
M: This is a customer announcement. Visit our great kitchen sale on the ground floor. Saucepans for twelve ninety-nine, Cookery books for three ninety-nine. Thank you for shopping at Madisons.
5
W: This is a message for all passengers on flight FH453 to Madrid. Please go to gate 23 immediately. That's flight FH453. Please go to gate 23 immediately. Thank you.

Unit 7 Recording 5
January, February, March, April, May, June, July, August, September, October, November, December

Unit 7 Recording 6
H=Game show host J=John
H: OK, John. Are you ready?
J: Yes, I'm always ready! I love this game.
H: Good. Let's start. Do you work from home?
J: No, never.
H: Do you have meetings?
J: Yes, but not often.
H: Do you give presentations?
J: Yes, sometimes - in schools, for example.
H: Do you call customers?
J: No, never. I don't have customers.
H: Do you write reports?
J: Yes, I do. I usually write three or four reports a week.
H: Do you take work home?
J: No, not usually.
H: Do you travel abroad?
J: No, never.
H: Do you answer the phone.
J: Yes, quite often.
H: Do you work outside?
J: Yes, very often.
H: Are you an engineer?
J: No, I'm not.
H: Are you a teacher?
J: No, I'm not.
H: Oh!! What is he?

Unit 7 Recording 7
1 I usually have a meeting on Monday morning.
2 I often take work home.
3 I don't usually answer the phone.
4 I don't often give presentations.

Unit 7 Recording 8
M=Michelle S=Sarah
M: Good morning, Sarah!
S: Morning, Michelle. Nice weekend?
M: Yes, thank you. And you?
S: Good, thanks.
M: Oh, Sarah, when is Mr Wu's visit?
S: Let me see. Mr Wu's visit is the 8th of June.
M: What's the date today?
S: It's the 6th of June.
M: Are there any other visits this month?
S: Yes, there are. There's Mrs King on the fourteenth of June.
M: Mrs King - the 14th of June.
S: And there's Miss Brown on the 24th of June.

M: The 24th of June. Is that all?
S: No, there's one more. It's Mr Rogers.
M: Mr Rogers – he's the BIG BOSS from the US! He's very important! When is his visit?
S: The 6th of June.
M: The 6th of Ju... But that's today.
S: Oh yes! Hello, Sarah Walker speaking.
... Oh hello Mr Rogers. ... You're in reception
... That's lovely. ... See you in five minutes
... Goodbye. That's Mr Rogers. He's in reception.
M: Arrrghhhh!

Unit 7 Recording 9

1 first, second, third, fourth, fifth, sixth, seventh, eighth, ninth, tenth
2 eleventh, twelfth, thirteenth, fourteenth, fifteenth, sixteenth, seventeenth, eighteenth, nineteenth, twentieth
3 twenty-first, twenty-second, twenty-third, twenty-fourth, twenty-fifth, twenty-sixth, twenty-seventh, twenty-eighth, twenty-ninth, thirtieth

Unit 7 Recording 10

M=Michelle R=Mr Rogers K=Ms. Khan
M: Please, come in. Sit down. What would you like to drink? Tea? Coffee?
R: I'd like a coffee, please.
K: I'd like a cup of tea, please.
M: Would you like milk and sugar?
R: No thank you.
K: Milk, no sugar, please.
M: Would you like a biscuit?
R: Yes, please.
K: No, thank you.

Unit 7 Recording 11

M=Michelle R=Mr Rogers A=Aisha Khan
M: OK, this is the canteen. Are you hungry?
R/A: Yes.
M: Good. OK, the drinks are here on the right. There are snacks next to the drinks. There's mineral water, orange   juice ... etc. There are some starters next to the snacks. Would you like a starter?
R: Err, no thank you. I'd like a salad.
M: OK. There's a salad bar in the middle of the canteen.
A: I'd like some fruit.
M: The fruit is next to the salad. And there are some desserts next to the cash tills.
R: Great. Thank you.

Unit 7 Recording 12

R=Receptionist D=Dodek
R: Good morning.
D: Good morning. I'm here to see Martina Hafner.
R: What's your name, please?
D: Dodek Nowak.
R: How do you spell that?
D: N – O – W – A – K.
R: OK, Mr Nowak. Take the lift to the third floor. Turn right. Miss Hafner's office is the third door on the left.
D: Thank you.
R: You're welcome.

R=Receptionist J=Jennifer
R: Good morning.
J: Good morning. I have a meeting with Lorda Romero.
R: What's your name, please?
J: Jennifer Wood.
R: Jennifer – Wood. OK, Mrs Wood. Take the lift to the third floor. Turn right. Mrs Romero's office is the second on the right.
J: Thank you. Where are the toilets, please?
R: There's a toilet on the third floor, next to the lift.

R=Receptionist J=Jemma
R: Good afternoon.
J: Good afternoon. I'm here to see Patrick Swinton.
R: Do you have an appointment?
J: Yes, I do.
R: What's your name, please?
J: My name's Jemma Hayes.
R: How do you spell Hayes?
J: H – A – Y – E – S.
R: OK, Ms Hayes. Mr Swinton's office is on the third floor. Take the lift and turn right. It's the first door on the left.
J: Thank you.

Unit 8 Recording 1

1 go to the theatre   2 eat out
3 play chess   4 go swimming
5 play football   6 go for a walk
7 watch TV   8 go sightseeing
9 read a book   10 play tennis
11 go cycling   12 do exercise

Unit 8 Recording 2

G=Gary A=Annie
A: Gary.
G: Yes?
A: Are you happy?
G: Happy?
A: Yes. Are you happy?
G: Yes. I'm happy.
A: I'm not. We never go out.
G: Oh.
A: We never go to the cinema. We don't often eat in restaurants. We never do exercise. We always watch television.
G: But I like watching television.
A: Gary!

Unit 8 Recording 3

G=Gary A=Annie
G: OK. Turn the TV off. Come on – choose a hotel with me.
A: A hotel?
G: Yes, for next weekend.
A: Oh. OK.
G: Right. Look at this one. The Langston Hotel? There's a golf course and there are tennis courts. It's great! I like playing golf.
A: Hmm. I want to go sightseeing. Look! What do you think of this one? The New Metro Hotel. There's got a swimming pool. You like swimming and I like going sightseeing.
G: I don't like going sightseeing. I want to do some exercise. Now this is good. Blue Sea Hotel. You can swim in the sea and you can walk in the countryside. We like swimming and walking.
A: I can't swim.
G: But you want to learn.
A: That's true. OK. Blue Sea Hotel it is.
G: Great. Now, is there a television at the Blue Sea Hotel?

Unit 8 Recording 4

M=Man W=Woman
M: bedroom
W: a) mirror b) bed c) wardrobe
M: bathroom
W: d) bath e) toilet f) basin
M: kitchen
W: g) cooker h) sink i) washing machine j) fridge
M: living room
W: k) sofa l) lamp m) coffee table n) armchair
M: garage
W: o) car

M: garden
W: p) bicycle

Unit 8 Recording 5

P=Paul J=Jo
P: Hi Jo. How are you?
J: Oh hi Paul. I'm fine. How are you?
P: Oh, so-so. It's my sister's wedding next week. I want to buy her a really nice present but I can't find one.
J: I can help.
P: Really?
J: Sure. OK. What does she like doing?
P: Well, she likes doing things at home ... she likes watching TV ... she's likes cooking ... Oh, and she like modern furniture. Her husband likes furniture, too.
J: Have they got an armchair?
P: Yes, they have.
J: Have they got a lamp?
P: Yes, they have.
J: Has your sister got a wardrobe for her clothes?
P: No, she hasn't.
J: Aha!
P: But my parents want to buy a wardrobe for her clothes.
J: Oh! Have they got a bed?
P: Yes, they have.
J: Has she got a bicycle?
P: No, she hasn't.
J: Aha!
P: But he's got a bicycle and she uses it.
J: Oh dear. I know!
P: What?
J: It's always a good wedding present.
P: What?
J: Give them ...

Unit 8 Recording 6

M=Man W=Woman 1
M: I live with my wife in a small house. We've got a bedroom, a living room, a kitchen and a bathroom. We've got a small garden – it's beautiful. But we haven't got a garage. My husband's got a car. He drives to work every day. I haven't got a car. I can't drive. But I've got a bicycle.
W: I live in my sister's house. She's got four bedrooms and two living rooms. She's got a TV in her bedroom. She watches TV in bed. But she hasn't got a TV in the living room. She's got a sofa and a big armchair in the living room. She's got a big cooker in the kitchen – it's great. We like cooking. She hasn't got a microwave oven. She doesn't like them.

Unit 8 Recording 7

M: Hi, Alda. How are you?
A: Fine thanks. And you?
M: Fine, thanks. I've got a new job!
A: Hey, that's great! How about dinner next Friday? We can celebrate.
M: Good idea. Which restaurant do you want to go to?
A: How about Sinatra's?
M: Where's that?
A: It's in Alderton.
M: Hmm, it's not very near. What about Wasabi?
A: What food do they serve at Wasabi?
M: Japanese food.
A: How big is it? I like small restaurants.
M: It's quite big.
A: What about Carlitto's? My friend is the manager there.
M: Who is your friend?
A: Thomas.
M: Oh yes. OK – Carlitto's is nice.

Tapescripts

Unit 8 Recording 8
W=Waiter A=Alda

W: Hello. Carlitto's Restaurant.
A: Hello. I'd like to book a table for Friday evening.
W: Certainly, madam. How many people?
A: Two.
W: What time?
A: 8 o'clock, please.
W: I'm sorry, we've only got 7 o'clock or 9 o'clock.
A: OK. 9 o'clock, please.
W: Smoking or non-smoking?
A: Non-smoking, please.
W: And what name, please?
A: Alda Pierce.
W: OK, that's fine Ms. Pierce. See you on Friday.
A: Thank you. Goodbye.

Unit 8 Recording 9
1 pork 2 chocolate 3 seafood
4 pasta 5 fish 6 beef 7 potatoes
8 lamb 9 cheese 10 rice

Unit 8 Recording 10
W=Waiter A=Alda M=Mark

W: Hello, madam. Do you have a reservation?
A: Yes. My name is Alda Pierce.
W: Ms. Pierce. A table for two?
A: That's right.
W: Come with me, please.
W: Are you ready to order?
M: Yes. I'd like fish soup, please, and lamb chops.
W: Certainly, sir. And for you madam?
A: Can I have seafood cocktail, please, and vegetable pasta bake.
W: Certainly. What would you like to drink?
M: A mineral water, please.
W: Still or sparkling?
M: Still, please.
A: I'd like an orange juice, please.
W: Certainly, madam.
M: Look! It's 11:30.
A: Really? It's late.
M: Yes, it is. Excuse me. Can I have the bill, please?
W: Of course.

Unit 9 Recording 1
1963 1946 1981 1977 1957 1912 2002
1990

Unit 9 Recording 2
Sputnik in Space 1957
Charles and Di: Royal Wedding 1981
First ipod in Shops 2002
Titanic Disaster 1912
Nelson Mandela Free 1990
Martin Luther King: I have a dream 1963
Juan Peron: President of Argentina! 1946
Elvis Presley is dead 1977

Unit 9 Recording 3
I was an actor.
You were a singer.
He was happy.
She was born in 1982.
It was great.
We were singers.
They were rich.

Unit 9 Recording 4
H=Host M=Mark T=Trudy J=Josh

H: OK. This game is called 'Who am I?' This is how we play. I say sentences about a famous person from the past, but I don't say the name. You guess the name. But remember you've got just one guess so don't get it wrong. Are you ready Mark?
M: I'm ready.
H: Are you ready Trudy?
T: I'm ready.
H: Are you ready Josh?
J: I'm ready.
H: OK. Let's play 'Who am I?'
For 10 points: I was born in 1940 in the UK.
For 9 points: My parents were Julia and Alfred.
For 8 points: I was quite tall and very thin.
For 7 points: I was a singer and I was famous for my music.
For 6 points: I was friends with …
Yes, Josh. Do you know the answer?
J: Is it Sir Paul McCartney?
H: No Josh. It isn't Paul McCartney. You're out of this game.
J: Oh no!
H: OK. Let's continue.
For 6 points: I was friends with Paul McCartney.
For 5 points: I was from Liverpool.
For 4 points: I was married to Cynthia Powell in my 20s.
For 3 points: I was married to Yoko Ono in my 30s. Yes, Trudy.
T: Is it …

Unit 9 Recording 5
J=Jasmine C=Cristof I=Isabella

J: OK. Your go, Cristof.
C: Four! One, two, three, four. My first teacher!
I: OK, Cristof, your first teacher. Forty-five seconds. Starting NOW!
C: OK, my first teacher was Mrs Lloyd. She was about fifty years old.
J: Was she a good teacher?
C: She was a good teacher but I wasn't a good student.
I: Were you her favourite student?
C: I wasn't her favourite student. Francoise was her favourite student.
J: Was Francoise your friend?
C: Yes, she … Oh no!
J: Bad luck, Cristof. OK, Isabella, your go.
I: Two! One, two. Your last meal at a restaurant.
J: OK, Isabella. Your last meal at a restaurant. Forty-five seconds. Starting NOW!
I: OK, my last meal at a restaurant was last week at Carluccio's.
C: Oh – that's great.
I: Yes, and Oh no!
J: Bad luck Isabella. OK, my go. Five! One, two, three, four, five. My last holiday.
C: OK, Jasmine. Your last holiday, forty-five seconds, starting NOW!
J: My last holiday was two years ago. It was a Greek island called Santorini.
C: Were you with your parents?
J: I wasn't with my parents. I was with my friend, Helen.
I: Was it a good holiday?
J: It was a very good holiday. The hotel was very nice.
I: Were there any tourist attractions? Castles, palaces, cathedrals?
J: There weren't any castles or palaces but there were some beautiful beaches.
I: Was the weather nice?
J: It was great. Sunny and hot …
C: Time's up! That's forty-five seconds. Well done Jasmine.
I: Yes, well done. Your go again.

J: Oh great! Six! One, two

Unit 9 Recording 6
1 I was a **good stu**dent.
2 I **wasn't very** intelligent.
3 Was **she** a **good tea**cher?
4 **Who** was your **best friend**?

Unit 9 Recording 7
1 You were my **best friend**.
2 You **weren't** a **good stu**dent.
3 Were you **happy** at school?
4 **Who** were your **favourite tea**chers?

Unit 9 Recording 8
1 vacuum the house 2 clean the bathroom 3 wash the dishes 4 do the laundry 5 iron a shirt 6 cook dinner

Unit 9 Recording 9
1
AS=Aunt Sally J=Jeff

AS: Hello Jeff. How are you?
J: Fine thank you, Aunt Sally.
AS: Look at you. You're so tall.
J: I'm thirty-nine Aunt Sally!
AS: Oh yes, of course.
J: How was your flight?
AS: Awful. Awful. There wasn't any coffee. There wasn't a film. And the air stewards weren't attractive!
J: Aunt Sally!
AS: Now, Jeff. Could you carry my suitcases?
J: Oh dear …
2
J=Jeff B=Billy

J: So, how was school, Billy?
B: It was great!
J: Were you good for your teacher?
B: No! I was very bad! It was funny. Daddy, can I have chocolate for dinner?
J: No, you can't. Oh dear …
3
K=Karen J=Jeff

K: Hello Jeff.
J: Hello darling. How was your day?
K: It was ok. What's for dinner?
J: Spaghetti.
K: OK. Can I turn on the TV?
J: Oh dear …

4
F=Friend J=Jeff

F: So Jeff. How was your week?
J: It wasn't very good. My Aunt Sally is here, my son is …
F: Oh baby! What's the matter? Jeff, could you pass the milk.
J: Yes, of course. Oh dear …

Unit 9 Recording 10
1 science 2 music 3 art 4 sport
5 maths 6 languages

Unit 9 Recording 11
Louise: My school was called William Morris High School. It was in Oxford. I was there from 1981 to 1986. It was a good school but I wasn't a good student. I was good at sport and art but I was very bad at maths and science and languages. My favourite lesson was art. My teacher was Mr Little and he was great. My best friend was Sarah Jenkins. She was in my class and she was fun!

Unit 10 Recording 1
1 You lose your wallet/purse.
2 A thief steals your mobile phone.
3 You stay in bed all day.
4 You win the lottery.
5 You get married.
6 You find €10 on the street.
7 A police officer arrests you.
8 You move to a new house.
9 You break your arm.
10 You meet your favourite actor.

Unit 10 Recording 2
wanted asked moved started finished
lived played worked cooked closed
talked arrested listened walked

Unit 10 Recording 3
1 Pope Julius II wanted a new ceiling in The
Sistine Chapel. He asked Michelangelo
to paint the ceiling of the Sistine Chapel.
Michelangelo started it in 1508. He
finished it in 1512.

2 Marcel Duchamp was an artist. He was
born in 1887. He lived in Paris and he
played chess with his brothers. In 1914
he moved to New York. He worked in a
library in New York. In 1918 he moved to
Argentina.

Unit 10 Recording 4
The story of the Mona Lisa (Part 2)
The Mona Lisa **moved to** Versailles and then
to the Louvre. In 1800 Napoleon **moved it**
to his bedroom but it **didn't stay** there. Four
years later it was back in The Louvre.
Then, on August the 21st, 1911, the Louvre
closed its doors. There was a big problem.
The Mona Lisa wasn't there! Who was the
thief? The police **talked to** lots of people.
They **talked to** Picasso. Was he the thief?
He wasn't. But they **didn't talk** to Vencenzo
Peruggia.

Unit 10 Recording 5
1 It was a good week for ... actor Romero
Cline, 43. He went to Las Vegas last week
and he met Monica Hawkins, a waitress,
in a fast food restaurant. Three days later,
they got married.

2 It was a good week for ... Mr and Mrs Blatt
from the UK. They had fish for dinner and
they found three gold coins inside the fish.
'The fish was £3.50' said Mrs Blatt, 'but
the gold coins are £1,000 each!'

3 It was a bad week for ... Emiliana Rotman
from Sweden. She won £14 million on the
Euro lottery but she lost her ticket. 'Never
mind' said Emiliana, 'That's life.'

4 It was a bad week for ... pop group *Gilt*.
Gilt's concert was last Friday but the
tickets said 'Saturday'. "Only five people
came" said Sia Kahn, *Gilt's* singer. "They
took photos and bought a T-shirt but it
wasn't a good day."

Unit 10 Recording 6
Get down to LOVELY ELECTRONICS today.
Low, low, low prices on hundred of items.
A fantastic DVD player: was €149. Sale price
€119!
A great laptop computer:was €1399. Sale
price €1050!
A beautiful washing machine: was €625. Sale
price €465!
Hurry, hurry, hurry. Sale ends soon.

A great LCD TV: was €2189. Sale price €1750!
A new fridge: was €505. Sale price €427!
And a fantastic cooker: was €469. Sale price
€325!
Remember, our sale ends today so hurry,
hurry, hurry down to Lovely Electronics.

Unit 10 Recording 7
A cool B competitive C shy D funny
E confident F friendly

Unit 10 Recording 8
The Fisherman
Mishima was a fisherman. He was an old
man and he was quite shy. He lived alone in
a small house on the beach. He went fishing
in his small boat every day. He was poor, but
he was happy. One day, Mishima's two sons,
Nobu and Akio, visited him. Nobu and Akio
worked in the city. Mishima, Nobu and Akio
went fishing in Mishima's little boat.
"Listen, brother," said Akio, "there is a job
vacancy in my company. Please, come and
work for me."
"Brother," said Nobu, "your offer is very
funny. My company is bigger than your
company. Please, come and work for me?"
"It's true," said Akio, "your company is
bigger than my company. But I am a manager
and you are not. My job is better than your
job. Please, come and work for me."
"It's true," said Nobu, "your job is better
than my job. But I like my job. My company is
friendly. I am happier than you. Please, come
and work for me."
"It's true," said Akio, "you are happier than
me. But I am more intelligent than you."
"It's true," said Nobu, "you are more
intelligent than me. But my wife is ..."
"Enough!" shouted Mishima. "Now listen to
me. I am a fisherman. I am not competitive
but the sea is my company and it's the
biggest company. I work outdoors in the sun
and the rain. My job is the best job. Every
morning I look out of my window and I see
the sea and the sky and my little boat, and
I am the happiest person in the world. And I
am the most intelligent person in this boat.
Why? Because I don't want more and more
and more, like you two. I am happy with my
life. So, do you, my sons, want to work for
me?"
Nobu looked at Akio and Akio looked at
Nobu. Then they looked at their father.
"Yes, father," said Akio, "I want to work with
you."
"Yes, father," said Nobu, "I want to work with
you."
"Well," said Mishima, "that's unfortunate
because there aren't any job vacancies."

Unit 10 Recording 9
Legg: Thank you everyone. Thank you. Last
night, at about 11 o'clock, someone killed Sir
Rufus Montgomery. The killer is one of you
four!
Please, be quiet. BE QUIET! We know two
things. Number 1: Sir Rufus died between 10
o'clock and 11 o'clock last night. Number 2:
the killer is one of you four.
BE QUIET! Now, Julia Montgomery. Who do
you think is the killer?
Julia: It was Rachel! She's the killer.
Legg: Rachel. Are you the killer?
Rachel: Me? It wasn't me. It was Emily!
Legg: Emily. Are you the killer?
Emily: It wasn't me. I'm not the killer. It was
Cecil!
Legg: Cecil. Are you the killer?
Cecil: No. It wasn't me. It was Julia!

Vokabelliste

Unit 1

Lead-in

arrival [əˈraɪvəl] Ankunft

Good morning. [gʊd ˈmɔːnɪŋ] Guten Morgen.

Hello./Hi. [həˈləʊ, he-, haɪ] Hallo./Hi.

Welcome to Easton Hotel. [ˌwelkəm tʊ ˌiːstən həʊˈtel] Willkommen im Hotel Easton.

Thank you. [ˈθæŋk jʊ] Danke.

Nice to meet you. [ˌnaɪs tə ˈmiːt jʊ] Nett, Sie kennen zu lernen.

Nice to meet you, too. [ˌnaɪs tə ˌmiːt juː ˈtuː] Ich finde es auch nett, Sie kennen zu lernen.

What's your name? [ˌwɒts jɔː ˈneɪm] Wie heißen Sie?

Lesson 1.1

check in to a hotel [tʃek ɪn tʊ ə həʊˈtel] in ein Hotel einchecken

zero [ˈzɪərəʊ] null

one [wʌn] eins

two [tuː] zwei

three [θriː] drei

four [fɔː] vier

five [faɪv] fünf

six [sɪks] sechs

seven [ˈsevən] sieben

eight [eɪt] acht

nine [naɪn] neun

ten [ten] zehn

listen [ˈlɪsən] zuhören

say [seɪ] sagen, nennen

room [ruːm, rʊm] Zimmer, Raum

number [ˈnʌmbə] Zahl, Nummer

Mr Smith [ˌmɪstə ˈsmɪθ] Herr Smith

Miss Jones [mɪs ˈdʒəʊnz] Fräulein Jones

Mrs/Ms Jones [ˌmɪsɪz ˈdʒəʊnz, ˌmɪz] Frau Jones

grammar [ˈgræmə] Grammatik

greeting [ˈgriːtɪŋ] Begrüßung

good [gʊd] gut

morning [ˈmɔːnɪŋ] Morgen

afternoon [ˌɑːftəˈnuːn] Nachmittag

evening [ˈiːvnɪŋ] Abend

night [naɪt] Nacht

speak [spiːk] sprechen

Lesson 1.2

airport [ˈeəpɔːt] Flughafen

greet someone [ˈgriːt ˌsʌmwʌn] jemanden begrüßen

letter [ˈletə] Buchstabe

country, countries [ˈkʌntri, ˈkʌntriz] Land, Länder

Argentina [ˌɑːdʒənˈtiːnə] Argentinien

India [ˈɪndiə] Indien

Germany [ˈdʒɜːməni] Deutschland

Japan [dʒəˈpæn] Japan

Italy [ˈɪtəli] Italien

Poland [ˈpəʊlənd] Polen

the UK [ðə juː ˈkeɪ] Großbritannien

Australia [ɒˈstreɪliə] Australien

Brazil [brəˈzɪl] Brasilien

the US [ðə juː ˈes] die US

city [ˈsɪti] Stadt

pronunciation [prəˌnʌnsiˈeɪʃən] Aussprache

lifelong [ˈlaɪflɒŋ] lebenslang

learn [lɜːn] lernen

read [riːd] lesen

He's from Russia. [hiːz frəm ˈrʌʃə] Er kommt aus Russland.

false [fɔːls] falsch

Lesson 1.3

introduce someone [ˌɪntrəˈdjuːs ˌsʌmwʌn] jemanden vorstellen

start a conversation [stɑːt ə ˌkɒnvəˈseɪʃən] ein Gespräch beginnen

common [ˈkɒmən] allgemein üblich, gewöhnlich

phrase [freɪz] Redewendung

Sorry. [ˈsɒri] Entschuldigung./ Verzeihung

No, thank you. [ˌnəʊ ˈθæŋk jʊ] Nein, danke.

Yes, please. [jes ˈpliːz] Ja, bitte.

Pardon? [ˈpɑːdn] Wie bitte?

Excuse me, ... [ɪkˈskjuːz mi] Entschuldigung, ...

people [ˈpiːpəl] Leute

This is Paul. [ðɪs ɪz ˈpɔːl] Das ist Paul.

question [ˈkwestʃən] Frage

Where are you from? [ˌweər ə jʊ ˈfrɒm] Woher kommen Sie?

I'm from ... [ˈaɪm frəm] Ich komme aus ...

Turkey [ˈtɜːki] Türkei

Communication

communication [kəˌmjuːnɪˈkeɪʃən] Kommunikation

find [faɪnd] finden

phone number [ˈfəʊn ˌnʌmbə] Telefonnummer

dial [ˈdaɪəl] wählen

Mexico [ˈmeksɪkəʊ] Mexiko

Spain [speɪn] Spanien

China [ˈtʃaɪnə] China

Unit 2

Lead-in

life [laɪf] Leben

mother [ˈmʌðə] Mutter

father [ˈfɑːðə] Vater

wife [waɪf] Ehefrau

husband [ˈhʌzbənd] Ehemann

daughter [ˈdɔːtə] Tochter

son [sʌn] Sohn

sister [ˈsɪstə] Schwester

brother [ˈbrʌðə] Bruder

phone [fəʊn] Telefon

mobile phone [ˌməʊbaɪl ˈfəʊn] Handy, Mobiltelefon

email [ˈiːmeɪl] E-Mail

address [əˈdres] Adresse

computer [kəmˈpjuːtə] Computer

website [ˈwebsaɪt] Internetseite

passport [ˈpɑːspɔːt] (Reise)Pass

first name [ˈfɜːst neɪm] Vorname

surname [ˈsɜːneɪm] Nachname

photo [ˈfəʊtəʊ] Foto

Lesson 2.1

family [ˈfæməli] Familie

give information (about) [gɪv ɪnfəˈmeɪʃən] Informationen geben (über)

basic [ˈbeɪsɪk] grundlegend

eleven [ɪˈlevən] elf

twelve [twelv] zwölf

thirteen [ˌθɜːˈtiːn] dreizehn

fourteen [ˌfɔːˈtiːn] vierzehn

fifteen [ˌfɪfˈtiːn] fünfzehn

sixteen [ˌsɪkˈstiːn] sechzehn

seventeen [ˌsevənˈtiːn] siebzehn

eighteen [ˌeɪˈtiːn] achtzehn

nineteen [ˌnaɪnˈtiːn] neunzehn

twenty [ˈtwenti] zwanzig

thirty [ˈθɜːti] dreißig

forty [ˈfɔːti] vierzig

fifty [ˈfɪfti] fünfzig

sixty [ˈsɪksti] sechzig

seventy [ˈsevənti] siebzig

eighty [ˈeɪti] achtzig
ninety [ˈnaɪnti] neunzig
talk (about) [ˈtɔːk] reden (über)
age [eɪdʒ] Alter
How old is she? [haʊ ˈəʊld ɪz ʃi] Wie alt ist sie?
She's sixty-two years old. [ʃiz ˌsɪksti tuː jɪəz ˈəʊld] Sie ist zweiundsechzig Jahre alt.
Who's she? [ˈhuːz ˈʃiː] Wer ist sie?
friend [frend] Freund(in)
It's OK. [ɪts ˌəʊ ˈkeɪ] Es ist in Ordnung.

Lesson 2.2
personal details [ˌpɜːsənəl ˈdiːteɪlz] persönliche Details
ask (for) [ɑːsk] fragen (nach)
great [greɪt] großartig
bad [bæd] schlecht
awful [ˈɔːfəl] furchtbar, schrecklich
What's your address? [ˌwɒts jɔːr əˈdres] Wie lautet Ihre Adresse?
spell [spel] buchstabieren
How do you spell that? [ˌhaʊ dʊ jʊ ˈspel ðæt] Wie schreibt man das?

Lesson 2.3
other [ˈʌðə] andere, übrige
write [raɪt] schreiben
short [ʃɔːt] kurz
Canada [ˈkænədə] Kanada
teacher [ˈtiːtʃə] Lehrer(in)
job [dʒɒb] Beruf, Stelle
accountant [əˈkaʊntənt] Buchhalter(in)
actor [ˈæktə] Schauspieler(in)
engineer [ˌendʒɪˈnɪə] Ingenieur(in)
artist [ˈɑːtɪst] Künstler(in)
student [ˈstjuːdənt] Student(in), Kursteilnehmer(in)
manager [ˈmænɪdʒə] Geschäftsführer(in)
sales assistant [ˈseɪlz əˌsɪstənt] Verkäufer(in)
police officer [pəˈliːs ˌɒfɪsə] Polizist(in)
doctor [ˈdɒktə] Arzt/Ärztin
picture [ˈpɪktʃə] Bild
What's his job? [ˌwɒts hɪz ˈdʒɒb] Was macht er beruflich?

Communication
my favourite ... [maɪ ˈfeɪvərɪt] mein(e) Lieblings-...

singer [ˈsɪŋə] Sänger(in)
film [fɪlm] Film
book [bʊk] Buch
restaurant [ˈrestərɒnt] Restaurant

Unit 3
Lead-in
travel [ˈtrævəl] reisen
castle [ˈkɑːsəl] Schloss, Burg
cathedral [kəˈθiːdrəl] Kathedrale, Dom
palace [ˈpæləs] Palast
museum [mjuːˈziəm] Museum
gallery [ˈgæləri] Gallerie
department store [dɪˈpɑːtmənt ˌstɔː] Kaufhaus
market [ˈmɑːkɪt] Markt
mountain [ˈmaʊntən] Berg
lake [leɪk] See
tourist attraction [ˈtʊərɪst əˌtrækʃən] Touristenattraktion
world [wɜːld] Welt

Lesson 3.1
with [wɪð, wɪθ] mit
simple [ˈsɪmpəl] einfach
holiday [ˈhɒlədi, -deɪ] Urlaub
old [əʊld] alt
modern [ˈmɒdn] modern
big [bɪg] groß
small [smɔːl] klein
beautiful [ˈbjuːtɪfəl] schön
ugly [ˈʌgli] hässlich
How are you? [haʊ ˈɑː jʊ] Wie geht es Ihnen/Euch?
fine [ˈfaɪn] gut, fein
attachment [əˈtætʃmənt] (E-Mail)Anhang
car [kɑː] Auto
Love ... [lʌv] Liebe Grüße ...
capital [ˈkæpɪtl] Hauptstadt
house [haʊs] Haus
suitcase [ˈsuːtkeɪs, ˈsjuːt-] Koffer
backpack [ˈbækpæk] Rucksack
map [mæp] (Land)Karte
place [pleɪs] Ort

Lesson 3.2
thing [θɪŋ] Ding, Gegenstand
camera [ˈkæmərə] Fotoapparat, Kamera
skirt [skɜːt] Rock

(a pair of) shoes [ʃuːz] (ein Paar) Schuhe
(a pair of) trousers [ˈtraʊzəz] (eine) Hose
MP3 player [ˌem piː ˈθriː ˌpleɪə] MP3-Player
top [tɒp] Top
make [meɪk] machen, herstellen, bilden
regular [ˈregjʊlə] regelmäßig
woman [ˈwʊmən] Frau
ticket (to) [ˈtɪkɪt] Fahrkarte (nach)
between [bɪˈtwiːn] zwischen
and [ənd, ən] und

Lesson 3.3
tourist information [ˌtʊərɪst ɪnfəˈmeɪʃən] Touristeninformation
day of the week [ˌdeɪ əv ðə ˈwiːk] Wochentag
Monday [ˈmʌndi, -deɪ] Montag
Tuesday [ˈtjuːzdi, -deɪ] Dienstag
Wednesday [ˈwenzdi, -deɪ] Mittwoch
Thursday [ˈθɜːzdi, -deɪθɜːzdi, -deɪ] Donnerstag
Friday [ˈfraɪdi, -deɪ] Freitag
Saturday [ˈsætədi, -deɪ] Samstag
Sunday [ˈsʌndi, -deɪ] Sonntag
art [ɑːt] Kunst
open [ˈəʊpən] geöffnet, offen
from Tuesday to Sunday [frəm ˌtjuːzdi tə ˈsʌndi] von Dienstag bis Sonntag
closed [kləʊzd] geschlossen
on Mondays [ɒn ˈmʌndiz] montags
free [friː] kostenlos
top [adj] [tɒp] Spitzen-...
visitor [ˈvɪzɪtə] Besucher(in)
every year [ˌevri ˈjɪə] jedes Jahr
near [nɪə] in der Nähe von
on the River Thames [ɒn ðə ˌrɪvə ˈtemz] an der Themse
street [striːt] Straße
river [ˈrɪvə] Fluss
here [hɪə] hier
there [ðeə] da, dort
shop [ʃɒp] Geschäft, Laden
today [təˈdeɪ] heute

Communication
See you on Friday. [ˌsiː jʊ ɒn ˈfraɪdi] Bis Freitag.
food [fuːd] Essen, Lebensmittel
hot [hɒt] heiß

Vokabelliste

cold [kəʊld] kalt
new [njuː] neu
very ['veri] sehr
Mum [mʌm] Mama
Dad [dæd] Papa
Bye. [baɪ] Tschüs.

Üben und können
possession [pəˈzeʃən] Besitz

Tapescript
Can I help you? [kæn aɪ ˈhelp jʊ] Kann ich Ihnen helfen?

Unit 4

Lead-in
town [taʊn] (Klein)Stadt
chemist ['kemɪst] Apotheke, Drogerie
supermarket ['suːpəˌmɑːkɪt] Supermarkt
café ['kæfeɪ] Café
bookshop ['bʊkʃɒp] Buchhandlung
train station ['treɪn ˌsteɪʃən] Bahnhof
bus stop ['bʌs stɒp] Bushaltestelle
bank [bæŋk] Bank
cinema ['sɪnəmə] Kino
newsagent ['njuːzˌeɪdʒənt] Kiosk
car park ['kɑː pɑːk] Parkplatz
cashpoint ['kæʃpɔɪnt] Geldautomat
pub [pʌb] Kneipe

Lesson 4.1
Can I have an espresso, please? [kæn aɪ hæv ən eˈspresəʊ pliːz] Kann ich bitte einen Espresso haben?
order ['ɔːdə] bestellen
drink [drɪŋk] Getränk
guide [gaɪd] Führer
coffee ['kɒfi] Kaffee
instant coffee [ˌɪnstənt 'kɒfi] Pulverkaffee
black [blæk] schwarz
white [waɪt] weiß
iced coffee [ˌaɪst 'kɒfi] Eiskaffee
sugar ['ʃʊgə] Zucker
milk [mɪlk] Milch
orange juice ['ɒrəndʒ dʒuːs] Orangensaft
mineral water ['mɪnərəl ˌwɔːtə] Mineralwasser

sandwich ['sænwɪdʒ] Sandwich, belegtes Brot
a piece of cake [ə ˌpiːs əv 'keɪk] ein Stück Kuchen
salad ['sæləd] Salat
a cup of tea [ə ˌkʌp əv 'tiː] eine Tasse Tee
chicken ['tʃɪkən] Huhn
ham [hæm] Schinken
small [smɔːl] klein
medium ['miːdiəm] mittel-...
large [lɑːdʒ] groß
chocolate ['tʃɒklɪt] Schokolade
Certainly./Sure ['sɜːtnli, ʃɔː] Sicher.
Anything else? [ˌeniθɪŋ 'els] Noch etwas?
price [praɪs] (Kauf)Preis
one pound [ˌwʌn 'paʊnd] ein Pfund
two dollars [ˌtuː 'dɒləz] zwei Dollar
three euros [ˌθriː 'jʊərəʊz] drei Euro
That's forty-two thirty, please. [ðæts ˌfɔːti tuː 'θɜːti pliːz] Das macht 42,30, bitte.
Eat in or take away? [ˌiːt 'ɪn ɔː ˌteɪk əˈweɪ] Zum hier Essen oder zum Mitnehmen?

Lesson 4.2
understand [ˌʌndəˈstænd] verstehen
What is on sale? [ˌwɒt ɪz ɒn 'seɪl] Was steht zum Verkauf?
antique [ˌænˈtiːk] Antiquität
tourist ['tʊərɪst] Tourist
two kilometres [ˌtuː 'kɪləmiːtəz, kɪˈlɒmɪtəz] zwei Kilometer
only ['əʊnli] nur
clothes [kləʊðz, kləʊz] Kleidung
popular ['pɒpjʊlə] beliebt
What kind of ...? [ˌwɒt kaɪnd əv] Welche Art von ...?
colour ['kʌlə] Farbe
orange ['ɒrəndʒ] orange
yellow ['jeləʊ] gelb
brown [braʊn] braun
red [red] rot
green [griːn] grün
blue [bluː] blau
coat [kəʊt] Mantel
dress [dres] Kleid
bag [bæg] Tasche
hat [hæt] Hut
T-shirt ['tiː ʃɜːt] T-Shirt
How much is it? [haʊ 'mʌtʃ ɪz ɪt] Wie viel kostet es?

It's four pounds fifty. [ɪts ˌfɔː paʊndz 'fɪfti] Es kostet vier Pfund fünfzig.
How much are they? [haʊ 'mʌtʃ 'ɑː ðeɪ] Wie viel kosten sie?
shirt [ʃɜːt] Hemd
jumper ['dʒʌmpə] Pullover
bracelet ['breɪslɪt] Armband

Lesson 4.3
around [əˈraʊnd] ringsherum, rundum
irregular [ɪˈregjʊlə] unregelmäßig
person ['pɜːsən] Person
man [mæn] Mann
men [men] Männer
baby ['beɪbi] Baby, Säugling
babies ['beɪbiz] Babys, Säuglinge
child [tʃaɪld] Kind
children ['tʃɪldrən] Kinder
women ['wɪmɪn] Frauen
wives [waɪvz] (Ehe)Frauen
adult ['ædʌlt, əˈdʌlt] Erwachsene(r)
single ['sɪŋgəl] einfache Fahrt
return [rɪˈtɜːn] Rückfahrt
or [ə, ɔː] oder
a packet of aspirin [ə ˌpækɪt əv 'æsprɪn] eine Packung Aspirin
pay by credit card [ˌpeɪ baɪ 'kredɪt kɑːd] mit Kreditkarte zahlen
sign [saɪn] unterschreiben
a pint [ə 'paɪnt] Pint (0,57 Liter)
beer [bɪə] Bier
dry [draɪ] trocken
wine [waɪn] Wein
enter ['entə] (hier:) eingeben
survive [səˈvaɪv] überleben
show [ʃəʊ] (an)zeigen
shopping ['ʃɒpɪŋ] Einkauf

Communication
opposite ['ɒpəzɪt] gegenüber
next to ['nekst tə, tʊ] neben
on King Street [ɒn 'kɪŋ striːt] in der King Straße
something ['sʌmθɪŋ] etwas
You're welcome. [jɔː 'welkəm] Gern geschehen.
know [nəʊ] wissen
I'm sorry. [aɪm 'sɒri] Es tut mir leid.
Never mind. [ˌnevə 'maɪnd] Das macht nichts.

Üben und können
useful ['juːsfəl] nützlich

Tapescript
for example [fər ɪɡ'zɑːmpəl]
 zum Beispiel
birthday ['bɜːθdeɪ] Geburtstag

Unit 5
Lead-in
south [saʊθ] Süden
north [nɔːθ] Norden
west [west] Westen
east [iːst] Osten
centre ['sentə] Mitte
in the north of [ɪn ðə 'nɔːθ əv]
 im Norden von
countryside ['kʌntrisaɪd] Land,
 ländliche Gegend
coast [kəʊst] Küste
building ['bɪldɪŋ] Gebäude
tree [triː] Baum
beach [biːtʃ] Strand
road [rəʊd] (Land)Straße
sea [siː] Meer
hill [hɪl] Hügel

Lesson 5.1
some [səm, sʌm] einige
description [dɪ'skrɪpʃən]
 Beschreibung
plants from all over the world
 [plɑːnt frəm ɔːl əʊvə ðə 'wɜːld]
 Pflanzen aus der ganzen Welt
outdoor theatre [aʊtdɔː 'θɪətə]
 Freilichttheater
It's called ... [ɪts kɔːld] Es heißt ...
famous ['feɪməs] berühmt
think [θɪŋk] denken
important [ɪm'pɔːtənt] wichtig
give an opinion [ɡɪv ən ə'pɪnjən]
 eine Meinung äußern
There are nice hotels in New York.
 [ðeər ə ˌnaɪs həʊtelz ɪn njuː 'jɔːk]
 Es gibt schöne Hotels in
 New York.
spice [spaɪs] Gewürz
a lot of [ə 'lɒt əv, ɒv] viele,
 eine Menge

Lesson 5.2
any ['eni] irgendwelche, alle, keine
in front of [ɪn 'frʌnt əv, ɒv] vor
in [ɪn] in

on [ɒn] auf
under ['ʌndə] unter
behind [bɪ'haɪnd] hinter
square [skweə] Platz
fountain ['faʊntən] Brunnen
news [njuːz] Nachrichten
receive [rɪ'siːv] erhalten
Is there a bank near here? [ɪz ðeər
 ə 'bæŋk nɪə ˌhɪə] Gibt es eine Bank
 in der Nähe?
nationality [ˌnæʃə'næləti]
 Nationalität
French [frentʃ] französisch
German ['dʒɜːmən] deutsch
Italian [ɪ'tæliən] italienisch
Indian ['ɪndiən] indisch
English ['ɪŋglɪʃ] englisch
England ['ɪŋglənd] England
Chinese [ˌtʃaɪ'niːz] chinesisch
Scottish ['skɒtɪʃ] schottisch
Scotland ['skɒtlənd] Schottland
Irish ['aɪərɪʃ] irisch
Ireland ['aɪələnd] Irland
Wales [weɪlz] Wales
Welsh [welʃ] walisisch
language ['læŋgwɪdʒ] Sprache
music ['mjuːzɪk] Musik

Lesson 5.3
cook [kʊk] kochen
general ['dʒenərəl] allgemein
ability [ə'bɪləti] Fähigkeit
course [kɔːs] Kurs
Welcome to ... ['welkəm tə, tʊ]
 Willkommen in ...
beginner [bɪ'ɡɪnə] Anfänger(in)
when [wen] wann
drive [draɪv] fahren
play [pleɪ] spielen
play golf [ˌpleɪ 'gɒlf] Golf spielen
play the piano [ˌpleɪ ðə pi'ænəʊ]
 Klavier spielen
swim [swɪm] schwimmen
use [juːz] benutzen
sing [sɪŋ] singen
dance [dɑːns] tanzen
can [kən, kæn] können
two o'clock [ˌtuː ə'klɒk] zwei Uhr
from two o'clock to four o'clock
 [frəm ˌtuː əklɒk tə 'fɔːr əklɒk]
 von zwei Uhr bis vier Uhr

in the afternoon/morning/evening
 [ɪn ðɪ ˌɑːftə'nuːn, 'mɔːnɪŋ, 'iːvnɪŋ]
 am Nachmittag/Morgen/Abend

Communication
bed [bed] Bett
breakfast ['brekfəst] Frühstück
blanket ['blæŋkɪt] Decke
shower ['ʃaʊə] Dusche
towel ['taʊəl] Handtuch
tea bag ['tiː bæg] Teebeutel
lamp [læmp] Lampe
fridge [frɪdʒ] Kühlschrank
kettle ['ketl] Kessel
television ['teləˌvɪʒən, ˌtelə'vɪʒən]
 Fernseher
time [taɪm] Zeit
double bed [ˌdʌbəl 'bed] Doppelbett
en-suite [ˌɒn 'swiːt] mit Bad/Dusche
 und WC
five past six [ˌfaɪv pɑːst 'sɪks]
 fünf nach sechs
quarter past four [ˌkwɔːtə pɑːst 'fɔː]
 viertel nach vier
half past seven [ˌhɑːf pɑːst 'sevən]
 halb acht
ten to nine [ˌten tə 'naɪn] zehn vor
 neun

Üben und können
island ['aɪlənd] Insel
location [ləʊ'keɪʃən] Stelle, Ort

Tapescript
level ['levəl] Niveau, Stand

Unit 6
Lead-in
chart [tʃɑːt] Tabelle
box [bɒks] Kasten
put [pʊt] setzen, stellen, legen
correct [kə'rekt] richtig
thin [θɪn] dünn
good-looking [ˌgʊd 'lʊkɪŋ]
 gut aussehend
tall [tɔːl] groß, hochgewachsen
fat [fæt] dick
short [ʃɔːt] klein, kurz
happy ['hæpi] glücklich
young [jʌŋ] jung
rich [rɪtʃ] reich
poor [pɔː] arm
unhappy [ʌn'hæpi] unglücklich
intelligent [ɪn'telɪdʒənt] intelligent

Vokabelliste

check [tʃek] überprüfen
test [test] testen
word [wɜːd] Wort
partner ['pɑːtnə] Partner(in)
opposite ['ɒpəzɪt] Gegenteil
sentence ['sentəns] Satz
quite [kwaɪt] ziemlich

Lesson 6.1

second ['sekənd] Sekunde
interview ['ɪntəvjuː] Interview
present ['prezənt] Gegenwart
like [laɪk] mögen
She is called Cynthia. [ʃiː ɪz kɔːld 'sɪnθɪə] Sie heißt Cynthia.
answer ['ɑːnsə] (be)antworten
fashion ['fæʃən] Mode
draw [drɔː] zeichnen
football team ['futbɔːl ˌtiːm] Fußballmannschaft
complete [kəm'pliːt] ergänzen
look at ['luk ət, æt] ansehen
each [iːtʃ] jede/r/s (einzelne)
more [mɔː] mehr
below [bɪ'ləu] unten
above [ə'bʌv] oben
page [peɪdʒ] Seite
tell [tel] sagen, erzählen
category ['kætəgəri] Kategorie
repeat [rɪ'piːt] wiederholen
time of day [ˌtaɪm əv 'deɪ] Tageszeit
italics [ɪ'tælɪks] Kursiv-, Schrägdruck
again [ə'gen, ə'geɪn] wieder
pair [peə] Paar
list [lɪst] Liste
do an interview [ˌduː ən 'ɪntəvjuː] ein Interview führen

Lesson 6.2

make friends [meɪk 'frendz] Freundschaft schließen
continue [kən'tɪnjuː] fortsetzen
someone ['sʌmwʌn] jemand
know [nəu] kennen
vocabulary [və'kæbjuləri, vəu-] Wortschatz
activity [æk'tɪvəti] Tätigkeit
architect ['ɑːkɪtekt] Architekt(in)
sales rep. ['seɪlz rep] Vertreter(in)
designer [dɪ'zaɪnə] Designer(in)
reporter [rɪ'pɔːtə] Reporter(in)
chef [ʃef] Küchenchef(in)

builder ['bɪldə] Bauunternehmer(in)
gap [gæp] Lücke
sell [sel] verkaufen
build [bɪld] bauen
design [dɪ'zaɪn] entwerfen, gestalten
do [duː] machen, tun
add [æd] hinzufügen
another example [əˌnʌðər ɪg'zɑːmpəl] noch ein Beispiel
match [mætʃ] zuordnen
mark [mɑːk] kennzeichnen
true [truː] wahr, richtig, zutreffend
false [fɔːls] falsch
on business [ɒn 'bɪznəs] geschäftlich
office building ['ɒfɪs ˌbɪldɪŋ] Bürogebäude
on holiday [ɒn 'hɒlədi, -deɪ] im Urlaub
show interest [ˌʃəu 'ɪntrəst] Interesse zeigen
etc. = et cetera [et 'setərə] usw.
really ['rɪəli] wirklich
magazine article [ˌmægə'ziːn ˌɑːtɪkəl] Zeitschriftenartikel
talk (to) [tɔːk] sprechen (mit)
best friends [ˌbest 'frendz] beste Freunde
same [seɪm] gleich
accountant [ə'kauntənt] Buchhalter(in)
in a lot of ways [ɪn ə 'lɒt əv weɪz] in vieler Hinsicht
different ['dɪfərənt] unterschiedlich, verschieden
young-at-heart [jʌŋ ət 'hɑːt] im Herzen jung
over sixty [ˌəuvə 'sɪksti] über sechzig
group [gruːp] Gruppe

Lesson 6.3

daily ['deɪli] täglich
routine [ruː'tiːn] Routine
underlined [ˌʌndə'laɪnd] unterstrichen
present ['prezənt] Geschenk
get up [get 'ʌp] aufstehen
have a shower [hæv ə 'ʃauə] duschen
every ['evri] jede/r/s
start work [ˌstɑːt 'wɜːk] (mit der Arbeit) anfangen

watch TV [ˌwɒtʃ tiː 'viː] fernsehen
fast [fɑːst] schnell
breakfast ['brekfəst] Frühstück
finish ['fɪnɪʃ] beenden
go to bed [ˌgəu tə 'bed] ins Bett gehen
early ['ɜːli] früh
change [tʃeɪndʒ] verändern
yoga ['jəugə] Yoga
biker ['baɪkə] Radfahrer(in)
aunt [ɑːnt] Tante
musician [mjuː'zɪʃən] Musiker(in)
form [fɔːm] Form
brunch [brʌntʃ] Brunch, Gabelfrühstück
midnight ['mɪdnaɪt] Mitternacht
member ['membə] Mitglied
describe [dɪ'skraɪb] beschreiben
song [sɒŋ] Lied
hear [hɪə] hören
line [laɪn] Zeile
letter ['letə] Brief
life [laɪf] Leben
now [nau] nun, jetzt

Communication

tick [tɪk] abhaken
tie [taɪ] Krawatte
flower ['flauə] Blume
saucepan ['sɔːspən] Kochtopf
wallet ['wɒlət] Brieftasche
cookery book ['kukəri buk] Kochbuch
candle ['kændl] Kerze
pen [pen] Füller, Kugelschreiber
occupation [ˌɒkju'peɪʃən] Beruf
company ['kʌmpəni] Firma
work long hours [ˌwɜːk lɒŋ 'auəz] lange arbeiten
married ['mærid] verheiratet
dictionary ['dɪkʃənəri] Wörterbuch
part [pɑːt] Teil
close [kləuz] schließen

Üben und können

together [tə'geðə] zusammen
desk [desk] Schreibtisch
for lunch [fə 'lʌntʃ] zum Mittagessen

Tapescript

home [həum] Zuhause, Daheim
Time is up. [ˌtaɪm ɪz 'ʌp] Die Zeit ist um.

(on the) floor [flɔː] (auf dem) Boden
Oh dear. [əʊ ˈdɪə] Ach, du liebe Zeit.

Unit 7
Lead-in
factory [ˈfæktəri] Fabrik
hospital [ˈhɒspɪtl] Krankenhaus
university [juːnəˈvɜːsəti] Universität
school [skuːl] Schule
call centre [ˈkɔːl ˌsentə] Call Center
waiter [ˈweɪtə] Kellner(in)
PA (personal assistant) [ˌpɜːsənəl əˈsɪstənt] Assistent(in) der Geschäftsleitung
nurse [nɜːs] Krankenschwester, Pfleger
lecturer [ˈlektʃərə] Dozent(in)
teacher [ˈtiːtʃə] Lehrer(in)

Lesson 7.1
written [ˈrɪtn] geschrieben
spoken [ˈspəʊkən] gesprochen
instruction [ɪnˈstrʌkʃən] Anweisung
polite [pəˈlaɪt] höflich
Sit down. [ˌsɪt ˈdaʊn] Setzen Sie sich.
Hold the line. [ˌhəʊld ðə ˈlaɪn] Bleiben Sie am Apparat.
Be quiet [bi ˈkwaɪət] Seien Sie still.
Turn off your mobile phone. [ˌtɜːn ɒf jɔː ˌməʊbaɪl ˈfəʊn] Schalten Sie Ihr Handy aus.
Come in. [ˌkʌm ˈɪn] (Kommen Sie) Herein.
Don't come in. [ˌdəʊnt kʌm ˈɪn] Kommen Sie nicht herein.
in class [ɪn ˈklɑːs] im Unterricht
announcement [əˈnaʊnsmənt] Ankündigung
sign [saɪn] Schild
notice [ˈnəʊtɪs] Mitteilung
succeed [səkˈsiːd] Erfolg haben
practise [ˈpræktɪs] üben
phone call [ˈfəʊn kɔːl] Anruf
prepare [prɪˈpeə] vorbereiten
lesson [ˈlesən] Unterrichtsstunde
teach [tiːtʃ] unterrichten
classroom [ˈklɑːs-rʊm, -ruːm] Klassen-, Kursraum
January [ˈdʒænjuəri, -njʊri] Januar
February [ˈfebruəri, ˈfebjʊri] Februar
March [mɑːtʃ] März

April [ˈeɪprəl] April
May [meɪ] Mai
June [dʒuːn] Juni
July [dʒuˈlaɪ] Juli
August [ˈɔːgəst] August
September [sepˈtembə] September
October [ɒkˈtəʊbə] Oktober
November [nəʊˈvembə, nə-] November
December [dɪˈsembə] Dezember
calendar [ˈkæləndə] Kalender
explain [ɪkˈspleɪn] erklären
reason [ˈriːzən] Grund

Lesson 7.2
presentation [ˌprezənˈteɪʃən] Präsentation
adverb [ˈædvɜːb] Adverb
frequency [ˈfriːkwənsi] Häufigkeit
how often [ˌhaʊ ˈɒfən, ˈɒftən] wie oft
something [ˈsʌmθɪŋ] etwas
board [bɔːd] Tafel
customer [ˈkʌstəmə] Kunde, Kundin
report [rɪˈpɔːt] Bericht
take (home) [teɪk] (mit nach Hause) nehmen
abroad [əˈbrɔːd] (ins) Ausland
outdoors [ˌaʊtˈdɔːz] draußen
always [ˈɔːlweɪz, -wɪz] immer
usually [ˈjuːʒuəli, ˈjuːʒəli] normalerweise
often [ˈɒfən, ˈɒftən] oft
never [ˈnevə] nie
mistake [mɪˈsteɪk] Fehler
pronounce [prəˈnaʊns] aussprechen
request [rɪˈkwest] Bitte, Aufforderung
note [nəʊt] Notiz, kurze Mitteilung
Thanks. [θæŋks] Danke.
Many thanks. [ˌmeni ˈθæŋks] Vielen Dank.
tomorrow [təˈmɒrəʊ] morgen

Lesson 7.3
visitor [ˈvɪzɪtə] Besucher(in)
place of work [ˌpleɪs əv ˈwɜːk] Arbeitsplatz
date [deɪt] Datum
visit [ˈvɪzɪt] Besuch
colleague [ˈkɒliːg] Kollege, Kollegin
Act out the conversation. [ˌækt aʊt ðə ˌkɒnvəˈseɪʃən] Spielen Sie das Gespräch vor.

the first of September [ðə ˌfɜːst əv sepˈtembə] der erste September
the second of July [ðə ˌsekənd əv dʒuˈlaɪ] der zweite Juli
the third of April [ðə ˌθɜːd əv ˈeɪprəl] der dritte April
the ninth of February [ðə ˌnaɪnθ əv ˈfebruəri, ˈfebjʊri] der neunte Februar
the twentieth of May [ðə ˌtwentiəθ əv ˈmeɪ] der zwanzigste Mai
When is your birthday? [ˌwen ɪz jɔː ˈbɜːθdeɪ] Wann ist Dein Geburtstag?
What would you like to drink? [ˌwɒt wʊd jʊ ˌlaɪk tə ˈdrɪŋk] Was möchten Sie trinken?
biscuit [ˈbɪskɪt] Keks
Read the conversation aloud. [ˌriːd ðə kɒnvəˌseɪʃən əˈlaʊd] Lesen Sie das Gespräch laut vor.
soup [suːp] Suppe
fruit [fruːt] Obst, Frucht
vegetable [ˈvedʒtəbəl] Gemüse
main course [ˌmeɪn ˈkɔːs] Hauptgericht
dessert [dɪˈzɜːt] Nachtisch
starter [ˈstɑːtə] Vorspeise
drink [drɪŋk] Getränk
snack [snæk] Imbiss
staff [stɑːf] Personal
canteen [ˌkænˈtiːn] Kantine

Communication
lift [lɪft] Fahrstuhl
floor [flɔː] Etage
receptionist [rɪˈsepʃənɪst] Empfangsdame
appointment [əˈpɔɪntmənt] Termin
mean [miːn] bedeuten
toilet [ˈtɔɪlət] Toilette
plan [plæn] Plan

Üben und können
chips [tʃɪps] Pommes frites
selection [səˈlekʃən] Auswahl

Tapescript
Can I speak to Mr Flynn, please? [kən aɪ ˌspiːk tə ˌmɪstə ˈflɪn ˌpliːz] Kann ich bitte Herrn Flynn sprechen?
Can he call you back? [kən hi ˌkɔːl jʊ ˈbæk] Kann er Sie zurückrufen?
I'm afraid he's in a meeting this morning. [aɪm əˌfreɪd hiz ɪn ə ˈmiː

tɪŋ ðɪs ˌmɔːnɪŋ] Ich fürchte, er ist heute Morgen in einer Konferenz.

immediately [ɪˈmiːdiətli] sofort

on the right/left [ɒn ðə ˈraɪt, ˈleft] auf der rechten/linken Seite

Turn right/left [ˌtɜːn ˈraɪt, ˈleft] Biegen Sie rechts/links ab.

Unit 8

Lead-in

leisure activity [ˈleʒər ækˌtɪvəti] Freizeitbeschäftigung

go cycling [ˌgəʊ ˈsaɪklɪŋ] Rad fahren

eat out [ˌiːt ˈaʊt] Essen gehen

(play) chess [tʃes] Schach (spielen)

go sightseeing [ˌgəʊ ˈsaɪtˌsiːɪŋ] Besichtigungen machen

go for a walk [ˌgəʊ fər ə ˈwɔːk] spazieren gehen

theatre [ˈθɪətə] Theater

do exercise [ˌduː ˈeksəsaɪz] Fitnessübungen machen

without [wɪðˈœaʊt] ohne

go swimming [ˌgəʊ ˈswɪmɪŋ] Schwimmen gehen

Lesson 8.1

why [waɪ] warum

He wants to go to the cinema. [hi ˌwɒnts tə ˌgəʊ tə ðə ˈsɪnəmə] Er will ins Kino gehen.

available [əˈveɪləbəl] verfügbar

go out [ˌgəʊ ˈaʊt] ausgehen

problem [ˈprɒbləm] Problem

(in) brackets [ˈbrækɪts] (in) Klammern

bicycle [ˈbaɪsɪkəl] Fahrrad

boring [ˈbɔːrɪŋ] langweilig

exciting [ɪkˈsaɪtɪŋ] aufregend

difficult [ˈdɪfɪkəlt] schwierig

interesting [ˈɪntrəstɪŋ] interessant

This is fun. [ðɪs ɪz ˈfʌn] Das macht Spaß.

easy [ˈiːzi] leicht

Lesson 8.2

possess [pəˈzes] besitzen

furniture [ˈfɜːnɪtʃə] Möbel

park [pɑːk] parken

kitchen [ˈkɪtʃən] Küche

washing machine [ˈwɒʃɪŋ məʃiːn] Waschmaschine

basin [ˈbeɪsən] Waschbecken

coffee table [ˈkɒfi ˌteɪbəl] Kaffeetisch

sofa [ˈsəʊfə] Sofa

fridge [frɪdʒ] Kühlschrank

bath [bɑːθ] Badewanne

armchair [ˈɑːmtʃeə] Sessel

lamp [læmp] Lampe

cooker [ˈkʊkə] Herd

wardrobe [ˈwɔːdrəʊb] Garderobe, Kleiderschrank

sink [sɪŋk] Spüle

mirror [ˈmɪrə] Spiegel

wedding [ˈwedɪŋ] Hochzeit

suggestion [səˈdʒestʃən] Vorschlag

idea [aɪˈdɪə] Idee

living room [ˈlɪvɪŋ ruːm, -rʊm] Wohnzimmer

bedroom [ˈbedrʊm, -ruːm] Schlafzimmer

microwave oven [ˌmaɪkrəweɪv ˈʌvən] Mikrowellenherd

flat [flæt] Wohnung

technology [tekˈnɒlədʒi] Technologie

quiz [kwɪz] Quiz

score [skɔː] Punktestand

point [pɔɪnt] Punkt

paper [ˈpeɪpə] Papier

GPS device [ˌdʒiː piː ˈes dɪˌvaɪs] Navigationsgerät

newspaper [ˈnjuːsˌpeɪpə] Zeitung

magazine [ˌmægəˈziːn] Zeitschrift

digital camera [ˌdɪdʒɪtl ˈkæmərə] Digitalkamera

camcorder [ˈkæmˌkɔːdə] Camcorder

Lesson 8.3

suggest [səˈdʒest] vorschlagen

celebrate [ˈseləbreɪt] feiern

Which restaurant ...? [ˌwɪtʃ ˈrestərɒnt] Welches Restaurant ...?

What food ...? [ˌwɒt ˈfuːd] Was für ein Essen ...?

serve [sɜːv] servieren, anbieten

local [ˈləʊkəl] örtlich

taste [teɪst] Geschmack

book [bʊk] buchen, reservieren

How many people? [ˌhaʊ meni ˈpiːpəl] Wie viele Personen?

What time? [wɒt ˈtaɪm] Um welche Zeit?

menu [ˈmenjuː] Speisekarte

fish [fɪʃ] Fisch

lamb [læm] Lamm

chop [tʃɒp] Kotelett

seafood [ˈsiːfuːd] Meeresfrüchte

pasta [ˈpæstə] Nudeln

still/sparkling mineral water [ˌstɪl ˈmɪnərəl ˌwɔːtə, ˌspɑːklɪŋ] Mineralwasser ohne / mit Kohlensäure

reservation [ˌrezəˈveɪʃən] Reservierung

bill [bɪl] Rechnung

salt [sɔːlt] Salz

pepper [ˈpepə] Pfeffer

enter [ˈentə] hineingehen, betreten

cheese [tʃiːz] Käse

beef [biːf] Rind fleisch

pork [pɔːk] Schweinefleisch

prawns [prɔːnz] Garnelen

potato(es) [pəˈteɪtəʊs] Kartoffel(n)

rice [raɪs] Reis

ice cream [ˌaɪs ˈkriːm] Eiscreme

Communication

postman [ˈpəʊstmən] Postbote postbotin

winner [ˈwɪnə] Gewinner(in)

and so on [ənd ˈsəʊ ɒn] und so weiter

Üben und können

sleep [sliːp] schlafen

maths [mæθs] Mathe

just [dʒəst, dʒʌst] nur

special offer [ˌspeʃəl ˈɒfə] Sonderangebot

far [fɑː] weit

Tapescript

next weekend [ˌnekst wiːkˈend, ˈwiːkend] nächstes Wochenende

Come on. [kʌm ˈɒn] Na los.

choose [tʃuːz] (aus)wählen

golf course [ˈgɒlf kɔːs] Golfplatz

tennis court [ˈtenɪs kɔːt] Tennisplatz

Smoking or non-smoking? [ˌsməʊkɪŋ ɔː ˈnɒn ˌsməʊkɪŋ] Raucher oder Nichtraucher?

See you on Friday. [ˌsiː jʊ ɒn ˈfraɪdi] Bis Freitag.

Are you ready to order? [ɑː jʊ ˌredi tʊ ˈɔːdə] Möchten sie jetzt bestellen?

What about...? [ˈwɒt əbaʊt] Wie steht's mit...?

How about...? [ˈhaʊ əbaʊt] Wie wär's mit...?

Unit 9

Lead in

past [pɑːst] Vergangenheit

space [speɪs] Weltraum

royal ['rɔɪəl] königlich

dream [driːm] Traum

president ['prezɪdənt] Präsident

dead [ded] tot

headline ['hedlaɪn] Schlagzeile

disaster [dɪ'zɑːstə] Katastrophe

guess [ges] raten

Lesson 9.1

statement (about) ['steɪtmənt]
  Behauptung, Aussage (über)

history ['hɪstəri] Geschichte

text [tekst] Text

meaning ['miːnɪŋ] Bedeutung

He was born on 8th January. [hi
  wəz ˌbɔːn ɒn ði ˌeɪtθ əv 'dʒænjuəri]
  Er wurde am 8. Januar geboren.

She was born in 1963. [ʃi wəz ˌbɔːn
  ɪn ˌnaɪntiːn sɪksti 'θriː] Sie wurde
  1963 geboren.

They were poor. [ðeɪ wə 'pɔː]
  Sie waren arm.

parents ['peərənts] Eltern

driver ['draɪvə] Fahrer(in)

quote [kwəʊt] Zitat

dreamer ['driːmə] Träumer(in)

princess [ˌprɪn'ses] Prinzessin

model ['mɒdl] Model

prince [prɪns] Prinz

fighter ['faɪtə] Kämpfer(in)

strong [strɒŋ] stark

feel [fiːl] fühlen

icon ['aɪkɒn] Ikone

pianist ['piːənɪst] Klavierspieler(in)

life [laɪf] Leben

marriage ['mærɪdʒ] Ehe

century ['sentʃəri] Jahrhundert

childhood ['tʃaɪldhʊd] Kindheit

game [geɪm] Spiel

in bold [ɪn 'bəʊld] fett gedruckt

Lesson 9.2

negative ['negətɪv] Veneinung

description [dɪ'skrɪpʃən]
  Beschreibung

two years ago [tuː 'jɪəz əˌgəʊ]
  vor zwei Jahren

yesterday ['jestədi, -deɪ] gestern

last night/week [ˌlɑːst 'naɪt, 'wiːk]
  letzte Nacht/Woche

last month [ˌlɑːst 'mʌnθ] letzten
  Monat

last year [ˌlɑːst 'jɪə] letztes Jahr

flight [flaɪt] Flug

remember [rɪ'membə] erinnern

(past) experience [ɪk'spɪəriəns]
  (frühere) Erfahrung

meal [miːl] Mahlzeit

Well done! [ˌwel 'dʌn] Gut gemacht!

Bad luck. [ˌbæd 'lʌk] Pech gehabt.

Time's up. [ˌtaɪmz 'ʌp] Die Zeit
  ist um.

Your go. [jɔː 'gəʊ] Du bist dran.

expression [ɪk'spreʃən] Ausdruck

Lesson 9.3

permission [pə'mɪʃən] Erlaubnis

housework ['haʊswɜːk] Hausarbeit

vacuum ['vækjuəm, -kjʊm]
  staubsaugen

clean [kliːn] reinigen, säubern

dishes ['dɪʃɪz] Geschirr

iron ['aɪən] bügeln

housewife ['haʊswaɪf] Hausfrau

stay [steɪ] bleiben

crazy ['kreɪzi] verrückt

househusband ['haʊsˌhʌzbənd]
  Hausmann

childcare ['tʃaɪldkeə]
  Kinderbetreuung

look (after) [lʊk] aufpassen (auf)

do the laundry [ˌduː ðə 'lɔːndri]
  die Wäsche machen

expensive [ɪk'spensɪv] teuer

stranger ['streɪndʒə] Fremde(r)

agree [ə'griː] zustimmen

How was your day? [ˌhaʊ wəz jɔː
  'deɪ] Wie war Dein Tag?

carry ['kæri] tragen

Could you pass the milk? [kʊd jʊ
  ˌpɑːs ðə 'mɪlk] Könntest du mir die
  Milch geben?

Communication

science ['saɪəns] Wissenschaft

subject ['sʌbdʒɪkt] Unterrichtsfach

Üben und können

composer [kəm'pəʊzə]
  Komponist(in)

politician [ˌpɒlə'tɪʃən] Politiker(in)

Tapescript

wrong [rɒŋ] falsch

ready ['redi] fertig

Let's play. [lets 'pleɪ] Lass(t) uns
  spielen.

He was married to Cynthia. [hi
  wəz ˌmærɪd tə 'sɪnθiə] Er war mit
  Cynthia verheiratet.

She was good at horse-riding and
  painting. [ʃi wəz ˌgʊd ət ˌhɔːs
  raɪdɪŋ ən 'peɪntɪŋ] Sie war gut im
  Reiten und Malen.

similar (to) ['sɪmələ] ähnlich, gleich

weather ['weðə] Wetter

sunny ['sʌni] sonnig

darling ['dɑːlɪŋ] Liebling

What's the matter? [ˌwɒts ðə 'mætə]
  Was ist los?

air steward ['eə ˌstjuːəd]
  Flugbegleiter(in)

attractive [ə'træktɪv] attraktiv

funny ['fʌni] lustig

Unit 10

Lead in

win [wɪn] gewinnen

arrest [ə'rest] festnehmen

lose [luːz] verlieren

steal [stiːl] stehlen

break [breɪk] brechen

move [muːv] umziehen

purse [pɜːs] Geldbörse

thief [θiːf] Dieb(in)

all day [ˌɔːl 'deɪ] den ganzen Tag

lottery ['lɒtəri] Lotterie

get married [get 'mærɪd] heiraten

respond [rɪ'spɒnd] antworten

Lesson 10.1

story ['stɔːri] Geschichte

narrative ['nærətɪv] Erzählung

event [ɪ'vent] Ereignis

most of them ['məʊst əv ðəm]
  die meisten von ihnen

but [bət, bʌt] aber

painting ['peɪntɪŋ] Bild, Gemälde

of course [əv 'kɔːs] natürlich

about four years [əbaʊt ˌfɔː 'jɪəz]
  ungefähr vier Jahre

later ['leɪtə] später

king [kɪŋ] König

ceiling ['siːlɪŋ] (Zimmer)Decke

chapel ['tʃæpəl] Kapelle

Vokabelliste

library ['laɪbrəri, -bri] Bibliothek,
  Bücherei
ending ['ɛndɪŋ] Endung
column ['kɒləm] Spalte

Lesson 10.2

summary ['sʌməri]
  Zusammenfassung
news [njuːz] Nachrichten
They got married. [ðeɪ gɒt 'mærid]
  Sie heirateten.
That's life. [ˌðæts 'laɪf] So ist das
  Leben.
concert ['kɒnsət] Konzert
ticket ['tɪkɪt] (Eintritts)Karte,
  (Tipp)Schein
gold [gəʊld] golden
coin [kɔɪn] Münze
inside [ɪn'saɪd, 'ɪnsaɪd] in Inneren
crossword ['krɒswɜːd]
  Kreuzworträtsel
high [haɪ] hoch
thousand ['θaʊzənd] Tausend
advert ['ædvɜːt] Werbeanzeige

Lesson 10.3

fisherman ['fɪʃəmən] Fischer
because [bɪ'kɒz, bɪ'kəz] weil
explanation [ˌeksplə'neɪʃən]
  Erklärung
catch [kætʃ] fangen
make money [ˌmeɪk 'mʌni]
  Geld verdienen
relax [rɪ'læks] sich entspannen
grandson ['grændsʌn] Enkel
sleep [sliːp] Schlaf
energy ['enədʒi] Energie
be in love [bi ɪn 'lʌv] verliebt sein

Communication

kill [kɪl] töten
die [daɪ] sterben
killer ['kɪlə] Mörder(in)
mile [maɪl] Meile; 1,6 km
suspect ['sʌspekt] Verdächtige(r)
butler ['bʌtlə] Butler
maid [meɪd] Hausmädchen
secretary ['sekrətəri] Sekretär(in)
note [nəʊt] Notiz

Üben und können

newly-weds ['njuːli wedz]
  Frischverheiratete
compare [kəm'peə] vergleichen
quantity ['kwɒntəti] Menge

Tapescript

back [bæk] zurück
then [ðen] dann
low prices [ˌləʊ 'praɪsɪz]
  niedrige Preise
item ['aɪtəm] Gegenstand
hurry ['hʌri] sich beeilen
soon [suːn] bald

A–Z Vokabelliste

ability 5.3
about four years 10.1
above 6.1
abroad 7.2
accountant 2.3
accountant 6.2
Act out the conversation. 7.3
activity 6.2
actor 2.3
add 6.2
address 2 L/in
adult 4.3
adverb 7.2
advert 10.2
afternoon 1.1
again 6.1
age 2.1
agree 9.3
air steward 9 T/s
airport 1.2
all day 10 L/in
always 7.2
and 3.2
and so on 8 C/a
announcement 7.1
another example 6.2
answer 6.1
antique 4.2
any 5.2
Anything else? 4.1
appointment 7 C/a
April 7.1
architect 6.2
Are you ready to order? 8 T/s
Argentina 1.2
armchair 8.2
around 4.3
arrest 10 L/in
arrival 1 L/in
art 3.3
artist 2.3
ask (for) 2.2
at home 9 S/f
attachment 3.1
attractive 9 T/s
August 7.1
aunt 6.3
Australia 1.2
available 8.1
awful 2.2
baby, babies 4.3
back 10 T/s
backpack 3.1
bad 2.2
Bad luck. 9.2
bag 4.2
bank 4 L/in
basic 2.1
basin 8.2
bath 8.2
be in love 10.3
Be quiet 7.1
beach 5 L/in
beautiful 3.1

because 10.3
bed 5 C/a
bedroom 8.2
beef 8.3
beer 4.3
beginner 5.3
behind 5.2
below 6.1
best friends 6.2
between 3.2
bicycle 8.1
big 3.1
biker 6.3
bill 8.3
birthday 4 T/s
biscuit 7.3
black 4.1
blanket 5 C/a
blue 4.2
board 7.2
book 2 C/a, 8.3
bookshop 4 L/in
boring 8.1
box 6 L/in
bracelet 4.2
(in) brackets 8.1
Brazil 1.2
break 10 L/in
breakfast 5 C/a, 6.3
brother 2 L/in
brown 4.2
brunch 6.3
build 6.2
builder 6.2
building 5 L/in
bus stop 4 L/in
but 10.1
butler 10 C/a
Bye. 3 C/a
café 4 L/in
calendar 7.1
call centre 7 L/in
camcorder 8.2
camera 3.2
can 5.3
Can he call you back? 7 T/s
Can I have an espresso, please? 4.1
Can I help you? 3 T/s
Can I speak to Mr Flynn, please? 7 T/s
Canada 2.3
candle 6 C/a
canteen 7.3
capital 3.1
car 3.1
car park 4 L/in
carry 9.3
cashpoint 4 L/in
castle 3 L/in
catch 10.3
category 6.1
cathedral 3 L/in
ceiling 10.1
celebrate 8.3
centre 5 L/in

century 9.1
Certainly./Sure 4.1
change 6.3
chapel 10.1
chart 6 L/in
check 6 L/in
check in to a hotel 1.1
cheese 8.3
chef 6.2
chemist 4 L/in
chicken 4.1
child 4.3
childcare 9.3
childhood 9.1
children 4.3
China 1 C/a
Chinese 5.2
chips 7 Ü/k
chocolate 4.1
choose 8 T/s
chop 8.3
cinema 4 L/in
city 1.2
classroom 7.1
clean 9.3
close 6 C/a
closed 3.3
clothes 4.2
coast 5 L/in
coat 4.2
coffee 4.1
coffee table 8.2
coin 10.2
cold 3 C/a
colleague 7.3
colour 4.2
column 10.1
Come in. 7.1
Come on. 8 T/s
common 1.3
communication 1 C/a
company 6 C/a
compare 10 Ü/k
complete 6.1
composer 9 Ü/k
computer 2 L/in
concert 10.2
continue 6.2
cook 5.3
cooker 8.2
cookery book 6 C/a
correct 6 L/in
Could you pass the milk? 9.3
country, countries 1.2
countryside 5 L/in
course 5.3
crazy 9.3
crossword 10.2
(a) cup of tea 4.1
customer 7.2
Dad 3 C/a
daily 6.3
dance 5.3
darling 9 T/s
date 7.3

daughter 2 L/in
day of the week 3.3
dead 9 L/in, 10 C/a
December 7.1
department store 3 L/in
describe 6.3
description 5.1, 9.2
design 6.2
designer 6.2
desk 6 Ü/k
dessert 7.3
dial 1 C/a
dictionary 6 C/a
die 10 C/a
different 6.2
difficult 8.1
digital camera 8.2
disaster 9 L/in
dishes 9.3
do 6.2
do an interview 6.1
do exercise 8 L/in
do the laundry 9.3
doctor 2.3
Don't come in. 7.1
double bed 5 C/a
draw 6.1
dream 9 L/in
dreamer 9.1
dress 4.2
drink 4.1, 7.3
drive 5.3
driver 9.1
dry 4.3
each 6.1
early 6.3
east 5 L/in
easy 8.1
Eat in or take away? 4.1
eat out 8 L/in
eight 1.1
eighteen 2.1
eighty 2.1
eleven 2.1
email 2 L/in
ending 10.1
energy 10.3
engineer 2.3
England 5.2
English 5.2
en-suite 5 C/a
enter 4.3, 8.3
etc. = et cetera 6.2
evening 1.1
event 10.1
every 6.3
every year 3.3
exciting 8.1
Excuse me, ... 1.3
expensive 9.3
(past) experience 9.2
explain 7.1
explanation 10.3
expression 9.2
factory 7 L/in
false 1.2, 6.2

family 2.1
famous 5.1
far 8 Ü/k
fashion 6.1
fast 6.3
fat 6 L/in
father 2 L/in
February 7.1
feel 9.1
fifteen 2.1
fifty 2.1
fighter 9.1
film 2 C/a
find 1 C/a
fine 3 C/a
finish 6.3
first name 2 L/in
fish 8.3
fisherman 10.3
five 1.1
five past six 5 C/a
flat 8.2
flight 9.2
(on the) floor 6 T/s, 7 C/a
flower 6 C/a
food 3 C/a
football team 6.1
for example 4 T/s
for lunch 6 Ü/k
form 6.3
forty 2.1
fountain 5.2
four 1.1
fourteen 2.1
free 3.3
French 5.2
frequency 7.2
Friday 3.3
fridge 5 C/a, 8.2
friend 2.1
from Tuesday to Sunday 3.3
from two o'clock to four
  o'clock 5.3
fruit 7.3
funny 9 T/s
furniture 8.2
gallery 3 L/in
game 9.1
gap 6.2
general 5.3
German 5.2
Germany 1.2
get married 10 L/in
get up 6.3
give an opinion 5.1
give information (about) 2.1
go cycling 8 L/in
go for a walk 8 L/in
go out 8.1
go sightseeing 8 L/in
go swimming 8 L/in
go to bed 6.3
gold 10.2
golf course 8 T/s
good 1.1
Good morning. 1 L/in

good-looking 6 L/in
GPS device 8.2
grammar 1.1
grandson 10.3
great 2.2
green 4.2
greet someone 1.2
greeting 1.1
group 6.2
guess 9 L/in
guide 4.1
half past seven 5 C/a
ham 4.1
happy 6 L/in
hat 4.2
have a shower 6.3
He wants to go to the cinema. 8.1
He was born on 8th January.
  9.1
He was married to Cynthia.
  9 T/s
headline 9 L/in
hear 6.3
Hello ./ Hi. 1 L/in
here 3.3
He's from Russia. 1.2
high 10.2
hill 5 L/in
history 9.1
Hold the line. 7.1
holiday 3.1
home 6 T/s
hospital 7 L/in
hot 3 C/a
house 3.1
househusband 9.3
housewife 9.3
housework 9.3
How about ...? 8 T/s
How are you? 3.1
How do you spell that? 2.2
How many people? 8.3
How much are they? 4.2
How much is it? 4.2
how often 7.2
How old is she? 2.1
How was your day? 9.3
hurry 10 T/s
husband 2 L/in
I'm afraid he's in a meeting
  this morning. 7 T/s
ice cream 8.3
iced coffee 4.1
icon 9.1
idea 8.2
I'm from ... 1.3
I'm sorry. 4 C/a
immediately 7 T/s
important 5.1
in 5.2
in a lot of ways 6.2
in bold 9.1
in class 7.1
in front of 5.2
in the afternoon/morning/

evening 5.3
in the north of 5 L/in
India 1.2
Indian 5.2
inside 10.2
instant coffee 4.1
instruction 7.1
intelligent 6 L/in
interesting 8.1
interview 6.1
introduce someone 1.3
Ireland 5.2
Irish 5.2
iron 9.3, 9 S/f
irregular 4.3
Is there a bank near here?
  5.2
island 5 Ü/k
Italian 5.2
italics 6.1
Italy 1.2
item 10 T/s
It's called ... 5.1
It's four pounds fifty. 4.2
It's OK. 2.1
January 7.1
Japan 1.2
job 2.3
July 7.1
jumper 4.2
June 7.1
just 8 Ü/k
kettle 5 C/a
key 9 S/f
kill 10 C/a
killer 10 C/a
king 10.1
kiss 6 S/f
kitchen 8.2
know 4 C/a, 6.2
lake 3 L/in
lamb 8.3
lamp 5 C/a, 8.2
language 5.2
large 4.1
last month 9.2
last night/week 9.2
last year 9.2
later 10.1
learn 1.2
lecturer 7 L/in
leisure activity 8 L/in
lesson 7.1
Let's play. 9 T/s
letter 1.2, 6.3
level 5 T/s
library 10.1
life 2 L/in, 6.3, 9.1
lifelong 1.2
lift 7 C/a
like 6.1
line 6.3
list 6.1, 8.2
listen 1.1, 6 L/in
living room 8.2
local 8.3

location 5 C/a
look (after) 9.3
look at 6.1
lose 10 L/in
(a) lot of 5.1
lottery 10 L/in
Love ... 3.1
low prices 10 T/s
magazine 8.2
magazine article 6.2
maid 10 C/a
main course 7.3
make 3.2
make friends 6.2
make money 10.3
man 4.3
manager 2.3
Many thanks. 7.2
map 3.1
March 7.1
mark 6.2
market 3 L/in
marriage 9.1
married 6 C/a
match 6.2
maths 8 Ü/k
May 7.1
meal 9.2
mean 7 C/a
meaning 9.1
medium 4.1
member 6.3
men 4.3
menu 8.3
Mexico 1 C/a
microwave oven 8.2
midnight 6.3
mile 10 C/a
milk 4.1, 7.3
mineral water 4.1
mirror 8.2
Miss Jones 1.1
mistake 7.2
mobile phone 2 L/in
model 9.1
modern 3.1
Monday 3.3
more 6.1
morning 1.1
most of them 10.1
mother 2 L/in
mountain 3 L/in
move 10 L/in
MP3 player 3.2
Mr Smith 1.1
Mrs/Ms Jones 1.1
Mum 3 C/a
museum 3 L/in
music 5.2
musician 6.3
my favourite ... 2 C/a
narrative 10.1
nationality 5.2
near 3.3
negative 9.2
never 7.2

Never mind. 4 C/a
new 3 C/a
newly-weds 10 Ü/k
news 10.2
  5.2
newsagent 4 L/in
newspaper 8.2
next to 4 C/a
next weekend 8 T/s
Nice to meet you, too. 1 L/in
Nice to meet you. 1 L/in
night 1.1
nine 1.1
nineteen 2.1
ninety 2.1
No, thank you. 1.3
north 5 L/in
note 7.2, 10 C/a
notice 7.1
November 7.1
now 6.3
number 1.1
nurse 7 L/in
occupation 6 C/a
October 7.1
oder 4.3
of course 10.1
office building 6.2
often 7.2
Oh dear. 6 T/s
old 3.1
on 5.2
on business 6.2
on holiday 6.2
on King Street 4 C/a
on Mondays 3.3
on the right/left 7 T/s
on the River Thames 3.3
one 1.1
one pound 4.1
only 4.2
open 3.3
opposite 4 C/a, 6 L/in
or 4.3
orange 4.2
orange juice 4.1
order 4.1
ordinal number 7.3
other 2.3
outdoor theatre 5.1
outdoors 7.2
over sixty 6.2
PA (personal assistant) 7
  L/in
(a) packet of aspirin 4.3
page 6.1
painting 10.1
pair 6.1
palace 3 L/in
paper 8.2
Pardon? 1.3
parents 9.1
park 8.2
part 6 C/a
partner 6 L/in
passport 2 L/in

past 9 L/in
pasta 8.3
pay by credit card 4.3
pen 6 C/a
people 1.3
pepper 8.3
permission 9.3
person 4.3
personal details 2.2
phone 2 L/in
phone call 7.1
phone number 1 C/a
photo 2 L/in
phrase 1.3
pianist 9.1
picture 2.3
(a) piece of cake 4.1
(a) pint 4.3
place 3.1
place of work 7.3
plan 7 C/a
plants from all over the
  world 5.1
play 5.3
play chess 8 L/in
play golf 5.3
play the piano 5.3
point 8.2
Poland 1.2
police officer 2.3
polite 7.1
politician 9 Ü/k
poor 6 L/in
popular 4.2
pork 8.3
possess 8.2
possession 3 Ü/k
postman 8 C/a
potato 8.3
practise 7.1
prawns 8.3
prepare 7.1
present 6.1, 6.3
presentation 7.2
president 9 L/in
price 4.1
prince 9.1
princess 9.1
problem 8.1
pronounce 7.2
pronunciation 1.2
pub 4 L/in
purse 10 L/in
put 6 L/in
quantity 10 Ü/k
quarter past four 5 C/a
question 1.3
quite 6 L/in
quiz 8.2
quote 9.1
rat 8 S/f
read 1.2
Read the conversation
  aloud. 7.3
ready 9 T/s
really 6.2

reason 7.1
receive 5.2
receptionist 7 C/a
red 4.2
regular 3.2
relax 10.3
remember 9.2
repeat 6.1
report 7.2
reporter 6.2
request 7.2
reservation 8.3
respond 10 L/in
restaurant 2 C/a
return 4.3
rice 8.3
rich 6 L/in
river 3.3
road 5 L/in
room 1.1
routine 6.3
royal 9 L/in
salad 4.1
sales assistant 2.3
sales rep. 6.2
salt 8.3
same 6.2
sandwich 4.1
Saturday 3.3
saucepan 6 C/a
say 1.1
school 7 L/in
science 9 C/a
score 8.2
Scotland 5.2
Scottish 5.2
sea 5 L/in
seafood 8.3
second 6.1
secretary 10 C/a
See you on Friday. 3 C/a, 8
  T/s
selection 7 Ü/k
sell 6.2
send 9 S/f
sentence 6 L/in
September 7.1
serve 8.3
seven 1.1
seventeen 2.1
seventy 2.1
She is called Cynthia. 6.1
She was born in 1963. 9.1
She was good at horse-riding and painting. 9 T/s
She's sixty-two years old.
  2.1
shirt 4.2
(a pair of) shoes 3.2
shop 3.3
shopping 4.3
short 2.3
short 6 L/in
show 4.3
show interest 6.2
shower 5 C/a

sign 4.3, 7.1
similar (to) 9 T/s
simple 3.1
sing 5.3
singer 2 C/a
single 4.3
sink 8.2
sister 2 L/in
Sit down. 7.1
six 1.1
sixteen 2.1
sixty 2.1
skirt 3.2
sleep 8 Ü/k, 10.3
small 3.1, 4.1
Smoking or non-smoking?
  8 T/s
snack 7.3
sofa 8.2
some 5.1
someone 6.2
something 4 C/a, 7.2
son 2 L/in
song 6.3
soon 10 T/s
Sorry. 1.3
soup 7.3
south 5 L/in
space 9 L/in
Spain 1 C/a
speak 1.1
special offer 8 Ü/k
spell 2.2
spice 5.1
spoken 7.1
square 5.2
staff 7.3
start a conversation 1.3
start work 6.3
starter 7.3
statement (about) 9.1
stay 9.3
steal 10 L/in
still/sparkling mineral
  water 8.3
story 10.1
stranger 9.3
street 3.3
strong 9.1
student 2.3
subject 9 C/a
succeed 7.1
sugar 4.1, 7.3
suggest 8.3
suggestion 8.2
suitcase 3.1
summary 10.2
Sunday 3.3
sunny 9 T/s
supermarket 4 L/in
surname 2 L/in
survive 4.3
suspect 10 C/a
swim 5.3
take (home) 7.2
take a photo 9 S/f

A–Z Vokabelliste

talk (about) *2.1*
talk (to) *6.2*
tall *6 L/in*
taste *8.3*
tea bag *5 C/a*
teach *7.1*
teacher *2.3, 7 L/in*
technology *8.2*
television *5 C/a*
tell *6.1*
ten *1.1*
ten to nine *5 C/a*
tennis court *8 T/s*
test *6 L/in*
text *9.1*
Thank you. *1 L/in*
Thanks. *7.2*
That's life. *10.2*
That's forty-two thirty, please. *4.1*
the first of September *7.3*
the ninth of February *7.3*
the second of July *7.3*
the third of April *7.3*
the twentieth of May *7.3*
the UK *1.2*
the US *1.2*
theatre *8 L/in*
then *10 T/s*
there *3.3*
There are nice hotels in New York. *5.1*
They got married. *10.2*
They were poor. *9.1*
thief *10 L/in*
thin *6 L/in*
thing *3.2*
think *5.1*
thirteen *2.1*
thirty *2.1*
This is fun. *8.1*
This is Paul. *1.3*
thousand *10.2*
three *1.1*
three euros *4.1*
Thursday *3.3*
tick *6 C/a*
ticket (to) *3.2, 10.2*
tie *6 C/a*
time *5 C/a*
Time is up. *6 T/s*
time of day *6.1*
Time's up. *9.2*
today *3.3*
together *6 Ü/k*
toilet *7 C/a*
tomorrow *7.2*
top [adj] *3.3*
top *3.2*
tourist *4.2*
tourist attraction *3 L/in*
tourist information *3.3*
towel *5 C/a*
town *4 L/in*
train station *4 L/in*
travel *3 L/in*

tree *5 L/in*
(a pair of) trousers *3.2*
true *6.2*
T-shirt *4.2*
Tuesday *3.3*
Turkey *1.3*
Turn off your mobile phone. *7.1*
turn right/left *7 T/s*
twelve *2.1*
twenty *2.1*
two *1.1*
two dollars *4.1*
two kilometers *4.2*
two o'clock *5.3*
two years ago *9.2*
ugly *3.1*
under *5.2*
underlined *6.3*
understand *4.2*
unhappy *6 L/in*
university *7 L/in*
use *5.3*
useful *4 Ü/k*
usually *7.2*
vacuum *9.3*
vegetable *7.3*
very *3 C/a*
visit *7.3*
visitor *3.3, 7.3*
vocabulary *6.2*
waiter *7 L/in*
Wales *5.2*
wallet *6 C/a*
wardrobe *8.2*
wash *6 S/f*
washing machine *8.2*
watch TV *6.3*
We are fine. *3.1*
weather *9 T/s*
website *2 L/in*
wedding *8.2*
Wednesday *3.3*
Welcome to ... *5.3*
Welcome to (Easton Hotel.) *1 L/in, 5.3*
Well done! *9.2*
Welsh *5.2*
west *5 L/in*
What about...? *8 T/s*
What food ...? *8.3*
What is on sale? *4.2*
What kind of ...? *4.2*
What time? *8.3*
What would you like to drink? *7.3*
What's the matter? *9 T/s*
What's his job? *2.3*
What's your address? *2.2*
What's your name? *1 L/in*
when *5.3*
When is your birthday? *7.3*
Where are you from? *1.3*
Which restaurant ...? *8.3*
white *4.1*
Who's she? *2.1*

why *8.1*
wife *2 L/in*
win *10 L/in*
wine *4.3*
winner *8 C/a*
with *3.1*
without *8 L/in*
wives *4.3*
woman *3.2*
women *4.3*
word *6 L/in*
work long hours *6 C/a*
world *3 L/in*
write *2.3*
written *7.1*
wrong *9 T/s*
yellow *4.2*
Yes, please. *1.3*
yesterday *9.2*
yoga *6.3*
young *6 L/in*
young-at-heart *6.2*
Your go. *9.2*
You're welcome. *4 C/a*
zero *1.1*

Unit 1

Lesson 1.1

1a **1** I'm Mr Stewart. **2** Nice to meet you. **3** Wendy, this is Patrick. **4** Hello, I'm David Smith. **5** What's your name? **6** Welcome to Hotel Havana.

1b **1** b **2** d **3** a **4** c

2 **a** two **b** eight **c** one **d** four **e** five **f** seven **g** six **h** three **i** nine

3a **1** A: I'm Maggie May. **B: You're** in room 511. **2** A: I'm Ruby Tuesday. **B: You're** in room 147. **3** A: I'm Peggy Sue. **B:** in room 312.

3b **1** B I'm **A** You're **2** You're **3** B I'm **A** You're

3c **A:** Hello. Welcome to Hotel Massimo. **B:** Thank you. I'm Arturo Ricci. **A:** You're in room 520, Mr Ricci. **B:** Thank you.

Lesson 1.2

1 **1** a–j **2** b–d **3** i–y **4** m–s **5** q–u

2a **1** Italy **2** Poland **3** Mexico **4** Turkey **5** Spain **6** Russia

2b **1** Japan **2** Australia **3** Argentina **4** The UK **5** Germany **6** India **7** Brazil   Hidden country = Portugal

3 **1** He's from the UK. **2** She's from the US. **3** He's from Argentina. **4** He's from Japan. **5** She's from Germany. **6** He's from Brazil. **7** She's from India. **8** She's from Australia.

4 **1** He's from Brazil. He's in the US. **2** She's from India. She's in the UK. **3** He's from Argentina. He's in Japan. **4** He's from the USA. He's in Australia. **5** She's from Germany. She's in India. **6** She's from the UK. She's in Argentina.

Lesson 1.3

1a **1** Sorry. **2** Pardon? **3** No, thank you. **4** Nice to meet you. **5** Excuse me. **6** Yes, please.

1b **a** 5 **b** 4 **c** 2 **d** 1 **e** 3 **f** 6

2 **1** Susan, this is George. **2** Luis, this is Murat. **3** Hans, this is Olga. **4** Bill, this is Nicole.

3a **Tom:** Carol, this is Ali. **Carol:** Nice to meet you. **Ali:** Nice to meet you, too. **Carol:** Where are you from, Ali? **Ali:** I'm from the UK. **Carol:** Where are you from in the UK? **Ali:** I'm from London.

3b **1** are from **2** Where are **3** you from **4** A you from B from **5** A Where **B** from **6** A are from **B** I'm

3c **1** **You:** Where are you from in the US? **George:** I'm from Texas. **2** **You:** Where are you from? **Mahatma:** I'm from India. **3** **You:** Where are you from? **Eva:** I'm from Argentina. **4** **You:** Where are you from in Australia? **Cate:** I'm from Melbourne.

Unit 2

Lesson 2.1

1 **1** phone **2** address **3** website **4** first name **5** photo **6** mobile phone **7** surname **8** computer   hidden word – passport

2 **1** thirty-two   sixty-four **2** fifty-five   sixty six **3** fifty   forty **4** fifteen   fourteen **5** seventy-seven   eighty-four **6** fifty-four   sixty-three **7** sixty-four   eighty one

3 **1** Julia's my **2** Adel's my **3** Konrad's my **4** Konrad's my **5** Dieter's my **6** Adel's my **7** Julia's my **8** Dieter's my

4 **1** Who's Julia? **2** Who's Adel? **3** Who's Konrad? **4** Who's Konrad? **5** Who's Dieter? **6** Who's Adel? **7** Who's Julia? **8** Who's Dieter?

5 **1** s **2** z **3** z **4** z **5** s **6** z **7** z

Lesson 2.2

1 **1** good **2** awful **3** great **4** ok **5** bad

2 **1** She's good. **2** He's ok. **3** She's great. **4** He's bad. **5** She's awful.

3 **1** What's your address? **2** What's your phone number? **3** What's your mobile phone number? **4** How old are you? **5** Where are you from? **6** How do you spell that, please?

4 **1** What's your name? **2** How do you spell that, please? **3** How old are you? **4** Where are you from? **5** What's your address? **6** What's your phone number? **7** What's your mobile phone number?

5 **1** Are you from Germany? **2** My mobile phone number is 07060 987885. Please phone! **3** How old are you? **4** What's your name? **5** It's great!

Lesson 2.3

1 Senkrecht **1** police officer **2** artist **6** student **8** doctor Waagerecht **3** manager **4** actor **5** teacher **7** accountant **9** engineer **10** sales assistant

2 **1** He's a police officer. **2** She's an artist. **3** She's a manager. **4** He's an actor. **5** She's a teacher. **6** She's a student. **7** He's an accountant. **8** She's a doctor. **9** She's an engineer. **10** She's a sales assistant

3 **1** What's your favourite city? **b)** Las Vegas. **2** What's your favourite restaurant? **c)** Gerrard's Bistro, London. **3** Who's your favourite singer? **f)** Britney Spears. **4** What's your favourite film? **e)** Toy Story 2 **5** What's your favourite CD? **a)** Forty Licks, The Rolling Stones. **6** Who's your favourite actor? **d)** Al Pacino.

4 **1** He's **2** He's **3** He's **4** His **5** She's **6** He's **7** She's **8** She's **9** She's **10** Her **11** He's **12** He's

5 **1** his **2** His **3** he **4** He's **5** he **6** He's **7** his **8** He's **9** his **10** It's **11** her **12** Her **13** she **14** he's **15** she **16** She's **17** her **18** She's **19** her **20** It's

Unit 3

Lesson 3.1

Exercise 1 **1** castle **2** mountain **3** cathedral **4** museum **5** market **6** gallery **7** palace **8** lake

2 **1** E **2** B **3** D **4** C **5** F **6** A

3a **1** We're **2** Our **3** We're **4** They're **5** our **6** their **7** their

3b **1** **Henry Watson:** Their car is old. Our car is modern. **2** **Paul Jones:** Our family is big. Their family is small. **3** **Georgia Watson:** Their surname is Jones. Our surname is Watson. **4** **Katie Jones:** We're forty-two. They're thirty-eight.

Lesson 3.2

1 **1** a camera D **2** a top **3** a backpack B **4** a pair of trousers J **5** a book F **6** a skirt I **7** a pair of shoes C **8** a suitcase E **9** a map A **10** an MP3 player H

2a **1** I'm not Miss Carter, I'm Ms Carter. **2** It's not open today. **3** You're not a good singer. **4** She's not from the UK. **5** You aren't twenty-one, you're twenty-three. **6** I'm not from Germany. **7** You're not my friend. **8** She isn't my sister. **9** You aren't in room 324.You're in room 325.

2b **1** You're not a teacher. You're a student. **2** It isn't a skirt. It's a pair of trousers. **3** We aren't from the US. We're from the UK. **4** Vienna isn't a country. It's a city. **5** He's isn't your sister. He's your brother. **6** You're not fifteen. You're fifty. **7** They aren't open today. They're closed today. **8** She isn't an accountant. She's an engineer.

3a and 3b **a** two CDs. /z/ **b** three tops /z/ **c** four suitcases /iz/ **d** one pair of trousers /z/ **e** two pairs of shoes /z/ **f** two maps /s/ **g** two books /s/ **h** two passports /s/ **i** three mobile phones /z/ **j** two laptop computers /z/

Lesson 3.3

1 **1** Wednesday **2** Thursday **3** Friday **4** Monday **5** Saturday **6** Tuesday **7** Sunday

2 **1** b **2** a **3** b **4** a

3a **1** Are we near the gallery? **2** Is the museum open? **3** Are they from Italy? **4** Is she your friend? **5** Is the lake near here? **6** Are the department stores open today. **7** Are we in the York Hotel?

3b **1** Yes, we are. **2** No, it isn't. **3** Yes, they are. **4** No, she isn't. **5** Yes, it is. **6** No, they aren't. **7** Yes, we are.

4 **A:** Good morning. Can I help you? **B:** (1) Yes. Is the Tate Modern open today? **A:** (2) Yes, it is. **B:** (3) Good. Is it a museum? **A:** (4) No, it isn't. It's a gallery. **B:** (5) Is it free? **A:** (6) Yes, it is. **B:** (7) Is it near here? **A:** (8) Yes, it is. Here's a map.

Unit 4

Lesson 4.1

1 **1** book shop **2** pub **3** car park **4** café **5** chemist **6** cinema **7** bank **8** newsagent **9** bus stop

2 **1a** Chicken sandwich **1b** black coffee **1c** mineral water **2a** cappuccino **2b** salad **2c** mineral water **3a** sandwich **3b** piece of cake **3c** espresso

3 **1** Can I have an **2** Can I have a **3** Can I have a **4** Can I have two **5** Can I have a **6** Can I have two

4 **1** That's one euro ninety, please. **2** That's two dollars forty-five, please. **3** That's fifty cents, please. **4** That's six dollars twenty-nine, please. **5** That's three euros sixty cents, please. **6** That's ninety-nine cents, please.

5 **1** Hello. Can I help you? **2** Yes. Can I have a white coffee, please? **3** Certainly. Anything else? **4** No, thank you. **5** That's one euro, please. **6** Eat in or take away? **7** Eat in, please.

Lesson 4.2

1 **1** brown **2** white **3** orange **4** green **5** blue **6** black **7** yellow **8** red

2 **1** a hat **2** a dress **3** a coat **4** a bag **5** a shirt **6** a pair of trousers **7** a pair of shoes **8** a T-shirt

3 **1** these **2** that **3** these **4** that **5** this **6** those **7** this **8** those

4 **1** How much is that shirt? **2** How much are these? **3** How much is this hat? **4** How much is that jumper? **5** How much are those coats? **6** How much is this skirt? **7** How much are those trousers? **8** How much are these bags?

Lesson 4.3

1 **1** children **2** women **3** men **4** babies **5** people **6** wives

2 **1** Single or return? **2** pay by credit card **3** Sign **4** or **5** That's **6** Can I **7** PIN number

3 **1** No, they aren't. They're Arabella's shoes. **2** No, it isn't. It's Armand's coffee. **3** No, they aren't. They're Larisa's children. **4** No, it isn't. It's Dimitri's hat. **5** No, they aren't. They're Katarina's books. **6** No, it isn't. It's Giacomo's orange juice.

4 **1** I **2** P **3** P **4** I **5** P **6** P **7** I **8** P

Unit 5

Lesson 5.1

1a **1** north **2** east **3** south **4** west **5** centre

1b **1** buildings **2** beach **3** river **4** mountains **5** trees

2 **1** There's **2** there are **3** there's **4** There are **5** There's **6** there's **7** there are

3 **1** There are **2** There's **3** There are **4** There are **5** There's **6** There are

4 **1** a lot of **2** nothing **3** some **4** some **5** nothing **6** a lot of

Lesson 5.2

1 **1** in **2** opposite **3** in front of **4** behind **5** under **6** next to **7** near

2 **1** German **2** Indian **3** Welsh **4** Scottish **5** French **6** Italian **7** Irish **8** English **9** British

3 **1** Is there a chemist? Yes, there is. **2** Are there any banks? No, there aren't. **3** Is there a cinema? No, there isn't. **4** Are there any bookshops? Yes, there are. **5** Are there any newsagents? Yes, there are. **6** Is there a car park? Yes, there is.

4 **1** There's a car park. **2** There aren't any galleries. **3** There aren't any pubs **4** There's a supermarket. **5** There isn't a department store. **6** There isn't a train station. **7** There are two bookshops. **8** There aren't any museums.

Lesson 5.3

1 **1** dance **2** sing **3** play golf **4** play the piano **5** swim **6** use a computer **7** drive **8** cook

2 **1** can you **2** I can **3** They can **4** Can you speak **5** can **6** I can't **7** He can **8** Can he

3 **1** Leroy and Lena can use a computer. **2** Jo can't use a computer. **3** **A:** Can Simon sing? **B:** No, he can't. **4** Leroy and Lena can't sing. **5** **A:** Can Jo sing? **B:** Yes, she can. **6** Simon can use a computer. **7** **A:** Can Leroy and Lena play the piano? **B:** Yes, they can. **8** Jo can't play the piano. **9** Simon can play the piano.

4 **a** Five o'clock in the morning. **b** Three o'clock in the afternoon. **c** Eight o'clock in the evening. **d** Nine o'clock in the morning. **e** One o'clock in the afternoon. **f** Ten o'clock in the evening.

Unit 6

Lesson 6.1

1a **1** short **2** rich **3** old **4** happy **5** thin

1b **1** tall – short **2** unhappy – happy **3** fat – thin **4** poor – rich **5** young – old

2a **1** I like cappuccino. **2** I don't like museums. **3** I like French music. **4** I don't like Arsenal Football Club. **5** I like Leipzig. **6** I don't like Indian food. **7** I don't like espresso. **8** I like children.

2b **1** **A:** Do you like black coffee? **B:** Yes, I do. **2** **A:** Do you like the countryside? **B:** Yes, I do. **3** **A:** Do you like Chinese food? **B:** Yes, I do. **4** **A:** Do you like modern buildings? **B:** No, I don't. **5** **A:** Do you like salad? **B:** Yes, I do. **6** **A:** Do you like supermarkets? **B:** No, I don't. **7** **A:** Do you like department stores? **B:** Yes, I do. **8** **A:** Do you like American cars? **B:** Yes, I do.

3a **1** them **2** her **3** him **4** it **5** you **6** me

3b **1** We **2** us **3** They **4** them **5** She **6** her **7** He **8** him

Lesson 6.2

1 **1** designers **2** chefs **3** builders **4** sales reps **5** reporters **6** architects

2 **1** **Grace:** We like our jobs. They don't like their jobs. **2** **Grace:** We work in an office. They don't work in an office. **3** **Grace:** We don't sell cars. They sell cars. **4** **Grace:** We design cars. They don't design cars.

3a **1** do **2** What **3** do **4** Who **5** Where

3b **1** What do you do? **2** Who do you work for? **3** What do you design? **4** Where do you work? **5** Where do you live?

Lesson 6.3

1a **1** d **2** c **3** f **4** c **5** a **6** b **7** e

1b **1** get up **2** have a shower **3** start work **4** eat a sandwich **5** finish work **6** watch TV **7** go to bed

2 **1** She gets up at 10:30. **2** She has a shower at 10:45. **3** She starts work at 11:30. **4** She has a sandwich at 3 o'clock. **5** She finishes work at 5 o'clock. **6** She watches TV from 6 o'clock to 2:30. **7** She goes to bed at 2:30.

3 **1** He doesn't eat chocolate. **2** She doesn't like chicken. **3** William doesn't start work early. **4** Teresa doesn't get up at seven-thirty. **5** He doesn't go to bed late. **6** She doesn't finish work at five o'clock. **7** He doesn't watch TV every day.

4 **1** Yes, she does. **2** No, she doesn't. **3** Yes, she does. **4** No, she doesn't. **5** Yes, she does. **6** No, she doesn't.

Unit 7

Lesson 7.1

1 **1** d **2** g **3** h **4** c **5** a **6** e **7** b **8** f

2 **1** be quiet **2** sit down **3** don't watch TV **4** hold the line

5 don't look   6 come in

3 (3) Hold the line, please.   (6) Hello, Ms. Price.   (1) Good morning. Rordon Engineering.   (4) Jurgen Schmitt.   (5) Hello Mr Schmitt. This is Vanessa Price.   (2) Good morning. Can I speak to Jurgen Schmitt, please?

4a July 7   October 10   January 1   December 12   August 8   May 5   April 4   February 2   November 11   June 6   September 9   March 3

4b 1 April   2 July   3 January   4 August   5 February   6 September   7 December   8 May   9 June   10 October   11 March   12 November

Lesson 7.2

1a 1 call   2 answer   3 write   4 take   5 work   6 work   7 give   8 travel   9 have

1b a give presentations   b take work home   c work outdoors   d travel abroad   e call customers   f answer the phone   g have meetings   h work from home   i write reports

2a a always   b usually   c often   d sometimes   e not often/not usually   f never

2b 1 I never watch TV in the afternoon.   2 Maggie doesn't usually take work home.   3 We sometimes work outdoors.   4 Do you always go to bed at 11 o'clock?   5 He often plays golf on Sundays   6 They don't often travel abroad.

3 1 I don't often swim in the sea.   2 I'm sometimes late for work.   3 I never drive.   4 I usually sing and play the piano at family parties.   5 My manager doesn't usually answer the phone at work.   6 He is always happy on Friday afternoons.

Lesson 7.3

1 1st first   2nd second   3rd third   4th fourth   5th fifth   6th sixth   7th seventh   8th eighth   9th ninth   10th tenth

2 1 21st January   2 11th March   3 1st May   4 12th December   5 20th June   6 16th November   7 2nd September   8 3rd February

2a 1 What would you like to   2 I'd like a   3 Would you like   4 thank you   5 What would you like   6 I'd like

2b 1 A: Would you like a black coffee? B: No thank you.   2 A: Would you like a piece of cake? B: Yes, please.   3 A: Would you like a mineral water? B: No, thank you.   4 A: Would you like an orange juice? B: Yes, please.   5 A: Would you like a ham sandwich? B: No, thank you.

3 1 Starters   2 Soup   3 Main courses   4 Vegetables   5 Desserts   6 Fruit

Unit 8

Lesson 8.1

1a 1 chess   2 TV   3 theatre   4 golf   5 cycling   6 eat out   7 tennis   8 football   9 walk   10 book   11 swimming   12 sightseeing

1b 1 play chess   2 watch TV   3 go to the theatre   4 play golf   5 go cycling   6 eat out   7 play tennis   8 play football   9 go for a walk   10 read a book   11 go swimming   12 go sightseeing

2a 1 want   2 like   3 want   4 like   5 like   6 want   7 like   8 want

2b 1 being   2 working   3 finishing   4 to work   5 to go   6 working   7 to be   8 travelling   9 selling   10 to call

3a 1 easy   2 boring   3 fun   4 difficult   5 exciting   6 interesting

3b 1 boring   2 easy   3 interesting   4 difficult   5 exciting/fun

Lesson 8.2

1a 1 sofa   2 basin   3 bed   4 cooker   5 fridge   6 coffee table   7 wardrobe   8 sink   9 washing machine   10 armchair   11 bath   12 car   13 toilet   14 mirror

1b bathroom: basin, bath, toilet   bedroom: wardrobe, bed, mirror   kitchen: washing-machine, cooker, fridge, sink   living room: sofa, coffee table, armchair   garage: car

2a 1 've got   2 's got   3 hasn't got   4 've got   5 haven't got   6 've got

2b 1 's got   2 's got   3 hasn't got   4 's got   5 hasn't got   6 hasn't got

3a 1 Have you got   2 have   3 Have you got   4 haven't   5 Has your mother got   6 has

Lesson 8.3

1 1 What   2 Who   3 How   4 Where   5 Which   6 How   7 Who   8 Which

2 1 lamb   2 seafood   3 rice   4 chocolate   5 potato   6 pork   7 fish   8 cheese

3 1 like   2 How   3 time   4 See

4 1 reservation   2 table   3 Come   4 ready   5 like   6 have   7 drink   8 Still   9 bill

Unit 9

Lesson 9.1

1 1 nineteen eighty-two   2 two thousand and four   3 eighteen oh three   4 nineteen oh nine   5 nineteen seventy

2a 1 was   2 were   3 were   4 was   5 was   6 were

2b 1 were   2 were   3 was   4 were   5 was   6 was   7 were

3 1 Jeff and I were late for the party.   2 My son and daughter were at home.   3 I was a computer engineer.   4 You were my best friend.   5 We were in the garage.   6 Franz was my sister's best friend.   7 This book was really exciting.   8 They were at school today.   9 She was a university lecturer in London.   10 It was my favourite restaurant.

4 1 Einstein was born on 14th March, 1879.   2 Alfred Hitchcock was famous for his films.   3 Margaret Thatcher was friends with Ronald Reagan.   4 Martin Luther King and Spike Lee were born in Atlanta in Georgia.   5 Marilyn Monroe was married to Joe DiMaggio and Arthur Miller.   6 Lyndon Johnson was the President of America from 1963 to 1969.   7 Some of Nina Simone's music was similar to Billie Holliday's music.   8 Mikhail Glinka was a good singer.

Lesson 9.2

1 1 were   2 were   3 wasn't   4 was   5 was   6 was   7 was   8 were   9 were   10 were   11 weren't   12 was   13 was

2 1 Were   2 weren't   3 wasn't   4 Was   5 wasn't   6 Were   7 was   8 was   9 was   10 Was

3a 1 C   2 D   3 E   4 A   5 B

3b 1 yesterday evening   2 one/a week ago   3 last year   4 last night   5 last week   6 ten days ago   7 last month   8 yesterday morning

Lesson 9.3

1a 1 cook   2 do   3 vacuum   4 clean   5 iron   6 wash

1b A iron a shirt   B clean the kitchen   C do the laundry   D cook dinner   E vacuum the house   F wash the dishes

2 1 How was the flight?   2 How was school?   3 How was the party?   4 How was your weekend?   5 How was your holiday?

3a 1 Can I talk to you?   2 Can you cook dinner?   3 Could I open the window?   4 Can I sit down?   5 Could I work at home tomorrow?   6 Could I turn on your television?

3b 1 C   2 B   3 D   4 A   5 E

Unit 10

Lesson 10.1

1 1 meet   2 move   3 win   4 arrests   5 lose   6 find   7 steals   8 break

2 1 started   2 asked   3 cooked   4 wanted   5 listened   6 walked   7 arrested   8 worked

3a 1 was   2 started   3 didn't move   4 didn't stay   5 moved   6 loved   7 didn't love   8 didn't like   9 didn't stay

3b 1 A: Did Van Gogh stay in Paris? B: No, he didn't.   2 A: Did Van Gogh move to London? B: Yes, he did.   3 A: Did Van Gogh love Eugenie Loyer? B: Yes, he did.   4 A: Did Eugenie Loyer love Van

Gogh? **B:** No, she didn't. **5 A:** Did Van Gogh like his job? **B:** No, he didn't.

4 1 wanted /ɪd/ **2** liked /t/ **3** moved /d/ **4** talked /t/ **5** walked /t/ **6** closed /d/ **7** arrested /ɪd/ **8** listened /d/ **9** asked /t/ **10** finished /t/ **11** played /d/ **12** cooked /t/

Lesson 10.2

1a 1 got married **2** bought **3** went **4** saw **5** said **6** met **7** gave **8** found

1b 1 gave **2** came **3** took **4** met **5** had **6** arrested **7** started **8** said **9** moved **10** found **Hidden word** = get married

1c 1 won **2** got married **3** didn't go **4** said **5** didn't have **6** went **7** looked **8** was **9** bought **10** did he buy **11** didn't buy **12** bought

1d 1 Did you find your wallet? **2** Did Terry go out last night? **3** Did they buy a new car? **4** Did you love her? **5** Did Harry move to London? **6** Did you say 'Yes'? **7** Did you lose your passport on holiday? **8** Did we win the lottery?

2 1 two *thousand*, one *hundred* and fifty **2** one thousand and ten **3** nine hundred and eighty **4** fifteen thousand, six hundred and twelve **5** nine thousand, nine hundred and ninety-nine **6** eighty-six thousand, three hundred and twenty-one **7** one hundred and

fifteen thousand, two hundred and ninety **8** two hundred thousand, one hundred and nine

Lesson 10.3

1a 1 friendly **2** shy **3** competitive **4** confident **5** cool **6** funny

2a 1 Why is she in bed? **2** Why was he at home yesterday? **3** Why did I eat out last night? **4** Why does she finish work at one o'clock in the morning? **5** Why do they always take work home?

2b a – 4 b – 5 c – 1 d – 3 e – 2

3a 1 Pavarotti is taller than Carréras. **2** Domingo is the tallest of The Three Tenors. **3** Domingo is older than Carréras. **4** Pavarotti is the oldest of The Three Tenors. **5** Domingo is more famous than Carréras. **6** Pavarotti is the most famous of The Three Tenors. **7** Carréras is younger than Domingo. **8** Carréras is the youngest of The Three Tenors. **9** Pavarotti is shorter than Domingo. **10** Carréras is the shortest of The Three Tenors.

3b 1 Tokyo is the biggest city in the world. **2** France is bigger than the UK. **3** He's more confident than me. **4** Who's the coolest actor in the world? **5** This is Steve Martin's funniest film. **6** The fisherman is more intelligent than his sons.

Irregular verbs

Verb	Past Simple	Past Participle	Verb	Past Simple	Past Participle
be	was/were	been	leave	left	left
become	became	become	let	let	let
begin	began	begun	lose	lost	lost
break	broke	broken	make	made	made
bring	brought	brought	mean	meant	meant
build	built	built	meet	met	met
buy	bought	bought	pay	paid	paid
can	could	been able	put	put	put
catch	caught	caught	read/rid/	read/red/	read/red/
choose	chose	chosen	ride	rode	ridden
come	came	come	ring	rang	rung
cost	cost	cost	run	ran	run
do	did	done	say	said	said
draw	drew	drawn	see	saw	seen
drink	drank	drunk	sell	sold	sold
drive	drove	driven	send	sent	sent
eat	ate	eaten	show	showed	shown
fall	fell	fallen	sing	sang	sung
feed	fed	fed	sit	sat	sat
feel	felt	felt	sleep	slept	slept
find	found	found	speak	spoke	spoken
fly	flew	flown	spend	spent	spent
forget	forgot	forgotten	stand	stood	stood
get	got	got	steal	stole	stolen
give	gave	given	swim	swam	swum
go	went	gone/been	take	took	taken
grow	grew	grown	teach	taught	taught
have	had	had	tell	told	told
hear	heard	heard	think	thought	thought
hold	held	held	throw	threw	thrown
hurt	hurt	hurt	understand	understood	understood
keep	kept	kept	wear	wore	worn
know	knew	known	win	won	won
learn	learned/learnt	learned/learnt	write	wrote	written